IDEOLOGY AND SOCIAL CHANGE IN LATIN AMERICA

IDEOLOGY & SOCIAL CHANGE IN LATIN AMERICA

Edited by

June Nash
City College of the
City University of New York

Juan Corradi
New York University

Hobart Spalding, Jr.
Brooklyn College of the
City University of New York

GORDON AND BREACH

Copyright © *1977 by*

Gordon and Breach Science Publishers Inc.
One Park Avenue
New York, N.Y. 10016

Editorial office for the United Kingdom

Gordon and Breach Science Publishers Ltd.
41/42 William IV Street
London W.C.2

Editorial office for France

Gordon & Breach
7-9 rue Emile Dubois
Paris 75014

Library of Congress catalog card number 76-53711
ISBN 0 677 04170 5

TABLE OF CONTENTS

PART I: Emergence of Worker Consciousness

INTRODUCTION

Despite premature epitaphs, ideologies persist as modes of formulating and interpreting experience. In societies lacking a division of labor crystalized in classes, every member of the society is expected to conform to a shared world view. The price of unitary consciousness may be the suppression of dissent when the basis for consensual accord is weakened, thus limiting the ability to respond adaptively to change. In complex societies, ideologies sustain group boundaries defined by caste, class, race, and increasingly by sex as consciousness of discrimination rises. The universalistic aims of renaissance philosophy have foundered in the quagmire of unequal distribution of material resources, power, and aesthetic and spiritual outlets, and new ideologies have emerged as each of the disprivileged groups seeks to define a new consciousness of its oppression and awareness of its potential development.

Those who treat ideology as errors of the past, asserting that in the utopias which they would bring into existence via the revolution there would be no need for promoting "false consciousness," commit the same error as liberals in the nineteenth century who consigned all traditions, beliefs, understandings and myths inherited from the past to the realm of the irrational and considered as rational, scientific truth only those measures of value that could enter into the cost accounting of the free market. Any attempt to socialize consciousness is a step toward forging an ideology. This applies as much to the social scientist as to the pamphleteers, although the connection between particular interests and contingent constructs was less evident.

Starting with the premise that ideology is operative in social science in the selection of problems, in the overall approach, in the choice of methods, almost always in the image of man and society that social theories connote, and in the policy implications of the findings, we seek to further scientific objectivity by making ideological inputs explicit. Therefore we begin the anthology with an essay by Corradi, who argues that, in the case of Latin America, social science is embedded in networks of dependency through which the interests and world view of powerful nations, notably the United States, are asserted and transmitted. The struggle for scientific autonomy must, according to this view, see itself as part of the struggle for political liberation.

1

Juan Corradi's essay analyzes the relationship between idea structures and social structures. The roles of intellectuals and cultural elites are explored in connection with trends toward the evolution of international stratification. The salient features of Latin American intellectuals are discussed in the framework of dependency analysis. Examining the evolution of Latin American intellectual history, and especially the debate in modern studies of cultural dependence, he concludes that social science in Latin America is a case of unequal development and subordination of those countries vis-a-vis metropolitan areas. Only after consciousness of cultural dependence is recognized can a critical study of the conditions affecting the production of knowledge be undertaken. He directs attention to the sociology of knowledge as an empirical discipline that will promote research strategies in response to critiques of social science practice in both metropolitan centers and dependent countries.

The essays in this volume reflect the movement away from patron-client bonds of loyalty and exploitation to a statement of interests defined in the new relations of production. Proletarian consciousness occupies a special place in revolutionary movements because, as Marx foretold, it is in the recognition of their fate and the attempt to overcome it that worker revolt is translated into a political movement to attain a larger horizon for all humanity. Camus (1955) identified Sisyphus as the prototype of the rebellious proletariat, condemned to a life of hopeless and futile labor by the gods whom he defied. He brings the image of the toiling Sisyphus to life, the "body straining to raise the huge stone, to roll it and push it up a slope a hundred times over . . . the face screwed up, the cheek tight against the stone, the shoulder bracing the clay-covered mass, the foot wedging it, . . . the wholly human security of two earth-clotted hands," and then the moment of truth when the stone rolls down and Sisyphus leaves the heights and follows it down. That walk downward, Camus tells us, is the hour of consciousness. If he should accept that fate, he finds the absurd victory of Oedipus, Krilov, or Candide, aware of the futility of their acts but accepting that all is for the best in the best possible of worlds.

The absurdity of such a victory lies in the reduction of class issues to individual consciousness. Marx provided another answer; the proletariates become the redeemers when they grasp full consciousness of their social position and join in collective action to fight the system that condemns them to fruitless toil for the profit of the capitalist expropriators. Lukacs (who was marginal to Marxist circles of the twenties when they were dominated by economic determinism and who has regained

favor with a younger generation committed to expanding
their own consciousness and that of the working class)
spells out the dimensions of that redemption (1971):

> Seeing himself as proletariat, the worker
> immediately recognizes the nature of capitalism.
> His own liberation depends on transforming the
> system. Redemption is to reconquer for
> man that state where there is no longer difference
> between suppressor and suppressed . . . [where]
> the era characterized by the degradation of
> humanity through economic dependencies is
> abolished, [where] -- as Marx put it -- the
> blind forces of economic power will be broken
> and in its stead come to adequate rule which
> accords with human dignity.

Both Marx and Engels lived to despair of the
British working class fulfulling the historic mission
they had proclaimed in the Communist Manifesto. A
decade after its publication, Engels wrote to Marx:

> The English proletariat is becoming more and
> more bourgeois, so that the most bourgeois of all
> nations is apparently aiming ultimately at the
> possession of a bourgeois aristocracy, and a
> bourgeois proletariat as well as a bourgeoisie.
> For a nation which exploits the whole world
> this is of course, to a certain extent justified.
> (quoted in Lenin 1947: 709).

Capitalism, instead of creating its grave-diggers was
breeding a class of morticians, sharing in the profits
of imperialist expansion. The workers of England no
longer held the mental outlook as they "merrily share
the feast of England's monopoly of the colonies and the
world market" (op. cit., p. 709).

Recently workers in the metropolitan centers have
begun to lose their privileged position as capital is
invested in low wage and low tax industries in other
countries. Faced by unemployment and inflation, they
have been asked to bear the greater share of the burden
in government policies to overcome the chronic inflationary
stagnation of developed economies. With these changing
conditions, it is important to reassess working class
consciousness in the industrial centers as well as the
margins.

When we shift our view from the metropolitan
centers to the newly industrializing countries it is
almost like finding Marx's idealized working class
before the "fall from grace." Small sectors of organized
labor are a highly politically conscious group,
especially in urban areas or concentrated production
centers such as the mines and commercial plantations.
The following series of papers deals with empirical
situations in the development of proletarian consciousness
in these kinds of contexts in Latin America and the
Caribbean. The variables that enter into the formation
of ideology -- taken here to mean outlook on the
world -- and of ontology -- the proletarian self-image --
will be discussed in agricultural and industrial settings
to see what common themes can be found and what modes of
action result from these. The seeds of Marxist theory
have been sown in the new hemisphere since the turn of
the century but the new hybrids of communismo criollo
or of socialismo criollo have been cultivated in response
to the changed conditions. The new consciousness is
rising at a time when the most depressed sector of the
working class, the unskilled worker, is becoming "obsolete"
in capital intensive industries, a time envisioned by
Marx when he predicted that automation would become so
developed that "the worker appears superfluous . . ."
(Grundrisse der Kritik der Politischen Okonomie,
Rohentwurf ms., by Marx 1857-8 quoted in Bottomore 1972:
59-60). If labor elites fail to link their struggle to
the marginally employed, they will lose whatever gains
they made in the reformist period.
        In advanced capitalist centers the relatively
simple, straightforward models of class consciousness
have had to be constantly redefined since Marx. The
"classic" proletariat has largely escaped extreme deprivation; unionization and political reform have led to an
institutionalization of conflict; class consciousness
and militancy have been weakened, and in the long run
there has been a noticeable withdrawal of the working
class from politics. Even though the socially irresponsible
use of power based on corporate property continue to be
chiefly responsible for tensions, class conflict in
metropolitan societies has been displaced and contained.
In the light of these developments it is highly instructive
to study the determinants of class consciousness among
the working classes of Latin America to see whether
similar processes are at work there or whether other
factors are operative that make the revolutionary
performance of Marx's idealized proletariat more likely.
        Directing himself to the question of how and why
proletarian consciousness emerges, Thomas Greaves explores
the issue in Viru, Peru. Peasants, tied to local

communities, find identity in the "particularized jural
obligations and privileges as well as psychological
rewards" contingent to this while the proletariat identifies
with a class that extends beyond locality. The patron-
client relationship gives way to contractual forms binding
the worker to a job. The transition, beginning with the
upset of traditional economic systems after the onset of
world-wide depression in the thirties, generated a
proletarian consciousness in 1954. He nails this
process down to a set of proposals and actions taken by the
agricultural union and summarizes these in terms of a
series of propositions about the transformation.

Hobart Spalding's paper provides an historical
and comparative survey of organized labor in Latin
America. He distinguishes three periods: the formative
period, 1850 to 1914, an expansive and explosive period,
1914-1933, and a cooptive period beginning in the 1930s
and extending to our own day. The article concentrates
especially on events after 1930. The main concern of
Spalding's analysis is the various ideologies and devices
used to contain and coopt organized labor. Chile under
the Popular Front government, Brazil under Vargas, and
Argentina under Perón are analyzed in order to show that
even governments supposedly friendly to labor are not
always what they seem to be. Especially revealing is
the comparative analysis of labor mobilization by
populist regimes in Argentina and Brazil. Nationalism
and developmentalism are critically examined as ideologies
of containment. The paper sheds light upon the role of
ideologies, mobilization "from above," and political
cooption in the failure of organized labor to play a
revolutionary part in the way anticipated by Marxian
theory.

In another paper concerned with urban workers Peppe
raises the question of whether internal divisions in the
status of workers in the modern industrial sector of
Santiago, Chile negates class solidarity and an ideology
of political change. The results of his attitudinal
study indicate that workers do not show a special
propensity to shrink from those changes which would
alter their immediate work environment but that they give
less support than other workers to popular revolutionary
parties.

The case studies reflect the transition occurring
in rural as well as urban industrial settings that is
occurring with the penetration of the market economy.
The contrast is no longer the simplistic opposition in
the neo-Weberian formula of traditional-to modern. Rather
than that, we see an adaptation along many lines, with
cultural material from the past serving to ease the trauma
of change. Gratitude to the populist leaders and the
encrusted bureaucracy of peasants and industrial workers

who have made interstitial gains may inhibit progressive
developments in the direction of fundamental structural
change. Recent developments in those countries with
repressive military regimes reveal the need to break
from the dependency relations created in the period of
populiast reform. In the recent blocade of the highways
in Cochabamba, Bolivia, carried out by peasants and industrial workers in protest to rising prices and diminishing
wages in January 1974 the spontaneous action gave rise to
a new leadership that was not crippled by the dependency
to the central government shown by the old leaders of the
Movimiento Nacional Revolucionario. In the course of the
struggles, the peasants rejected the campesino-military
pact forged in the period of declining populist movement
as the new leaders responded to the changing power structure.
    The field work on which these essays are based
was carried out prior to the Chilean coup which signals
an intensification of military intervention as a means
to contain workers' movements. As Latin America enters
a phase of intensified class struggle, the resistence
against extreme forms of repression will forge new forms
of organization and of ideological expression.

BIBLIOGRAPHY

Camus, A.
    1955   The Myth of Sysiphus. New York: Vintage Press.

Bottomore, T.
    1972   "Class Structure and Social Consciousness,"
               Aspects of History and Class Conscience.
               I. Meszaros, ed. New York: Herder and Herder.

Lenin, V.I.
    1947   Selected Works in Two Volumes. Moscow: Foreign
               Language Press.

Lukacs, G.
    1972   History and Class Consciousness. London: Merlin
               Press.

CULTURAL DEPENDENCE AND THE SOCIOLOGY OF KNOWLEDGE: THE LATIN AMERICAN CASE*

Juan Eugenio Corradi

1 The Study of Ideology in Latin America

1.1 Traditional Interpretations

Traditional interpretations of the role of ideologies in Latin America -- especially of those operative during the struggles for independence and during the successive phases of "nationbuilding" and modernization -- suffered from a strong idealistic bias. They overemphasized what J.P. Nettl called the "problems of push." In other words, they were limited by an exclusive focus on the social consequences of idea-systems.

The liberal interpretation stressed the modernizing consequences of the adoption of Western ideas throughout the different stages of Latin American development, and complacently pointed to an alleged correlation between the adoption of modern Western Weltanschauungen and higher rates of development. On the other hand, nationalists of various shades denounced the role that the very same ideas and values played in furthering the subordination of Latin American societies to European, and later American, imperialism.

The polemic between liberals and nationalists shed little light on the understanding of the actual social structuring of ideas in Latin America, that is, on the "problems of pull." Starting with ideas as they presumably seek social attachment, these traditional interpretations pinned themselves to idea-systems as means of analysis. By that token, that is, by "descending from heaven to earth," traditional interpretations were themselves ideological.

1.2 Sociological Interpretations

The concern with social structure as a locus of ideas is of relatively recent date in Latin America. This approach has represented a step forward in the study of ideology in the region. Nonetheless, current sociological

---

* A version of this paper was presented at the VII World Congress of Sociology, Varna, Bulgaria, September, 1970.

interpretations have in turn been vitiated by an almost
exclusive focus on national society as the locus of
ideas, and have therefore neglected the international
context -- the world-historical totality that characterizes
development and under-development as interacting
opposites rather than as polar terms of an abstract
continuum.

It is only in recent years that an integrated
approach to Latin American development has been developed
which takes cognizance of the international context. The
new approach has shed light on the role of ideologies in
Latin American societies, has explained the limitations
of previous interpretations, and has revealed the
inadequacies of the theories of development underlying
them. Its central focus is the concept of dependence.

It is common to find in the available literature
on Latin American development frequent references to
discrepancies or "lags" between social structures and
idea-structures[1] -- for instance, a discrepancy between
traditional agrarian societies on the one hand, and the
urban liberal ideologies of their ruling elites during
certain periods, on the other. Such "lags" appear as a
result of a comparative analysis of Western-industrial
and Latin American development processes that is loaded
with questionable assumptions. The most conspicuous of
these is perhaps the adoption of the historical experience
of Western industrialization as a universal paradigm of
development. Considered from such perspective, the
structural peculiarities of Latin American societies and
their processes of change tend to appear as deviant
cases. Hypotheses are then brought to bear in order to
account for the "lags," "contradictions," and "discrepancies"
which a misled comparative analysis generates before the
eyes of the uncritical student. Favorite explanations
make reference to mechanisms of cultural diffusion and to
socio - psychological characteristics of different
recipient groups in the local societies. The accent is
bestowed on the lack of correspondence between ideas
and social reality, that is, on the alleged situational
inadequacy of ideologies and values.

The imputations of situational inedequacy so
frequent in the study of ideologies in Latin America
clearly stand or fall with the underlying conception of
modernization that sustains them -- especially with the
implicit "reading" of the historical evidence that they
contain. I shall examine in more detail the processes
involved in arriving at such imputations.

The first datum observed is the culture and
ideologies of developed societies, as well as the
mechanisms of their diffusion. A second datum observed

is the adoption of some of those ideologies by local elites. Then a judgment is made to the effect that the bearers of those ideologies behave in an illusory manner, being presumably unable to perceive the real problems facing their societies -- being, in other words, "alienated," a term which in this context suggests a psychological separation from one's own cultural milieu.

The imputation of situational inadequacy just described is obviously guided by standards of what is a "proper" sequence of development. And the implicit yardstick is usually nothing more than a hypostatized version of the processes of industrialization of some Western societies. The lack of historical specificity and the absence of a global perspective on the inter-connectedness of development and underdevelopment make this kind of analysis fruitless and misleading.

An integrated analysis shows, on the other hand, the consistency and situational adequacy of the very same ideologies and value-systems, on a depth level that is never reached by current interpretations. Since an integrated analysis derives the structural features of Latin American societies from the changing patterns of their dependence vis-a-vis developed societies, its interpretation of ideologies is two-pronged: on the one hand it investigates how dominant ideologies legitimize the dependence of Latin America on metropolitan powers; on the other, it investigates how they also legitimize the internal rule of classes and elites that occupy strategic positions in the networks of dependence within local societies.

1.2.1   The Study of Dependence as a
        New Framework of Analysis

The field of Latin American studies is presently undergoing a thorough overhauling of the categories of analysis of social and economic development. The recent work of many social scientists in the area seeks to integrate social and economic facts in a polemical framework of theory that runs counter to the "working truths" which form a major part of the conceptual apparatus used so far in the study of Latin American societies.[2] It is a timely undertaking, since the constant repetition of unexamined and extrapolated cliches in books and articles has given certain misleading conceptions a life of their own, turning them, despite growing evidence to the contrary, into dogmas, and surrounding the entire field with the aura of ideology.

        The main thrust of this effort has been to
examine how Latin American development has been related
to the principal aspects of world capitalist development
in each of its historical stages -- colonial, imperialist,
and neo-imperialist. These phases correspond to the
divisions of the epochs of capitalism into commercial-
mercantilist, industrial laissez-faire, and monopoly
capitalism. Focusing on the role of foreign investment
and finance in Latin America, these authors seek to
determine the structural feature of the system of
international stratification and their repercussions on
the structure of local societies. The force of their
argument lies in the rejection of widespread theses about
the "stages" of economic growth and modernization, their
universal and evolutionary assumptions, and the typologies
based on them. They substitute instead a conception of
development and underdevelopment as two poles of a
single historical process which extends to the present
and which penetrates every aspect of Latin American social
structures. Their goal is to unfold analytically the
process which gave rise to the structural tensions of
present-day societies in the region.[3] This has been
achieved by analyzing first the conquest and colonization
of Latin America in the context of commercial-capitalist
goals.

        The colonial stage is seen from this perspective
as an act of finance and investment which in turn wss
part of mercantile capitalist expansion designed to tap
natural and human resources, and to plow the proceeds
into metropolitan development and consumption. A
significant fact is that Europe provided only a small
portion of the initial capital necessary for the
development of the colonial resources. Most of this
capital came from the plundering of the colonial areas
and their inhabitants. Thus, from the very outset of
colonization, there was a capital flow from the colonies
to the metropolis, a process which would recur with
increasing intensity in the next stages of the unfolding
of underdevelopment in the region. This treatment of the
process of colonization seeks to destroy the myth of the initial unavailability of capital and resources in Latin
America, a situation which would seem -- if on gives
credit to conventional views -- to create a "need" for
foreign investment in traditional -- supposedly "feudal" --
societies unable to pull out of backwardness by their own
means. On the contrary, underdevelopment now appears as
a direct effect of European colonization in the context
of metropolitan commercial goals, which produced a most
severe structural distortion of the regional economies
of Latin America. The colonial system, by acting like a

pumping mechanism to draw surpluses and to channel them to
royal treasuries, set rigid obstacles to the internal
differentiation and to the self-sustained growth of those
economies. The international system secreted a specific
social order, maintained through foreign finance and
military force, which in turn further suppressed the
internal differentiation of markets and the development
of local industries. The only exceptions to this pattern
of dependence were spurts of local development linked to
the weakining of ties with metropolis during times of crisis
or war, a phenomenon that reappears during the 19th and
20th centuries within other contexts of international
control.

    With the triumph of the Industrial Revolution in
Europe and the dominance of Great Britain on the international scene, Latin America changed metropolitan masters.
The new patterns of dependence inaugurated by British
imperialism led to the accentuation and generalization of
the structural distortions in Latin American economies.
The colonial past provided a favorable starting-point for
new imperialist integration. The socio-economic structure
secreted by the period of colonial dependence paved the
way for the later incorporation of the area into the
network of British trade. The structure instituted by the
latter both inside Latin American countries and in terms
of their ties with the outside world,in turn favored the
absorption of their economies into a neo-imperialist
system under the hegemony of the United States. At each
stage of the "development of underdevelopment," as
Professor Frank calls this process, the configuration of
one system of international stratification has, like a
switchman, determined the tracks along which action has
been pushed by the dynamics of the successive domination.
Such dynamic was not, however, smooth and without
resistance. At each stage of the process it involved the
suppression of different possibilities of autonomous
development.

    The analysis which I could only briefly outline
above reveals a search for new ways to organize and interpret data which has been hitherto grossly disregarded by
different sociological and economic "schools" of development and modernization. Moreover, it seeks to tell the
story of Latin American backwardness from a critical Latin
American viewpoint. Finally, the analysis sheds light on
a basic general problem, namely the role of advanced
capitalism in maintaining and reinforcing underdevelopment
in the Third World. Until the middle of the 20th century,
the usual mechanisms of control and economic dependence
were mainly loans, financial ties, the penetration of some
extractive industries by foreign concerns, and also the

foreign development and control of social overhead and infrastructural facilities in most Latin American countries. During the second half of the century, the emergence of American capitalism as a major world force has inaugurated a new pattern of dependence in the area, under the aegis of multinational corporations.[4]

The arguments advanced by Latin American students of dependence are most persuasive in their treatment of the conjunctural and sporadic spurts of industrialization and semi-autonomous development which took place in Latin America as a result of metropolitan crises. This has been amply documented by Latin American economic research. Each metropolitan crisis gave Latin America a respite from financial and other ties. This relaxation of the mechanisms of external dependence allowed the temporary growth of national industries, which were later taken over or squeezed out of competition by the resumption of foreign capital's penetration once the metropolitan crises were over. This situation repeats itself during and after each major international crisis -- the World Wars and the Depression. The end of the Korean conflict marks the end of those sporadic attempts at autonomous development and marks the wholesale penetration of American capital in the region. It is symbolized by the demise of nationalist "developmental" regimes in some of the major countries of the area. The present period of wholesale satellization culminates -- according to these authors -- in the regional integration of Latin American countries. In its political aspects, it entails the recrudescence of militarism under the umbrella of hemispheric alliances. On the other hand, the ever increasing indebtedness of these states vis-a-vis metropolitan centers makes it necessary to establish a series of international financial stabilizers and institutions. Since the latter are more or less direct tools of the foreign policy of the advanced capitalist West, economic "assistance" becomes a weapon of deterrence in international power politics. They further serve to "persuade" the recipient nations to create a "favorable climate" for foreign investment, by instituting orthodox policies. Such policies, however favorable they may prove to multinational corporations, are hardly compatible with social and political stability within Latin American countries. They generate strong resistance on the part of rural and urban masses which could ordinarily sweep out of power any government committed to instituting them which was also publicly accountable for its actions. Hence military interventions and the reinforcement of dictatorship as well as stepped-up foreign "assistance" for "internal security."

The new approach is not simply a renovated version of standard theories of imperialism. Much as these theories might still be relevant, their shortcoming lies in that they have interpreted the processes of imperialist expansion

from the standpoint of the metropolitan powers. The study
of dependence offers instead an analysis of those processes
from the standpoint of the target areas. Whereas current
theories of imperialism focus on capitalist expansion as
an external cause of backwardness, the developing theory
of dependence focuses on the constitution of dependent
social structures[5]. The task is to analyze the social
structures of Latin America and their processes in terms
of changes that have taken place in the more inclusive
system of international stratification. Social structures
and idea-structures can then be studied as substructures
of this more inclusive system. In other words, what is
being developed is a theory of dependent capitalism.

The function of ideologies and the corresponding
behavior of their bearers can now be studied in terms of
the position of different groups in the networks of
dependence[6]. At any given moment, these ideologies
reflect a twofold condition -- national and international
at the same time. To use an example; the adoption of
European liberalism by Latin American elites during the
19th century no longer appears as a mere consequence of
"cultural diffusion," or as the expression of the
"alienation" of those elites vis-a-vis their own socio-
cultural reality, but rather as the expression of the very
concrete interests of a clsss of latifundist agrarian
producers allied with mercantile urban groups for the
purpose of commercializing their primary products in the
international market. The concrete tenets of liberal
ideology, such as "free trade", the free navigation of
rivers, the stress on private property, etc., were all
important tools for subordinating the productive structure
of local society to the needs of the capitalist world
market. The same tenets were also instrumental in the
struggle against obsolete forms of Spanish colonial
domination and in the elimination of pre-capitalist forms
of production. The dominant position achieved by liberal
ideologies during the latter part of the 19th century
reflected the success of landowners in turning to commercial agriculture geared to the needs of the world markets,
the viability of their alliances with other sectors of
Latin American societies -- such as urban intermediaries --
and the consolidation of their interests against other
groups -- lower or rival classes. Their oligarchic version
of the liberal state was an effective political tool of
domination. The receptivity of these elites to Western
values and ideas expressed their interest in maintaining
their dependent ties to metropolitan centers -- a situation
from which they largely derived their privileges. Moreover, the diffusion of European patterns of culture
furthered the consumption of manufactures that could not
be produced locally as a result of the overspecialization

to which Latin American economies were subjected. In
this manner, the ideological field characteristic of a
certain period expresses the meeting of external and internal interests in the same social structure.

2 Ideologies and Cultural Dependence

The foregoing remarks aimed at showing the heuristic superiority of the concept of dependence in approaching the study of ideology in Latin America. I shall now
enter more directly into this field[7].

The patterns of cultural dependence have changed
following the different modes of insertion of Latin
American societies in the evolving international system
of stratification and the structures which this insertion
generated. Studies of Latin American dependence often
distinguish between different periods of development,
each one determining different structural peculiarities
for these societies. The processes of "nation-building"
correspond to the period of the outward growth of Latin
American economies, i.e., the period of the expansion of
exports of their primary products, under the coincident
or successive hegemony of England and the United States,
externally, and internally, under the hegemony of an
oligarchy of agrarian and commercial groups. Liberalism
prevailed and the ideological climate was by and large
optimistic and oriented towards the reception of European
culture. Since the expansion of European -- above all
British -- capitalism entailed the corresponding expansion
of local exports; and insofar as the internal differentiation of Latin American societies had not yet reached the
point in which other groups could challenge the historical
project of the oligarchies, the latter were able to maintain their privileged position through the political
medium of semi-liberal institutions. The consciousness
of dependence was largely non-existent and backwardness
was perceived as the result of internal obstacles to
westernization.

The consolidation and the very success of the pattern
of outward growth soon led, however, to the internal
differentiation of Latin American societies. Urbanization,
massive immigration in some countries, the emergence of
middle sectors and of a rudimentary working class as a
result of subsidiary industrialization, determined the
appearance of a larger variety of outlooks and ideologies,
and led to the emergence of new types of intellectuals,
and to the organization of oppositional movements of some
consequence. While liberalism crystallized into
positivism -- thus reflecting the consolidation of the
processes of "nation-building" -- oppositional and reactive
ideologies made their first appearance: nationalism,

socialism, americanism, and a sort of intellectual spiritual-
ism and elitism called <u>arielismo</u>. The social structure
was now perceived as susceptible to crises. Converging
with these developments, the pole of dominance of the international economy shifted -- particularly after World War
I -- to the United States. The economic leadership of
America -- in many cases a direct competitor with Latin
American export economies -- made dependence a much less
automatic guarantee of economic growth in the subcontinent.
      Up to that point the dominant elites had managed
to establish a political organization fitted both to the
internal needs of oligarchic rule and to the external
demands of the world market. The "liberal-oligarchic"
state had served their requirements and a liberal and
humanistic culture had sanctioned their rule, as long as
there was no political mobilization of other groups in
their societies. Yet, as has already been mentioned, the
very operation of this system within the established international division of labor had stimulated social change
and internal differentiation. Especially in those
countries in which -- by contrast to enclave economies --
the productive process was under the control of a local
ruling class, the growth of exports, the income it
generated, the expansion of services derived from finance
and commercialization, the need for labor power, coupled
with a centralized structure of land ownership, were all
factors that led to massive immigration, rapid urbanization,
and the emergence of sizable middle sectors. On the other
hand, international conjunctures that weakened the ties
of dependence, such as wars and international economic
crises, stimulated the development of local industries on
an import-substitution basis.[8] This pattern of industrialization served to satisfy the internal demand for
manufactured goods in already complex societies. In this
climate, nationalist ideologies became more prevalent.
It was no longer the early reactive nationalism of
traditionalist groups -- usually landed groups that had
failed to turn to commercial agriculture -- but a bourgeois, "developmental" nationalism which would later
assume in some countries, strong populist features. The
new nationalism was the expression of an urban middle
class making a bid for social and political hegemony
through a complicated system of class alliances whenever
international conjunctures debilitated the grip of metropolitan economies, and by implication weakened the oligarchies. In countries like Argentina and Brazil, the
nationalist project became part of movements of mass
mobilization which tried to incorporate internal migrants
and other previously marginal groups in the political system.

Despite the aforementioned trends, nationalist and populist ideologies never coalesced into a new "official culture," even in those countries in which nationalist-populist regimes came to power. In a similar manner, these regimes failed to establish a new state organization capable of replacing the increasingly obsolescent liberal-oligarchic institutions. The ambiguity of these political movements, their bonapartist features and confused ideologies are all symptoms of the inability of national industrial groups and related political elites to offer a viable alternative to the preceding model of economic growth. The ideological ambiguity was in this sense consistent with the impossiblity of realizing an autonomous project of development. At best, the policies of those groups helped pave the way for a new pattern of dependence characteristic of the present constellation.

Beginning in the 50's, and gaining increasing force thereafter, basic changes took place in the direction and character of Latin American development. The central feature of this process has been the internationalization of the internal markets developed during the period of semi-autonomous industrialization. The agents of this "internationalization" are the large multinational corporations. In several countries the internal markets are sufficiently important in terms of generated income so as to allow the establishment of modern industry. This makes possible a certain pattern of economic growth, at the least in terms of capital accumulation and industrial diversification of not at all in terms of increasing popular, let alone national, participation in the fruits of such growth. Under these conditions, foreign investment is directed toward manufacturing activities, modernizing the economy and increasing its control over the new productive processes. Both the flow of capital and the lines of decision-making "pass through" the metro-politan centers, particularly the United States.[9]

In the new context of dependence, ideologies of national development have lost dominant positions as "official" ideologies and have instead joined the camp of oppositional ideologies. They have been officially replaced by <u>desarrollismo</u> ("developmentalism"), that is, by an ideology that stresses the technical aspects of development and modernization, and suppresses the reference to the political control of these processes. In other words, the new dominant ideologies tend to substitute technological or instrumental considerations for political analysis and action. The political aspects are treated in a specialized, "value-neutral" manner, so as to neutralize the implications of the perception of foreign domination over essential productive processes. On the

wake of the failure of bourgeois groups to effect a course
of autonomous development, and gripped by the fear of
more radical revolutionary, alternatives, desarrollismo
appears as perhaps the only functional ideology within
the limits of the "possible consciousness" of dominant
classes and ruling elites in today's Latin America.

The foregoing is no more than a cursory review of
dominant ideologies in Latin America from the viewpoint
of a changing pattern of dependence. I shall presently
approach in more detail one central aspect of dominant
ideologies today, namely scientism and its functions.

2.1 Social Change and Scientific Self-Understanding.

The decade of the 50's brought important changes
in the tasks and functions of Latin American intellectuals.
In some countries, the fall of populist regimes opened
new paths to intellectual development. Populism had
produced a serious rupture in the process of communication
between intellectuals and popular sectors. It had displaced intellectuals as potential leaders of the mobilized
masses and instituted instead bureaucratic manipulation
topped by charismatic leadership.[10] The dissociation of
the intellectuals from popular sectors was never overcome
thereafter: popular antiintellectualism and intellectual
antipopulism are still active as complementary opposites.
The experience of populism broke a fairly well established
tradition among Latin American intellectuals, namely, the
preoccupation with political leadership and public issues.

The collapse of populist regimes imposed a new
intellectual climate one of the central features of which
was the reorganization of universities on a modern basis.
Important groups of intellectuals devoted their efforts
to updating the circuits of production and transmission
of knowledge, in an effort to catch up with the levels
of international science,[11] and meet the standards
developed in advanced industrial societies. Their effort
of institutional reorganization coincided in several
ways with the modernizing goals and with the assumptions
of desarrollismo. Many intellectuals abandoned the old
pretension of interpreting or leading movements and
redefined their roles. To them, what was at stake was
the creation of a scientific basis that would enable
Latin American countries to develop the economic and
technological "engines" of social change. In this way,
scientists became an articulate group structured around
a specific cultural project. "Scientism" is a term
which has been frequently used to refer to their actual
and perceived cultural policies.

We have already seen how desarrollismo substitutes
technical ind instrumental considerations for a concern
with political control over the processes of development.
It is complemented by scientism in that the latter provides methods and results geared to facilitate technical
manipulation, and neutralizes the value concerns of
inquiry by disguising the connection between knowledge
and interests.

Dependent, or reflex, modernization,[12] and the
depoliticization of thought are central features of the
cultural renovation sought by Latin American scientism.
The transplant of social science to Latin America is in
that respect a paradigmatic case of scientism in a context
of dependence.[13]

The intellectuals who sought to introduce the ideals
of scientific sociology in Latin America have been quite
effective in redefining the role of intellectuals and in
restructuring the order of priorities and the concerns
of knowledge in the area. They belong to a larger group
of scientists who helped to institutionalize modern
disciplines in Latin America. The group was characterized
by a solid scientific training, by the desire to pull
their countries out of economic stagnation, by a high
degree of rationality, and by great effectiveness as
teachers, researchers, and cultural entrepreneurs.
They organized significant research centers, covering
virtually the entire gamut of modern disciplines, from
mathematics to political science.[14] This group of
modernizing scientific intellectuals was quite heterogeneous in terms of specific values and political per-
suations, but in a very general sense they were left-
wing liberals, often assuming militant reformist positions
in university politics. The cultural renovation which
they brought about provoked the resistance of a sizable
and well entrenched traditional sector of the academy.
This resistance, coupled with the fact that many of the
"modernizers" assumed strongly dissident positions
vis-a-vis the status quo, earned them a somewhat undeserved
reputation as radicals. In actual fact, a close look at
their academic and research activities reveals a self-
image that tries strongly to emulate the outlook of their
counterparts in advanced industrial societies.[15]

The faculties of science organized during this
period in some of the larger Latin American countries
offer good examples of the "ideological field" then pre-
vailing. Those institutions were often attacked by
traditional academic groups who saw in them a dangerous
political experiment. On the other hand, radical students
often accused scientists of disregarding urgent issues
for the sake of an abstract and borrowed scientific ideal.

The latter criticism derived from the fact that, in
order to update the scientific level of research
proficiency, theories, methods, equipment, funds, and
even teaching personnel were transplanted from advanced
centers, especially from the United States. As Gino
Germani remarked, "the country of origin is also the
he emonic country in the continent and one of the dominant
ones in the world scene."[16] This was the field of
conflicting interests within which the modernizing
scientists had to carry out their activities. They
founded, with varying degrees of success, a professional
academic environment in each country based on the consensus
about the validity of the scientific method. This emphasis
on scientific rules of procedure served as a principle of
self-definition; they were the scientific vanguard, as
opposed to an entire host of pre-scientific intellectuals
whom they regarded as relics of the past. The dichotomy
between traditionalism and modernity, which the theories
of development popular at the moment imposed with simplistic confidence, also pervaded the Latin American
intellectual milieux. Scientism came to reinforce the
stereotype of Latin American thinkers as enemies of
modernization and technical progress. Today we know to
what extent this image did not correspond to the facts
and to what extent it constituted an ideological counter-
image.[17] In the face of student criticism -- which
suggested that behind scientific modernization stood a
subtle form of cultural colonization scientific intellectuals asserted time and again their faith in the universality
of the scienfific method as the sole guarantee of objectivity
in producing knowledge whose validity was beyond all
interests. The self-image thus projected by scientists
offered an aseptic and optimistic description of the development of scientific knowledge. This simplified self-image
was itself derived from the self-understanding of the
sciences developed in the United States and other centers
of research. Such self-understanding is "scientistic" in
that it reduces the problems posed by the concrete
practice of research as a social process, to formal problems, presumably soluble through the correct application
of rules of scientific procedure.[18] Scientific work and
ideological interests appear, from this perspective as
irreducible entities, in theory as well as practice. The
scientific method is the sole safeguard of objectity and
the only criterion of relevance. The distortion of
objectivity is attributed to subjective factors that are
eventually corrected through the intersubjective practice
of research and scientific communication. The production
of scientific knowledge is then perceived as an autonomous,
cumulative, and self-corrective process. Scientism is

ideological precisely to the extent that it transforms an empirically hypothetical statement into an axiom:

> "Precisely, the character of science as a
> social process, which is based not on isolated
> efforts (the work of each researcher), but on
> the result of a cooperative activity, the product
> of which is the body of scientific propositions
> (provisionally) included by virtue of certain
> norms that constitute the criteria of validation
> and rejection, enables to transcend the relativism
> derived from attachments to values."[19]

The refusal to treat this description as a verifiable (and falsifiable) hypothesis, and its adoption instead as an article of faith, testify to the illusory and ideological character of scientism. The latter blends precisely what it avowedly abhors to mix, namely, descriptive and normative statements.

The laboratory or the research center replace the old ivory tower as the illusory refuge of knowledge from extra-theoretical interests. Ideological interferences are perceived as coming from the outside. Otherwise, the social practice of research presumably provides its own correctives, as a system of rigorous action and communication, based on explicit rules of procedure which are universally accepted by the community of scientists. Knowledge would then presumably advance unhampered by virtue of an immanent mechanism, leaving on the wayside the remnants of ideologies. From this standpoint, "value-neutral" scientists challenged the pursuits of politically committed thought. Yet this self-understanding of scientific praxis bears the hallmark of ideology plus the additional defect of maskerading as anti-ideology.

The scientistic self-understanding of the sciences does not analyze scientific praxis in concrete terms, but rather in terms of its desired goals. It is reluctant to face the implications of a sociology of science and presents in its stead a reconstructed logic of inquiry. Scientism thus analyzes a social process -- the production of scientific knowledge -- as if it were a formal-logical development. This is tantamount to a refusal to consider the pragmatic dimension of scientific communication and action -- questions of scientific policies, choice of subjects, selection of methods and approach, the connotative aspects of scientific discourse -- problems which are not understandable, let alone soluble, by recourse to the formal rules of a reconstructed logic of inquiry. Objectivity is not, for scientism, an empirical social problem. By this token it contradicts its own tenets and becomes vulnerable to an immanent critque.

The scientistic self-understanding of science per-
forms several important functions. The illusion of
objectivism and the fetishism of the scientific method
promote the fiction that unhampered dialogue is possible
everywhere and at any time -- at least among scientists.
On the one hand, this fiction (false consciousness) has
a protective function, for most sciences lack the means
for dealing with the risks that appear once the connection
of knowledge and social interests has been comprehended
on the level of self-reflection. This situation might
appear justifiable in the case of the natural sciences,
but it becomes inexcusable in the case of the social
sciences, the concepts and methods of which are indeed
pertinent to self-reflection. The illusion of objectivity
protects against the crudest forms of relativism and
irrational regression. On the other hand, this illusion
protects the ideological implications of certain scientific practices from critical examination and leaves the
emancipatory potentialities of rational inquiry in a
frozen state. With regard to Latin America, the scientistic
illusion offered to its adherents the opportunity of feeling
positively immersed in the process of social change without
having to assume any concrete political commitment. Science
reduced to method was identified tout court with modernization. Hence the intimate connection of scientism with
desarrollismo.
      The events of recent years have nevertheless
exploded the scientistic delusion. The concrete practice
of research has been compromised by obvious international
political interests -- a situation that has rendered the
fragility of the methodological asepsis painfully obvious
as a safeguard of objectivity or even integrity.[20] Scientific activity has been exposed as a far less autonomous
and self-corrective mechanism than scientistic theses
pretended. The very innocence of those theses has been
questioned. True, from everyday experience we know that
ideas serve often enough to furnish our actions with
justifying motives in place of the real ones. What is
called rationalization at this level is called ideology
at the level of collective action. In both cases the
manifest content of statements is falsified by consciousness' unreflected tie to human interests, despite its
illusion of automony. The discipline of trained thought
thus correctly aims at excluding such interests. Yet
the aforementioned crises have revealed to what extent
the available routines developed by science to guard
against the subjectivity of opinion fail to counter the
uncontrolled influence of interests on a deeper level,
which derives less form the individual than from the
objective situation of social groups. Episodes such as

the well-publicized scandal of Project Camelot showed
how little the sociology of knowledge had affected the
standards of self-reflection of social scientists. At
the same time, the sharpening of social and political
conflicts in several countries has led to the dismantling
of research centers, the dispersion of research teams, and
finally, the direct military intervention in universities
by regimes which, ironically, proclaim a desire to de-
politicize knowledge.[21] The decade of the 70's opens
with great uncertainty about the viability of scientistic
ideals in Latin America. In any case, recent experiences
have imposed on the consciousness of many Latin American
scientists dilemmas and contradictions that have hitherto
remained obscure.

In more concrete terms, "scientism" refers today
to the condition of those Latin American scientists who
are adapted to the international scientific market --
itself dominated by highly developed branches of knowledge -- and who have abandoned the concern for the social
and cultural implications of their activities in the
context of Latin American dependence. They devote their
efforts to specialized research, accepting the goals and
standards established by international centers.[22] Some
important consequences follow from this situation. One
of them is that scientism reinforces cultural and other
forms of dependence in Latin America. The situation of
dependence finds expression both in the internal development of scientific research and organization in each
country, and also in the international "brain drain"
from dependent to metropolitan areas.[23] "Scientistic"
scientists in Latin American countries tend to become
perpetually frustrated. Those devoted to basic research
and who aspire to enter the higher circles of international
scientific communities are often frustrated by innumerable
institutional and cultural obstacles in their countries:
from outright suspicion or lack of official encouragement
to absence of funds and equipment as well as permanent
insecurity. In seeking to escape these frustrations, many
develop intimate ties with foreign institutions operating
abroad or in situ, the priorities of which are by no
means consonant with the best interests of Latin American
countries. Other scientists have lowered their standards
and have become gatherers of data for processing elsewhere or else apply locally the results of research done
elsewhere. They tend to be more thoroughly "deintellec-
tualized" than basic researchers, in the sense of being
specialized scientific workers. The intellectual predica-
ment is strikingly parallel to the economic constellation
of dependence: Latin American countries become producers
of raw data and exporters of qualified scientific personnel.

The earlier scientistic optimism concerning the progressive functions of scientific modernization has therefore
become much more tentative and qualified. Both the sharpening of conflicts and the particular contradictions of
the scientist's role-set have led many to impose on their
activities new standards of self-reflection and therefore
to approach with interest the problems of the sociology
of knowledge.
        Some have developed these concerns as a result of
a critical examination of the current organization of
teaching and research. In 1964, a Latin American sociologist stressed the fact that the social sciences in the
area were limited to gathering data which were later
processed outside Latin America, more often than not
guided by considerations of political or economic domination.[24] In this sense, Latin America was being transformed -- according to that report -- into a data export
center. The development of research since then has lent
more support to this contention.[25] In other cases, the
critical self-reflection of scientists has been triggered
by their general opposition to the status quo. Those who,
among scientists, are seriously concerned with the radical
overhauling of social structures in Latin America, have
recently proposed a new order of priorities for scientific
work, so as to bring it more in accordance with a revolutionary political project. What emerges is a cultural
orientation radically opposed to scientistic desarrollismo.
        A recent polemical essay by an Argentine mathe-
matician has concisely presented the dilemma that faces
those Latin American scientists who reject the established
social system.[26] They must either continue to work as
cogs in the system which they reject, or else substitute
political militancy for their intellectual concerns. A
possible third option consists of a sterile combination
of both activities. As a way out of this dilemma, radical
scientists have proposed the retooling or conversion of
science so that it may help to change the social system;
in other words, gearing the entire structure of research
towards the social, political, economic, add technological
aspects of radical change in both their theoretical and
practical aspects. The "politicization" of science which
they seek means the conceptual, theoretical, and methodological conversion of efforts in the light of new priorities. In this manner, the rebel scientists explicitly
reject the scientistic standards of value-neutrality which
they view as illusory anyhow. The conversion of which
they speak is not simply a redefinition of applied science
which could be accomplished by using the existing scientific tools so as to deal with national or regional
problems. It rather entails questioning the very

"universality" of scientific organization, by critically
analyzing the international scientific community as a
social system that sanctions topics of research, establishes priorities, defines which are the proper methods
and general approaches, and distributes resources and
prestige according to certain pre-established rules
themselves tied -- it is claimed -- unexamined interests.
The criticism thus reaches the very basis of the scientific leadership of some countries and the intellectual
dominance of certain branches of science. The alternative which they offer is a different assignment of
resources and a different allocation of priorities so as
to convert research towards goals that transcend the
established social organization. The critique touches
the foundation of today's technological culture:

> "A new social system formed in opposition to the
> existing one will conceivably show less interest
> in psychoanalysis, algebraic topology, and quantic
> electrodynamics, than in theories of education,
> the general ecological balance of the planet,
> creative imagination, or ethics."[27]

As opposed to traditional critiques of science,
this new intellectual rebellion proposes an alternative
use of technological achievements.
True, a new society will conceivably develop a new
science in terms of priorities, interests, approaches, and
methods. Yet how is it going to develop in the womb of
the present social organization, particularly in dependent
areas like Latin America? As long as this question remains
unanswered, the projects of scientific conversion will stay
trapped in utopia. Nonetheless, the very fact that an
utopian ideal should develop among scientists is itself
a symptom of a new cultural horizon -- the opening of a new
stage of scientific self-reflection. In what concerns
Latin America, it indicates that there are scientists who
do not renounce a view of the social totality and who
seek to establish problem-areas independently of dominant
powers. We should recall Baran's statement:

> "For what marks the intellectual and distinguishes
> him from the intellect workers and indeed from all
> others is that his concern with the entire histor-
> ical process is not a tangential interest but
> permeates his thought and significantly affects
> his work."[28]

The concern about the socio-historical "totality"
has today ceased to be, in Latin America, the monopoly of
the pensadores. In other words, side by side with the

"intellect workers," there are scientists who conceive
their responsibility as not simply knowing, but also
knowing how and for whom their knowledge matters.
     With regard to Latin American social science,
the development of new concepts and approaches that promise
a better understanding of the social structures and processes of the area has taken place -- as we have seen --
in opposition to the "working truths" prevalent in metropolitan countries. Therefore, the growth of substantial
sociological knowledge has gone hand in hand with a
sharpening of the standards of scientific self-reflection.
Today, the construction of theory in Latin America is
accompanied by a metatheoretical consciousness in many ways
more advanced than the current scientific self-understanding
of mainstream Western sociology.

3   Retrospect and Prospect

     I have so far surveyed the development of the study
of ideology in Latin America. It has been my contention
that the study of ideology has come to its proper focus
as a result of a better understanding, on the part of Latin
American social scientists, of the phenomenon of dependence.
I have also tried to show the ideological functions of
scientism within the context of the dependent culture of
Latin America, and pointed to some of the reactions it
has provoked. Now, insofar as scientism has been the main
mode of self-understanding social science in Latin America,
and insofar as social science in the area has recently
started to achieve theoretical autonomy against many of the
working truths of mainstream metropolitan approaches, the
perception of the relationship between science -- specifically social science --, ideology, and dependence has
attained greater sharpness than before and perhaps also
greater sharpness than elsewhere. As a result of this a
new interest has developed for such problems as the politics
of scientific research, the ideological dimensions of
sociology, and the sociology of scientific knowledge in
general. The interest for these problems is not exclusively
theoretical: its real aim is emancipatory self-reflection.
I believe that this interest has opened new prospects for
the sociology of knowledge with bearing well beyond the
limits of Latin America. I shall presently discuss its
bearing on the notion of ideology and the conception of
its proper study and then go on to indicate some of the
issues which a more vital and active sociology of knowledge
than what we have had so far might turn to in the future.

3.1 On the Concept of Ideology

As a result of what has been discussed above and throughout this paper, three distinct meanings of the concept of ideology have emerged: the positivist, the sociological, and the critical conceptions. I have implicitly criticized the first, and utizized the other two, conceptions.

Positivistic thought has usually defined "ideology" -- in contrast to "science" -- by characterizing it as erroneous knowledge. According to this conception, the confrontation of a given body of thought with the knowledge produced by the correct application of the scientific method determines whether such body of thought is ideological or not. In other words, positivism defines ideology as distorted thought. It partakes of all the difficulties and contradictions that were indicated in the case of scientism.

The sociological interpretation distinguishes ideology from science as systems of representations in terms of function rather than in terms of truth content. Ideology is defined as a system of representations for which the social-practical function is more central than the theoretical function. From a sociological standpoint, the distortion of thought is in principle independent from its ideological character. In this sense, the sociological interpretation is strictly "value neutral". An important variant of the sociological conception characterizes ideology not as a type of discourse or language, but as a specific level of signification of any discourse that is transmitted in a concrete social situation.[29] This characterization is derived from the observation that any message transmitted in a social situation inevitably carries, beyond its explicit, literal meaning, a configuration of suggestive or associative implications. "Ideology" refers then, to the connotative dimensions of discourse and the pragmatic aspects of communication in social situations.

The critical notion of ideology transforms the sociological perspective into an imputation of the "correctness" or the "alienation" of consciousness. It focuses on the coincidence and discrepancy between the historical self-knowledge of groups and the actual consequences of their actions.[30] Hence its preoccupation with the problem of "false consciousness." The critical perspective transcends "value neutrality." "Critical" means, in this context, the concern with going beyond the theoretic goal of social science -- the production of nomological knowledge -- to determine when theoretical statements grasp invariant regularities of social action as such and when they express frozen relations of dependence that can in principle be

transformed. Ideology is characterized as reification.
The critique of ideology therefore seeks to release the
subject from dependence on hypostatized powers, setting
off a process of self-reflection. The cognitive interest
is emancipatory and not exclusively theoretical.[31]

3.2 The Relevance and Problem-Areas of the Sociology of Knowledge

The word "relevance" is as frequent in use today
as it is ambiguous. In the light of previous remarks its
meaning becomes, however, more precise. I shall try to
characterize this relevance of the sociology of knowledge
in a set of propositions in the way of a summary of the
implications of what has been said so far.

3.2.1

The development and enormous success of scientific
research in our age has changed the character and functions
of ideology. Far from witnessing an end to ideologies --
as positivism and scientism would like us to believe -- we
see that the field of operation of ideology today "passes
through" science. It consists of all those options in the
construction of scientific messages that cannot be
decided upon in terms of the formal rules of scientific
procedure. This field is especially large in the case of
the social sciences, but it is operative in all the sciences
and constitutes their ideological aura. This field is
nevertheless amenable to empirical analysis. Such analysis
would focus on the conditions of the production of knowledge and on the decision-making processes leading to the
choice of the options mentioned above. Thus, my first
thesis is that, by considering objectivity as an empirical
social problem -- i.e., as the study of the conditions of
the social production of knowledge as determining factors
in the pragmatic dimensions of scientific discourse --
the sociology of knowledge finds its proper focus today as
an inquiry into the politics of science.

3.2.2

The development of social science has relegated the
sociology of knowledge to a specialized and peripheral
position. Historically this was the result of the late
development of social science, which borrowed heavily from
the scientific self-understanding of more advanced sciences.
In consequence, my second proposition is that, in order to
be able to approach the problem of ideology in a scientific age, the sociology of knowledge should first break
the dependence of social science on the self-understanding of

other disciplines. The starting point of research should
therefore be the sociology of sociology.

3.2.3

        The self-understanding of science has largely been
illusory because most sciences lack the means to compre-
hand the ties between knowledge and interests. Their
specialized knowledge and theoretical pursuit drive them
away from the perception of the conditions of production
of their truths. This is in principle not the case with
the social sciences, the concepts, approaches, and method
of which are indeed pertinent to an analysis of their own
processes of knowledge. This is one precise meaning of
the term "relevant": sociological concepts are meta-
theoretically relevant. This is what places the sociology
of knowledge at the center of relevance of social science:
it is the meeting ground of substantive knowledge and self-
reflection -- a situation which determines the uniqueness
os social science. My third thesis therefore is that the
sociology of knowledge should occupy a place in sociological
theory commensurate with its relevance as defined above.
        Perhaps the main thrust of these propositions is
the belief that the central task of the sociology of knowledge today should be the extension of the self-understanding
of scientific reason. Its ultimate relevance shall be
measured by its contribution to substituting enlightened
action for instrumental manipulation in established and
developing technological societies.

REFERENCES

1. Cf. J. Medina Echavarria, Consideraciones sociológicas
    sobre el desarrollo económico de América Latina,
    Buenos Aires: Solar/Hachette, 1964; G. Beyhaut, Raices
    contemporaneas de America Latina, Buenos Aires: EUDEBA,
    1965; and J. Lambert, América Latina: estructuras
    sociales e instituciones políticas, Barcelona: Ariel.
2. See the following: Andre Gunder Frank, "Sociology of
    Development and Underdevelopment of Sociology," in
    Catalyst, No. 5; 20-73 (1967); José Nun, "Los para-
    digmas de la ciencia politica: un intento de concep-
    tualización," Revista Latinoamericana de Sociología,
    2 (1): 67-97 (1966); Rodolfo Stavenhagen, "Siete tesis
    equivocadas sobre America Latina." Desarrollo indo-
    americano, 1 (4): 23-27 (1966); and Pablo Gonzalez
    Casanova, Las categorias del desarrollo economico y
    la investigación en ciencias sociales, México: Uni-
    versidad Nacional Autonoma, Instituto de Investigacions
    Sociales: 1967.

3. Cf. especially Andre Gunder Frank, Capitalism and Underdevelopment in Latin America, New York: Monthly Review Press, 1967, and Tulio Halperin Donghi, Historia contemporanea de America Latina, Madrid: 1969.
4. Cf. Celso Furtado, "U. S. Hegemony and the Future of Latin America," The World Today, Vol. 22, No. 9: 375-385 (1966).
5. See F. H. Cardoso and E. Faletto, Desarrollo y dependencia en América Latina, Mexico: Siglo XXI, 1969.
6. See Tomas A. Vasconi, "Cultura, ideología, dependencia y alienación," in La crisis del desarrollismo y la nueva dependencia, edited by the Instituto de Estudios Peruanos, Lima: Moncloa editores, 1969; and Fernando Uricoechea, Intelectuales y desarrollo en America Latina, Buenos Aires: Centro Editor de America Latina, 1969.
7. Cf. Cardoso & Faletto, op. cit., and Uricoechea, op. cit.
8. See M. C. Tavares, "Auge y declinacion de la industrialización sustitutiva en Brasil," Boletín economico de América Latina, Vol. 9, No. 1 (1964).
9. Cardoso & Faletto, op. cit., pp. 143, 155-156.
10. Cf. Uricoechea, op. cit., pp. 69 and ff.
11. Uricoechea, op. cit., pp. 73 ff. Cf. also Darcy Ribeiro, La universidad latinoamericana, Montevideo: CEAL and Departamento de Publicaciones de la Universidad de la Republica, 1968, esp. Chapters IV and V.
12. See Darcy Ribeiro, "Universities and Social Development," in S. M. Lipset and A. Solari, eds., Elites in Latin America, New York, Oxford University Press, 1967.
13. Cf. the publications of the Centro Latinoamericano de Pesquisas em Cienciais Sociais de Rio de Janeiro, esp. the following: Nos. 4, 8, 9, and 13 (1959-60). See also Johan Galtung, "Los factores socioculturales y el desarrollo de la sociología en América Latina," Revista Latinoamericana de Sociología, Vol. I (1): 72-101 (1965). Cf. also the transactions of the VII Latin American Congress of Sociology, Bogota: 1965, vol. I.
14. Cf. Darcy Ribeiro, La universidad latinoamericana, pp. 127 ff.
15. See especially Gino Germani, La sociología en la América Latina: Problemas y Perspectivas, Buenos Aires: EUDEBA, 1964.
16. Germani, op. cit., p. 7.
17. Cf. Gloria Cucullu, "El estereotipo del 'intelectual latinoamericano'. Su relación con los procesos económicos y sociales," Revista Latinoamericana de Sociología, 4 (1): 38-62 (1968).
18. See the review of Germani's book, op. cit., by Eliseo Veron in Conducta, estructura y comunicación, Buenos Aires: J. Alvarez, 1968, Chapter XI. Cf. also Juan E. Corradi, "The Sociology of Knowledge in Latin

America," VI World Congress of Sociology, Evian, 1966; and Theotonio Dos Santos, "El nuevo caracter de la dependencia," in La crisis del desarrolismo, op. cit., pp. 102 ff.

19. Germani, op. cit., p. 146.
20. See Gregorio Selser, Espionaje en América Latina. El Pentagono y las tecnicas sociologicas, Buenos Aires: Iguazu, 1966. Cf. also Juan E. Corradi and John David Ober, "Pax Americana and Pax Sociologica. Remarks on the Politics of Sociology," Catalyst, No. 2:41-54 (1966).
21. On the Brazilian case, see A. L. Machado Neto, "El derrumbe de la Universidad de Brasilia," in Darcy Rebeiro, op. cit., Appendix II. On the Argentine case, cf. Juan E. Corradi, "The Assault on Argentine Universities," Alternatives, California, Feb. 1967. See also Enrique Oteiza, "La emigracion de personal altamente calificado de la Argentina. Un caso de 'brain drain' latinoamericano," Instituto T Di Tella, CIE, Documento de Trabajo No. 14, esp. pp. 48 ff.
22. See especially Oscar Varsavsky, Ciencia, politica y cientificismo, Buenos Aires: CEAL, 1969, pp. 39 ff.
23. Cf. Glaucio Ary Dillon Soares and Mireya S. de Soares, "La fuga de los intelectuales," Aportes, Paris, No. 2, Oct. 1966.
24. Jorge Graciarena, "Algunas consideraciones sobre la cooperación internacional y el desarrollo reciente de la investigación sociológica," Revista Latino-americana de Sociología, 1 (2): 231-242 (1965).
25. Cf. Eliseo Veron, op. cit., p. 297.
26. Oscar Varsavsky op. cit.
27. Varsavsky, op. cit., p. 21.
28. Paul A. Baran, "The Commitment of the Intellectual," Monthly Review, May 1961, p. 12.
29. See Veron, Conducta, estructura y communicación, Chapters X and XI.
30. Cf. Jerzy Szacki, "Remarks on the Marxian Concept of 'False Consciousness'," The Polish Sociological Bulletin, No. 2, 1966.
31. See Jurgen Habermas "The Process of Knowledge and Human Interests: A General Perspective," Frankfurt: Suhrkamp Verlag, 1968. Mimeo. trans. by Jeremy Shapiro, reprinted in D. Emmet and A. MacIntyre, eds., Sociological Theory and Philosophical Analysis, New York: MacMillan, 1970.

THE ANDEAN RURAL PROLETARIANS [*]

Thomas C. Greaves

Especially since the 1930 appearance of Robert
Redfield's Tepoztlan, a Mexican Village, the ethnology
of peasants and other peoples of the agrarian countryside
has grown to sizeable dimensions. During the early years
of this growth such concepts as folk society, Great and
Little Traditions, and the folk-urban continuum--all
associated with Redfield--gained substantial influence,
and subsequent decline. But in other respects, Redfield's
views regarding rural non-tribal peoples are still very
much with us. One abiding aspect of the Redfield legacy,
not, of course, stemming solely from him nor universally
followed, is that these peoples tend to be labeled with
the single term, peasant. This practice has carried
with it the necessary implication that there is a certain
sameness about them, a characteristic homogeneity, that
warrants using a single label.
  Though the ethnography of such people since at
least the end of World War Two clearly depicts a plethora
of cultural and social diversity, those who have argued
that the agrarian countryside contains people not well
described as "peasants" have had to wage an up-hill
battle against the inclusiveness of that label. Articles
by Mintz distinguishing rural proletarians (1953), by
Fallers defining non-peasant African cultivators (1961),
and by Helms on "purchasers" (1969) are examples of
explicit efforts to undercut the pervasive assumption
that in the Third World anyone who is poor, uneducated,
farms and lives in the countryside must be a peasant
and is reasonably well described by that label. This
paper, though having its own objectives, is consistent
with these efforts. It singles out the sort of non-
peasant ruralite, the rural proletarian, limiting its
geographic purview to the Andean zone of South America.
  Anthropological knowledge of rural proletarians
since Mintz' pioneering contributions (1951, 1953, 1956)
has grown slowly and, in sharp contrast to peasant
studies, without developing a core of theorists identified
with the category. Articles and monographs have accumulated as ethnographers encountered peoples who seemed
aptly described as rural proletarians, but it has remained
until now to pull the literature together around a working
definition, to work out the distribution of such people,
to examine the reasonableness of the category in
delineating a generic and distinctive social type, and

[*]This article was first published in *Anthropological Quarterly*,
Vol. 45, No.2, pp 65-83 (April 1972).

to suggest hypotheses regarding the processes by which
they are formed.

A brief review of the world ethnographic literature
employing the term would reveal that attention paid to
them has been sporadic except for the Andean zone. Only
in that region has a significant corpus of ethnography
on them developed, though there, too, its growth has been
uneven and is not the produce of a long-term, broadly
shared research concern among Andeanists. Yet because
the category "rural proletarian" is recurringly used in
this literature and a part of the Andeanists' vocabulary,
one may draw together the available information on these
people for the Andes in terms of the goals outlined above.
In doing this, light may be shed on some more specific
problems. It is not self evident, for instance, which
occupational groups are included. Nor is it clear that
rural proletarians as such have much cultural distinc-
tiveness. Too, one wonders what contrasts are implied
between this category and such concurrent terms as
"migrant laborers," "Contemporary Quechua," "mestizos,"
"serfs," and, of course, "peasants." Clarifying these
issues should put us in a better position to evaluate
whether or not it is worth singling out Andean rural
proletarians as a particular or noteworthy variety of
people.

Definition and Distribution

What is a rural proletarian? Mintz's definition
serves as a good beginning point. He defines them as

> ...(1) landless and essentially property-
> less, lacking any means of production other
> than their own labor; (2) wage earners...;
> (3) predominantly store-buying since they
> cannot produce more than a small part of
> the basic commodities; ...[and] (4) pre-
> vailingly employed by corporate entities,
> rather than working for themselves or for
> an owner-employer with whom they maintain
> continuous face-to-face relations.
>
> (1956: 351-2).

Clearly all four characteristics are interrelated, the
first three being especially bound together.

Thus rural proletarians are primary producers
controlling neither significant financial capital nor the
major material means of production. They are wage-earners
--individuals who continuously gain their livelihood by
selling their labor for cash wages and supplements which
are then usually exchanged in a market economy for the
essentials of life.

But though the rural proletarian is fundamentally
a wage earner, not all wage earners are proletarians.
Wage earning occurs in a variety of Andean contexts, from
local paid-labor exchanges within small villages to the
rank and file of industrial behemoths. Those who are
proletarians will be employed by corporate enterprise,
though not always of large scale. This is by no means
an idle correlation. As Mintz's own research suggests,
corporate enterprises in rural areas are essential to
generating rural proletarians--that when attention is
directed to the process by which rural proletarians
emerge, one finds that corporate enterprise plays a
principal formative role.[1] A private capitalist corpo-
ration is the usual form, but this is not always the case.
Expropriated sugar plantations in Peru and Cuba continue
to support rural proletariats while being state owned.
So far, then, the rural proletarian is a wage earner
gaining his livelihood from corporate enterprise.

It should be noted here that wage earning within
a corporate enterprise will generally be on a full-time,
relatively permanent basis. Particularly the data from
Peru indicate that this generates a life style contrasting
sharply with that of people who combine some wage earning
with peasant subsistence activities, commonly through
seasonal migration. This contrast, which is accentuated
by Peruvian labor legislation strongly favoring the
permanent employee, is especially apparent where one finds
both permanent, proletarian labor and migratory laborers
engaged by the same enterprise (cf. Greaves 1967). Thus
the rural proletarian is the "landless laborer," the
"peón permanente," the "obrero de planilla," the resident
laborer.

As a third defining feature, the rural proletarian
is located in, not surprisingly, a rural area.[2] For the
strict typologies, their being rural will be the most
difficult to sustain. Some of the best examples of rural
proletarians, such as those on large sugar plantations,
find them aggregated in very large numbers. Even though
often located far from so-called "natural" towns and
cities, their residential nucleus often numbers many
thousands of people. Hence their status as rural people
becomes difficult to defend. But the very difficulty of
describing them as rural in fact discloses a feature of
great importance--their manifold relations with, and
similarities to, urban proletarians. I will return to
this presently.

We are thus provided with a minimal definition.
The three characteristics set forth - largely a recom-
bination of those given by Mintz - seem sufficient:
they are wage earners, basically full-time, associated
with corporate enterprise, and they are in some sense

(an uneasy one, to be sure) rural. All this is necessary
because in the literature the term rural proletarian has
been applied thus far only to agriculturalists, an
occupational attribute this minimal definition leaves
open. This is not contrived; there is nothing inherently
agrarian in the words, rural proletarian. Two points can
now be elaborated: one, that people outside agriculture
can be, and are, rural proletarians; and two, that the
significance of the category becomes more apparent when
we move away from this spurious focus on agriculture. A
review of the ethnographic evidence for rural proletarians
in the Andean area is now in order.

The agricultural proletarians are a useful beginning point since they are the ones labeled as such in the
Andean literature. The most prominent cases are the
rural proletarians of the large sugar plantations in the
coastal valleys of Peru. Solomon Miller (1964, 1967)
has done detailed work on the recently nationalized
estates near Trujillo, Patch (1959) has looked at similar
groups at Paramonga, and Collin Delavaud has provided
somewhat thinner data for the northern coast (1964).
Lang's brief paper on San Carlos (1965) extends the range
to the few sugar plantations in Ecuador. Delbert Fitchett
(1963: 181, 1966: 9-10) mentions that rice and cotton
plantations in Northern Peru can be farmed with proletarian labor, but by no means as consistently as are the
sugar plantations. No one has looked into the occasional
cattle ranches dotted along the coast; brief visits by
the author to Batan Grande above Chiclayo suggest that
they may be found there too, but closer observation is
necessary in order to be sure.

Recent work by Louis Faron (1967: 267-268), José
Matos Mar (1964) and Greaves (1968) shows that large-
scale agriculture carried on with proletarian labor is
not confined to the plantations on the Andean coast. At
least two structurally different types of smaller estates,
the coastal haciendas and the fundos, use permanently
employed wage laborers to carry on their direct cultivation, supplemented with other types of direct and
indirect labor.[3]

Except along the Pacific coast on the plantations,
coastal haciendas and fundos, agricultural proletarians
are difficult to discern. They are particularly hard to
pick out among cultivators in the Peruvian highlands.
Solomon Miller's study of Granadabama (cf. 1964, 1967),
for example, reports no group having the features of a
proletariat despite the fact that the estate had been
administered by a coastal sugar plantation for twenty-
eight years. Elsewhere in the literature, traditional
haciendas Vicos, Lauramarca, Capana, Chujuni, Cochela,
Panaschachi, those surveyed by Favre, and (in Ecuador)

Atahualpa and Colta Monja all reflect minor variations
on the standard highland model; no proletarians are
present.[4] Thus on the basis of the currently available
ethnography, the agrarian rural proletarians are reported
in significant numbers only on the coast, employed by
the plantations (particularly those cultivating sugar),
coastal haciendas and fundos.

It was noted above that wage-earning agricultural
workers are the only group to which Andeanists have
applied the term. However, there is no compelling reason
why this term cannot be extended to at least two other
groups of rural wage earners, the miners and the oil
workers. Certainly they fit the minimal definition set
out above. But more than that, one can show that they
have many more than the three minimal features in common
with, say, the plantation cortador de cana. Therefore,
Their inclusion will not only further our understanding
of the class we are dealing with, but also demonstrate
that the category is significant beyond the immediate
interests of research hinging on the three definitional
attributes.

Our knowledge of mining populations in the Andean
region is extremely limited. The very cursory overview
provided by Bourricaud (1962) at Cerro de Pasco, and
materials from the Kami, Siglo XX and Colquiri Mines of
Bolivia (Vasquez 1969, Nash 1970, Hickman and Brown 1971)
are the major highlights of the extant field work. To
justify the inclusion of the miners is essentially a
mechanical procedure, given the defining characteristics
set out above. One might question their rurality, since
the residential nucleus of plantations can also be very
large, the issue is not one of excluding the miners from
the category, but rather, of properly describing the
category itself. We shall deal with this problem later.

Parallel reasoning obliges us to include the oil
workers. In Peru our descriptions of them stem mainly
from the former I.P.C. operations at Talara (Patch 1958,
McIrwin 1969, and Arbazia, 1961, cited in McIrwin) but
data which corroborate their findings can be found in
studies by Havens and Romieux (1966) and Bernal (1969) at
Barrancabermeja in Colombia. We have, again, in the
petroleum workers a social group apparently quite similar
to the miners and the agrarian rural proletariat.

Thus the main groups enclosed by the three defining
criteria are the various agrarian proletarians, the miners
and the oil workers. While the reader might well suggest
other groups--the Peruvian anchovy fishermen, for instance
--this paper will be limited to the three already
described. But what can turn this from an exercise in
classification to a more productive effort is the fact
that these three groups manifest further, more significant

similarities. These additional features not only add
further descriptive detail, but also begin to tap the
distinctive configuration of qualities that makes the
Andean rural proletariat a productive focus of research.
The next section of this paper examines four such
similarities.

Features of the Andean Rural Proletarians

1. The rural proletariat consistently serves as a major
channel of social and spatial mobility, and does this in
two ways: by recruitment into the group, and through the
loss of members out of the group. For sugar plantations
recruitment into the proletariat has been analyzed in
detail by Miller (cf. 1965) and Patch (1959), and has also
been described for the coastal haciendas (Greaves 1967,
1968: 236-241), and more briefly treated by Hammel (1962),
Faron (1967), and Matos Mar (1964). Among the very
largest plantation, oil and mining companies, however,
mobility into the proletariat over the past fifteen years
has sharply diminished. Beginning with the late fifties
these corporations sought to reduce their labor forces as
the demands of unions and labor legislation became more
burdensome; even the sons of the proletarians are refused
jobs, much to the consternation of their unions (Miller
1964: 117-118, McIrwin 1969: 2). However, in smaller,
less industrialized enterprises - less visible but far
more numerous - the recruitment of highlanders still
flourishes.

The process of mobility is not limited to the
sources of rural proletarians, but extends to the many
who abandon their workmates each year. While worker
turnover seems to vary widely, field work from four
coastal haciendas at Viru on the Peruvian coast showed
staggering turnover rates, with about half of the proletarian labor force resigning and leaving every three
years. Further, those who resign tended to be the ones
recently recruited, indicating that for them the rural
proletarian status was a kind of mobility tube and not a
more permanent affiliation.[5] In the case of the larger
plantations and mines where management has quit hiring,
the mobility process is altered, but not eliminated. As
both McIrvin (1969) and Miller (1967) show, out-migration
shifts to the offspring of rural proletarians, unable to
secure work in their fathers' trade.

To say, however, that people who become rural
proletarians change and usually improve their relative
social status understates the magnitude and transforma-
tional qualities this shift commonly entails. A very
heavy component of those becoming Andean rural proletarians abandon a former status as "Indians," an identity

not only socially disvalued, but locally viewed as of
a different cultural and racial order. The rural
proletarians emphatically affirm their identity as cholos,
criollos or mestizos, terms defined as much by their not
being Indian as by traits of their own. To them, Indians
are innately inferior, servile under authority, psycho-
logically brutish, untrustworthy, morally undisciplined,
absurdly quaint, and incapable of generating their own
social progress. Paradoxically, most rural proletarians
are themselves former Indians, a fact revealed with
reluctance and not perceived as a common occurance. Thus
mobility for them amounts to more than incremental social
advantage. It requires a radical change of personal
identity and a denial of one's past. Patch (1959) has
called this process "Hispanization" and Miller (1965),
"proletarianization." In these and most other descriptions it is described as an acculturational process, that
those who transfer make a shift from Indian culture to
mestizo culture. Determining the magnitude of real
cultural difference is, I think, a more complex issue than
has been realized, but regardless of the degree to which
cultural change is involved, clearly the metamorphosis of
the individual as he moves from Indian to proletarian
status is sweeping and profound.

2. These features of the mobility process relate to a
second feature common to rural proletarians, that the
social milieu in which they live contains markedly different, sharply ranked social statuses juxtaposed to
their own. A useful example is provided by the coastal
hacienda. On these estates, found in the majority of
Peruvian coastal valleys, the proletarians are only one of
three components to the labor force. Marginal lands for
which management is reluctant to commit scarce and costly
development capital are cultivated indirectly by peasant
sharecroppers providing their own capital to bring the
land under plow. Rural proletarians view these people
as too tradition-bound, too concerned with family and
community, too divorced from the cultural mainstream, and
too poor by their standards, forfeiting the obvious
benefits of the proletarians' secularized, mobile, cash-
based life. While the peasant sharecroppers would be the
last to agree, rural proletarians perceive them to have
a decidedly inferior life-style. Another laboring group
is the contract laborers, Indians recruited in the highlands and brought down to the coast on short-term
contracts. Even though a majority of the proletarians
have Indian origins and first came to the estate as
contract laborers, the public view persists that Indian
contract laborers are innately inferior, too docile and
ignorant to ever form a union or demand better treatment,

and justly deserve the unpleasant sorts of work which the
unionized proletarians are happy to see allocated to them.
Within the coastal hacienda milieu the contract laborers
rank at the very bottom of the social scale. Above the
proletarians are two more types of people who are
similarly remote, the white-collar administrative group
and, at the apex, the elite landowner. That their worlds
are of sharply different constructions is clearly visible
in the often tragic misunderstandings underlying incidents
of labor conflict (cf. Greaves 1968: 281-304). Thus the
proletarian worker on the coastal hacienda lives in a
milieu of sharply defined, graded statuses, each perceived
not simply as a matter of occupation, but as a life-way
with its own customs, values, and psychological
dispositions.

The same status pluralism confronts the proletarian
of the mine, the plantation or the oil center, but with
differences of detail. The reported ethnography depicts
them in large population clusters numbering several
hundred to many thousands. Evidently in such large groups
the process of status transfer is slowed and provides many
intermediate "stopping points" between Indian and mestizo
configurations. Retaining Indian traits, however, is not
without costs, and as a general rule the higher one's
status within the proletarian community, the less one's
status, behavior and self-identity are described as
"Indian" (cf. Patch 1959: 508, Miller 1967: 202-206,
Hickman and Brown 1971: 362). Beyond the proletarian
group they are confronted with other statuses in the form
of a merchantile population, a large, internally graded
white-collar bureaucracy, and a union political hierarchy
which contains officials at great social remove from the
ordinary laborer. A rather different constellation of
statuses probably obtains in smaller, more remote mining
camps but no published ethnography is yet available. To
summarize this point, then, a second salient feature of
the rural proletarian as a class is that they are
consistently found in contexts of sharply distinguished,
ranked social statuses.

3. A third major characteristic of rural proletarians
concerns their reference groups. It is not surprising
that the labor union, which is becoming universal among
them, has been instrumental in establishing a self-
identity covered by the Spanish word, obrero. This word
links them in more than semantic terms with their cohorts
in other rural enterprises, and (of special significance)
with their counterparts in the city. They do not refer
to themselves as obreros rurales (rural workers), but
simply obreros (workers). And the compass of the term
coincides with the boundaries of their reference group.

To illustrate, the major parent union for wage laborers
on Peruvian coastal haciendas is now the Unión Sindical.
It has locals not only on haciendas and smaller properties, but also in urban industries such as bottling
plants and canning factories. The fact that the Unión
Sindical is able to appeal successfully for war chest
support from impoverished hacienda locals to support
urban strikers indicates with whom the rural proletarians
cast their lot. In the local idiom, they are indeed
"correligionarios".

Our prior difficulty in defining rural proletarians
as "rural" is germane here. That their reference group
carries with it no urban-rural distinction suggests that
defining them as rural may be irrelevant. We may be
dealing simply with those proletarians who happen to
reside in the countryside, an artifact of where research
has been done, rather than reflecting where the empirical
boundaries of the category lie. Unfortunately almost no
ethnographic information exists on the urban proletarians.
The reference group of those in rural areas may not be
reciprocated, and other features, too, may contrast.
One concludes that denoting them as rural may be
artifactual, but given the current paucity of information
one cannot tell.

We find also that the obrero identity carries with
it a more than subtle anti-campesino (anti-peasant)
flavor. It is significant in this regard that these
locals on the coastal haciendas dropped their affiliation
with the peasant-dominated Federación Nacional de
Campesinos del Perú (FENCAP) which had organized them,
for the all-obrero Unión Sindical as soon as overtures
were made (Greaves 1971: 6-7). FENCAP is now an almost
exclusively peasant syndicate organization by default and
little in evidence locally.[6]

The fact that their reference group is the obreros
as a class, transcending the rural-urban distinction, has
further implications. Their class consciousness as
obreros effectively generates a national orientation with
ideological foundations. It promotes their integration
into the national polity. One does not find here the
"defensive ignorance," the disposition to disengage, which
characterizes the classic peasant world, and that of some
urbanites. Thus, the pervasiveness of the obrero
reference group is a third major dimension of rural
proletarians, one which clearly serves as a powerful
element in knitting them together.[7]

4. This is relevant to a fourth characteristic, one
which again serves to underscore the significance of the
category, rural proletarian. Stemming from their class
identity, ideological underpinnings, and national

participation, their potential or actual role as an
interest group within national politics can be, and often
is, a powerful one. Certainly the Bolivian tin miners,
catalysts to the 1952 revolution, are the polar case.
In Peru the political role of the rural proletariat has
been less obvious, but anyone viewing national politics
in recent years will note that the actions of the sugar
workers and the oil workers are not to be neglected.
Especially with the current nationalization program,
these two organized laboring groups are playing integral
roles in shaping the emerging expropriated properties,
and will critically mold such procedures in the future.

Testing the Category: Syndicalist Peasants

At the juncture it is worthwhile considering the
status of the peasant syndicates, as described both in
Bolivia and in the La Convención region of Peru. There
are obvious differences between the peasant syndicates
and rural proletarians. Members of peasant syndicates
continue to farm land in a way which may be peasant, or
capitalist, but not proletarian. Wage labor is only a
part-time occupation, if it is engaged in at all.
Therefore our minimal definition disqualifies them as
rural proletarians.

Yet the real importance of these differences could
pale if they are highly similar otherwise. We have a
substantial corpus of useful and detailed descriptions of
peasant syndicates in the Bolivian highlands. Very
recently a few contributions have appeared dealing with
syndicates in Ecuador and southern Peru.[8] From these
materials one sees that like rural proletarians, peasant
syndicates have often participated in the national polity.
While there is great variation in degree, peasant
syndicates have some class awareness and have generated
regional and national political action. Class-based
ideologies and party organization have penetrated to the
local level. And one finds in Bolivia that peasant
syndicates and the mine unions have sometimes collaborated
to achieve mutual aims. Given these similarities, could
one argue that the peasant syndicates constitute another
form of the rural proletariat, a sort of variant of it?

The question is a deceptively simple one, raising
an issue that until now has remained covert in this paper.
That issue concerns the distinction between artificial
and natural categories and the conditions under which
grouping people together according to an abstract concept
is a productive effort. We have already noted that the
peasant syndicates do not conform to the minimal conditions of our definition of rural proletarians. If,

however, they were shown to be similar in terms of the
other features, then one would have to conclude that
the minimal conditions isolate a group whose significance
is likely to go little beyond that implied in the minimal
conditions themselves. If this is the case, then in
defining rural proletarians we have delimited largely an
"artificial category," a grouping "determined by super-
ficial resemblances or external criteria"(Hemple 1952:
52). While artificial categories can be useful to very
specific research--even such a category as people whose
names begin with A--few anthropologists would be long
content if we did not at least presume that our major
social groupings are, to some degree, natural categories
really existing "out there."

Explicitly or implicitly, most empirically minded
anthropologists presume that in the long run research
categories will achieve major and enduring theoretical
value only in so far as they approximate natural categories: that is, conceptual groupings whose boundaries
enjoy a high correspondence with empirically observed
trait discontinuities, and where a large number of
logically different features are found to share those
discontinuities. Ethnologists have classified human
variation into all sorts of categories, most of them
thought of as more natural than artificial. Hunter-
gatherers, tribes, pastoralists, and peasants are but a
few employed with the assumption that they come as close
to being natural categories as we have a right to expect
from cultural data. The question here, of course, is to
what degree "rural proletarian" is also a natural
category, "out there," as opposed to an artificial one
with a distinctive reality only in the head of its
definer?

The peasant syndicates of Bolivia and Peru offer
a crude and partial test of the "naturalness" of the rural
proletarian category. Granting that the four features
just reviewed are not exhaustive, at least it is a useful
beginning to see to what extent the features of the
peasant syndicates correspond to the four described here
as features of the rural proletarians. If the similarity
is high, it would suggest that the category rural proletarian may need to be re-cast or abandoned, except for
research particularly focused on those minimal features
selected at the outset: permanent wage-earners of rural-
based Andean corporations.

The first trait, social mobility in and out of
the group, was found to be high among the rural proletarians and embarked upon in an individual fashion. Somewhat
by contrast, becoming a member of the syndicalist
peasants, other than by birth, has been on a group basis.
After the 1952 Bolivian revolution, peasant syndicates

were quickly formed from pre-existing indigenous communities or from former private haciendas. In Peru the
sweeping invasion movement triggered by the Blanco
movement had a similar effect. The transformation in
both countries has been one of whole communities rather
than a piecemeal, individual phenomenon. It seems
plausible that the differing recruitment process has
probably produced somewhat divergent populations but
the evidence here is fragmentary.[9]

Mobility out of the peasant syndicate, particularly as described by the Buechlers (1970, 1971: 43-46)
seems more similar. Upward mobility consists of sequen-
tial steps along political, kin-based, and marketing
acquaintance networks. For the particularly successful
individual or his children this will eventually mean
removing his residence from the rural community to an
urban center. Thus while exiting from the peasant
syndicate status may be a more gradual transition than
for rural proletarians, the difference seems to be one
of degree rather than kind. The point of greater contrast
in terms of social mobility is the process of entry into
syndicate status, yet even here it is not the fact of
mobility, but its form, that varies.

The second feature, a social context of sharply
contrasting, ranked social statuses, seems to be a point
of more visible divergence between syndicate peasants and
rural proletarians. While there is internal status
variation in the syndicates, it in no way approximates
the sharply contrasting and ranked social identities daily
confronting rural proletarians.

There is mixed evidence for the third feature,
group consciousness. It would appear that in the syndicates such a class identity is more characteristic of the
leaders than the general membership and seems to decline
in areas removed from Bolivia's urban and political
centers. With increasing isolation identity seems to be
more locality-centered and less easily mobilized for
class-based goals (cf. Patch 1966, Heyduk 1971: 285-296).
In Peru, the degree of class consciousness of syndicate
peasants appears generally to be below that of their
Bolivian counterparts. The eventual dissipation of the
Blanquista movement, the abject failure of the de la
Puente-Lobaton call to arms in 1965, and the fragmentation
of the syndicate movement during these years as documented
in Borque's recent study (1971a) all indicate that while
fervent group consciousness is or has been an aspect of
the syndicalist peasants, the trait has been unstable and
usually operating at considerably weaker levels. The same
can be said of the fourth characteristic, national participation. In Bolivia it has thus far been stronger than
in Peru or in Ecuador, but in neither country does it
rival that of the proletarians.

Thus the correspondence between the syndicate peasants and the rural proletarians is far from perfect, but there is some overlap. The reader is as well equipped as the author to judge whether a re-casting or rejecting of the rural proletarian as a category is warranted. It is the latter's view that the comparison is an enlightening one, provoking one to wonder if there are not particular change forces and antecedent features common to both which account for the similarities, but that the contrasts are sufficient to justify a continuing research investment in rural proletarians as defined.

Continuing this view, the evidence suggests that we are seeing a number of ways in which people of peasant backgrounds are changing themselves. The rural Andean world is rapidly becoming the domain of the post-peasant. Some are indeed becoming rural proletarians, some are becoming urbanites, and those in the peasant syndicates have become some new formulation for which the term "peasant" is heuristically inept. It should be obvious enough that mobilized peasant syndicates are not composed of peasants at all.[10] Likewise, the colonists described by Casagrande and Thompson (1964) for Ecuador, and Hickman (1968) for Bolivia are no longer peasants, but neither are they rural proletarians.

Retrospect

To conclude, it is worthwhile reviewing several points offered in this paper. As a beginning, we probably know more about the rural proletarians in the Andean region than anywhere else and it is within these boundaries that the paper's scope is confined. Armed with a few minimal criteria, one finds that not only are agricultural workers on large estates included, but also miners and oil workers, and one supposes there may be still others. But what improves the attractiveness of this social category is that in looking at the groups encompassed by the minimal definition, we find that they held in common further, more significant characteristics. Consistently they are found to provide important mobility channels in terms of both recruitment and out-migration. This mobility usually entails a marked identity change, giving rise to a second characteristic, the fact that they are usually found in contexts of ranked, sharply distinct, status pluralism. Their reference groups are national in purview and class-oriented, as obreros particularly and not as campesinos. This brings them into the national arena on both political and social terms, where they are not only able to defend their own interests, but are making important contributions to national emergence as well.

It is, then, the present contention that the rural proletarians are a noteworthy group. They have attributes of a natural category. "Rural proletarian" is not just a heuristic construct, but has real social meaning on the ground. This augers for the continued usefulness in Andean ethnology of the category as defined. It suggests, too, that many people in the countryside are no longer well described by the word, "peasant," and have themselves developed several new social forms. One that bears watching is the rural proletariat.

APPENDIX

The following case occurred in October, 1966; its
sequence of events is presented here in outline form,
condensed from personal field notes:

During the morning shape-up one worker arrived some
ten minutes late, after all the gangs had been assigned.
The overseer reprimanded him for being late and suspended
him for the day. During the course of the work day word
began to circulate that a meeting would be held that
evening in the union hall to discuss the incident. The
meeting was held and it provided a stage for airing a
series of similar incidents that had been smoldering for
as long as a year. Speeches became increasingly fervent
and the unanimous consensus at the end of the meeting was
to demand the immediate dismissal of the overseer. This
demand was conveyed by the three ranking officers of the
union to the general administrator the following evening,
together with the open threat that a work stoppage (paro)
would be called if compliance was not forthcoming. At
shape-up the next morning the general administrator
announced that work should go on as usual, and that a
meeting would be held that evening at 5 p.m. with Don
Vicente, himself and the overseer present. The union
leaders agreed and the day's work began.
        During the afternoon Don Vicente, the general
administrator and the overseer conferred on the three
principal charges, the overseer explaining the circumstances of each. Two were cases of suspension for late
arrival and one alleged that the overseer physically
struck a worker with a stick without provocation. The
first two were routine late arrivals, and the third he
categorically denied, saying he knew nothing of the
charge.
        About 5:30 p.m. the union leaders, the workers
concerned in each charge, and various other members
arrived from the union hall and the meeting began. Don
Vicente sat at his desk, the general administrator and
the overseer sitting in chairs to one side. The workers,
who grew steadily to nearly thirty, stood in a large semi-
circle in front of them. Don Vicente asked what the
protests were, and then played the role of judge,
demanding order, questioning witnesses and clarifying the
facts. After some twenty minutes it was clear that the
facts were very confused, especially about the assault.
When another worker protested an incident that eventually
was discovered to have occurred nearly a year previously,
Don Vicente lost his temper. He launched a withering

deprecation of the workers for raising serious charges
when they could not agree on the facts. He had caught
several workers in gross exaggerations and he angrily
chastised them for slandering a man who did his work with
justice and competence. Then he abruptly ended the meeting, stalking out, declaring that the overseer was an
excellent man whom he would not fire simply because the
workers disliked him. The workers withdrew in disarray
and repaired to the union hall. There a workers' meeting
materialized, though no one had called a meeting and no
one presided. It began with most of those who attended
the confrontation with Don Vicente, all discussing the
course of the confrontation, trying to discover how they
had been so quickly undercut. Others joined in until
the hall was jammed and the officers began to address
their remarks to the audience as a whole. Tempers began
to rise. Diatribes against the hacienda (though not
against Don Vicente personally) competed for the
audience's approval and great applause rewarded the most
impassioned denunciations. The officers eventually
declared that a formal meeting of the membership would
be held the following evening after work to decide what
the union's response should be. Clearly the concensus
was not merely to call a work stoppage, but to declare
a strike (huelga).

The scheduled meeting the next day was not held
because one of the officers had gone to Trujillo the next
day to inform the Regional Secretary of the parent union
organization (La Unión Sindical) and the latter had asked
that the meeting be postponed for two days until he
could personally attend.

On the specified evening the meeting was held,
attended by the Regional Secretary, the full complement of
union officers, and a crowd of union members, wives and
other adults, and droves of children. The Regional
Secretary took charge. He asked for the charges to be
reviewed one by one, to determine the facts. He was
clearly disappointed that each one raised and explained
showed either no tangible abuse by the overseer, or was
buried in masses of conflicting testimony. Through
careful questioning it became clear that in the case of
the alleged assault, it was another worker who had wielded
the stick, not the overseer. The overseer had become
associated because the assaulted worker believed that the
overseer had ordered the second man to hit him, and then
had rephrased the scene with the overseer raising the
weapon. The man who had actually done the hitting was
queried and it was determined that he received no such
order from the overseer and was just settling a grudge
stemming from a drinking party the night before.

The Regional Secretary was visibly upset by the
dissipation of the union's case. The members attempted

a last-minute rally with impassioned calls for a strike,
putting the Secretary General in the embarrassing position
of having to take the side of the hacienda in order to
quell an obviously illegal and futile strike. He gave a
long speech urging that though the workers had suffered
many abuses, it should give the hacienda another chance.
The general administrator declared that the hacienda would
work out clear guidelines for penalizing late-arrivals at
shape-up to reinforce the conciliatory mood. The speech
of the Secretary General was long enough that it began to
bore the audience and as people began to drift away he was
able to close the meeting and depart for Trujillo. Other
than some bitter grumbling that the Secretary General had
abandoned the union cause, the following day was quiet and
the situation returned to normal.

FOOTNOTES

1. See especially Mintz (1956) and Miller (1967) for
    interpretations strongly predicated on this
    linkage. Much of the more general literature takes
    Marx as a reference point. An incisive review of
    Marx' position, a critique, and an alternate theory
    are provided by Darendorf (1958). Darendorf's book
    offers a variety of leads to a more precise empiri-
    cal delineation of the causal factors associating
    corporate enterprise with the emergence of a
    proletariat.

2. Mintz did not explicitly include "rural" as a charac-
    teristic of the rural proletarian.

3. While fundo may be used (as is "hacienda") to
    designate an agricultural holding of almost any
    size upon which the owner maintains a home, though
    he may not normally live in it, fundo may also be
    used to denote an estate which is smaller than a
    hacienda and which lacks a large dependent popula-
    tion, chapel, and other accoutrements of a socially
    complete environment for living. In this sense,
    fundos rarely range above 100 cultivated hectares,
    though size per se is not a crucial criterion. It
    is this latter meaning which is intended here. I
    have discussed the distinguishing features of these
    properties elsewhere in greater detail. (1968: 21-
    26, 422-434).

4. Appropriate citations are as follows: Vicos (Vasquez 1952, Holmberg 1961, Holmberg et al. 1965), Lauramarca (Kuczynski-Goddard 1946), Capana (Martinez 1963), Cujuni, Cochela and Panaschachi (Martinez 1967), Atahualpa (Crespi 1968), Colta Monja (Revilla and de Revilla 1965). A survey of the Peruvian Huancavelica zone is reported in Favre 1964. Changes have occurred on a number of these estates since the original ethnography was done. The transformation of Vicos by the Cornell-Peru Project, and the recent changes described at Lauramarca (Gall 1972) and Atahualpa (Crespi 1971) are cases in point. The implications of these changes are dealt with later in this paper.

5. Faron, however, found a very low turnover rate (less than one percent per year) for the Chancay Valley (1967: 271). Matos Mar's remarks on Chancay (1964: 373), while offering no figures, would seem to indicate a faster rate of movement in which those born in the highlands most heavily partici- pate. In any case, it is likely that turnover rates are sensitive to local factors and not uniform along the coast.

6. Bourque's recent contributions (1971a, 1971b) are especially useful in giving a recent picture of FENCAP.

7. The papers presented in the recent symposium, "The Genesis of Proletarian Consciousness" (American Anthropological Association 70th Annual Meeting, New York) are indicative of recent efforts to investigate these issues on an empirical level.

8. A basic bibliography would begin with (Bolivia) Patch 1966, Dandler 1969, Carter 1964, Buechler 1969, 1970, Heyduk 1971, Heath 1969; (Ecuador) Crespi 1971; and (Peru) Craig 1967, 1969, Borque 1971a, 1971b.

9. A particularly poignant statement reflecting the social and emotional magnitude of change in becoming syndicated peasants has been advanced by Gall (1971: 290).

10. The recent work of Bourque agrues for applying the term cholo, but this term has been used in such different ways that developing a consensus on a rigorous usage will be difficult (cf. Bourque 1971a: 22-25), Escobar 1964, Cotler 1967, Fried 1961, Scrimshaw 1971.

REFERENCES

Bernal, Segundo V.
   1969 -- Aspectos Sociologicos de Barrancabermeja para
            la Plan de Ordenamiento Urbano. Bogota: Uni-
            versidad de los Andes. Sección de Sociología.

Bourque, Susan C.
   1971a -- Cholification and the campesino: a study of
            three Peruvian peasant organizations in the
            process of societal change. Dissertation
            Series No. 21. Ithaca: Cornell University
            Latin American Studies Program.
   1971b -- El systema politico peruano y las organiza-
            ciones campesinas. Estudios Andinos 2, 2:
            37-60.

Bourricaud, Francois
   1962 -- "Sindicalismo y politica," Cuadernos (Paris).
            57: 32-42.

Buchler, Hans C.
   1969 -- "Land reform and social revolution in the
            northern Altiplano and Yungas of Bolivia."
            In Land Reform and Social Revolution in
            Bolivia. (Dwight B. Heath, Charles J. Erasmus
            and Hans C. Buechler, eds.). New York:
            Frederick A. Praeger, 169-240.
   1970 -- Processes of Bolivian syndicalism: a reinter-
            pretation of the relationship between social
            behavior and institutions. Paper presented
            at the 69th Annual Meeting of the American
            Anthropological Association, San Diego.

Buechler, Hans C. and Judith-Maria Buechler
   1971 -- The Bolivian Aymara. New York: Holt, Rinehart
            and Winston.

Carter, William E.
   1964 -- Aymara Communities and the Bolivian Agrarian
            Reform. University of Florida Monographs,
            Social Sciences, No. 24. Gainesville:
            University of Florida Press.

Casagrande, Joseph B.
   1969 -- "The implications of community differences for
            development programs: an Ecuadorean example."
            Paper delivered at the 28th Annual Meeting of
            the Society for Applied Anthropology, Mexico
            City.

Casagrande, Joseph B. and Stepehn I. Thompson
    1964 -- "Colonization as a research frontier: the
               Ecuadorean case." In Process and Pattern in
               Culture (Robert A. Manners, ed.). Chicago:
               Aldine. 281-325.

Collin Delavaud, Claude
    1964 -- "Consecuencias de la modernización de la
               agricultura en las haciendas de la costa norte
               del Peru," Revista del Museo Nacional (Lima).
               33: 259-281.

Cotler, Julio
    1967 -- La mecanica de la dominación interna y del
               cambio social en el Peru. Lima: Instituto de
               Estudios Peruanos.

Craig, Wesley W., Jr.
    1967 -- From Hacienda to Community: an Analysis of
               Solidarity and Social Change in Peru.
               Dissertation Series No. 6. Ithaca: Cornell
               University, Latin American Studies Program.
    1969 -- "Peru: The peasant movement of La Convención."
               In Latin American Peasant Movements (Henry A.
               Landsberger, ed.). Ithaca: Cornell University
               Press. 274-296.

Crespi, Muriel K.
    1968 -- The patrons and peons of Pesillo: a tradition-
               al hacienda system in highland Ecuador.
               Unpublished Ph.D. dissertation, University of
               Illinois, Urbana (Ann Arbor: University
               Microfilms).
    1971 -- Changing power relations: The rise of peasant
               unions on traditional Ecuadorian haciendas.
               Anthropological Quarterly 44,4: 223-240.

Dandler, Jorge H.
    1969 -- El Sindicalismo Campesino en Bolivia: Los
               Cambios Estructurales en Ucarena. Antropología
               Social No. 11. Mexico City: Instituto
               Indigenista Interamericano.

Darendorf, Ralf
    1958 -- Class and Class Conflict in Industrial Society.
               Stanford: Stanford University Press.

Escobar, Gabriel
    1964 -- El mestizaje en la región Andina: el caso del
               Peru. Revista de Indias (Madrid) 95-96: 197-
               219.

Fallers, Lloyd A.
    1961 -- Are African cultivators to be called
             "peasants"? Current Anthropology 2,2: 108-110.

Faron, Louis C.
    1967 -- "A history of agricultural production and local
             organization in the Chancay Valley, Peru." In
             Contemporary Change in Traditional Societies,
             Vol. III (Julian H. Steward, ed.). Urbana:
             University of Illinois Press. 229-294.

Favre, Henri
    1964 -- "Evolución y situación de las haciendas en la
             región de Huancavelica, Perú," Revista del
             Museo Nacional (Lima). 33: 237-258.

Fitchett, Delbert A.
    1963 -- "Defects in the Agrarian Structure as Obstacles
             to Economic Development: a Study of the
             Northern Coast of Peru." Unpublished Ph.D.
             dissertation, University of California at
             Berkeley, California (Ann Arbor: University
             Microfilms).
    1966 -- "Agricultural land tenure arrangements on the
             northern coast of Peru," Publication No. P3342
             (mimeo). Santa Monica: The Rand Corporation.

Fried, Jacob
    1961 -- The Indian and mestizaje in Peru. Human
             Organization 29, 1: 23-26.

Gall, Norman
    1971 -- Peru: The master is dead. Dissent (New York)
             June: 281-320.

Greaves, Thomas C.
    1967 -- "Descent to the coast: the labor supply of
             Peruvian coastal haciendas." Paper read at the
             66th Annual Meeting of the American Anthropo-
             logical Association, Washington, D. C.
    1968 -- "The Dying Chalan: Case Studies of Change on
             Four Haciendas of the Peruvian Coast." Unpub-
             lished Ph.D. dissertation, Cornell University,
             Ithaca, New York (Ann Arbor: University
             Microfilms).
    1971 -- Proletarians, patrons and clients in Viru.
             Paper presented at the 70th Annual Meeting of
             the American Anthropological Association,
             New York.

Hammel, Eugene A.
  1962 -- Wealth, Authority and Prestige in the Ica
          Valley, Peru. University of New Mexico Publi-
          cations in Anthropology No. 10. Albuquerque:
          University of New Mexico Press.

Havens, A. Eugene and Michel Romieux
  1966 -- Barrancabermeja: Conflictos Sociales en Torno
          a un Centro Petrolero. Bogota (Colombia):
          Ediciones Tercer Mundo y la Facultad de
          Sociologia, Universidad Nacional.

Heath, Dwight B.
  1969 -- "Bolivia: peasant syndicates among the Aymara
          of the Yungas - a view from the grass roots."
          In Latin American Peasant Movements (Henry A.
          Landsberger, ed.). Ithaca: Cornell University
          Press. 170-209.

Helms, Mary W.
  1969 -- Peasants and purchasers: preliminary thoughts
          on a differentation of intermediate societies.
          In Peasants in the Modern World. Phillip K.
          Bock, ed. Albuquerque: University of New
          Mexico Press. 69-74.

Hemple, Carl G.
  1952 -- Fundamentals of concept formation in empirical
          science. International Encyclopedia of Unified
          Science. Otto Neurath, ed. Vol. 2, No. 7.

Heyduk, Daniel
  1971 -- Huayrapampa: Bolivian Highland Peasants and
          the New Social Order. Dissertation Series No.
          27. Ithaca: Cornell University Latin American
          Studies Program.

Hickman, John M.
  1968 -- "Colonización y movilidad social en Bolivia,"
          American Indigena 28,2: 389-403.

Hickman, John M. and Jack Brown
  1971 -- Adaptation of Aymara and Quechua to the
          bicultural social context of Bolivian mines.
          Human Organization 30,4: 359-366.

Holmberg, Allan R.
  1961 -- "Changing community attitudes and values in
  (1960)   Peru: a case study in guided change." In
          Social Change in Latin America Today (Philip E.
          Moseley, ed.). New York: Vintage Books.

Holmberg, Allan R. et al.
    1965 -- "The Vicos case: peasant society in transi-
            tion,: The American Behavioral Scientist. 8,
            No. 7.

Kuczynski-Goddard, Maxime
    1946 -- "Un latifundio del sur: una contribución al
            conocimiento del problema social," América
            Indígena. 6,3: 257-274.

Lang, Norris G.
    1965 -- "Stratification and industrialization: a case
            study of an Ecuadorean sugar plantation."
            Proceedings of the 1965 Annual Spring Meeting,
            American Ethnological Society. Seattle:
            University of Washington Press.

Martinez, Hector
    1963 -- "La hacienda Capana," Peru Indigena. 10, 24-
            25: 37-64.
    1967 -- "Tres haciendas altiplanicas: Chujuni, Cochela
            y Panascachi," Peru Indigena. 26: 96-162.

Matos Mar, Jose
    1964 -- "Las haciendas del Valle de Chancay, Revista
            del Museo Nacional(Lima)." 33: 282-395.

McIrvin, Ronald R.
    1969 -- "Cultural continuity in the face of change:
            becoming an adult in a new context (Talara,
            Peru)." Paper read at the 28th Annual Meeting
            of the Society for Applied Anthropology,
            Mexico City.

Miller, Solomon
    1964 -- "The Hacienda and the Plantation in Northern
            Peru." Ph.D. dissertation, Columbia Universi-
            ty, New York, New York. (Ann Arbor: Univer-
            sity Microfilms; subsequently revised as
            Miller 1967).
    1965 -- "Proletarianization of Indian peasants in
            northern Peru," Transactions of the New York
            Academy of Sciences. Ser. II, 27: 782-789.
    1967 -- "Hacienda to plantation in northern Peru: the
            proletarianization of a tenant farmer society."
            In Contemporary Change in Traditional Soci-
            eties. Vol. III (Julian Steward, ed.).
            Urbana: University of Illinois Press. 134-
            225.

Mintz, Sidney W.
    1951 -- "Canamelar: the Contemporary Culture of a
              Puerto Rican Sugar Cane Plantation, 1876-1949."
              Ph.D. dissertation, Columbia University, New
              York, New York. (Ann Arbor: University Micro-
              films; subsequently revised as Mintz 1956).
    1953 -- "The folk-urban continuum and the rural
              proletarian community," American Journal of
              Sociology. 59,2: 136-143.
    1956 -- "Canamelar: The subculture of a rural sugar
              plantation proletariat." In The People of
              Puerto Rico (Julian H. Steward, ed.). Urbana:
              University of Illinois Press. 314-417.

Nash, June C.
    1970 -- Mitos y costumbres en las minas nacionalizadas
              de Bolivia. Estudios Andinos (LaPaz) 1,3:
              69-82.

Patch, Richard W.
    1958 -- "An oil company builds a town," American Uni-
              versities Field Staff, Reports Service; West
              Coast South America Series. 5, No. 2.
    1959 -- "The role of a coastal hacienda in the hispani-
              zation of the Andean Indians," American
              Universities Field Staff, Reports Service; West
              Coast South America Series. 6, No. 2.
    1966 -- "Change on the Altiplano," American Universi-
              ties Field Staff, Reports Service; West Coast
              South America Series. 13, No. 1.

Revilla, Arcenio and Ana B. de Revilla
    1965 -- "The hacienda Colta Monjas." In Indians in
              Misery. Ithaca: Cornell University, Depart-
              ment of Anthropology, and the Ecuadorean
              Institute of Agrarian Reform and Colonization.
              95-130.

Scrimshaw, Susan C.
    1971 -- A description of non-coresidential polygyny in
              Spanish Ecuador. Paper presented at the 70th
              Annual Meeting of the American Anthropological
              Association, New York.

Vásquez, Mario C.
    1952 -- "La antropología cultural y nuestro problema
              del Indio: Vicos, un caso de antropología
              aplicada," Peru Indígena. 2, Nos. 5-6: 7-157.
    1969 -- The Kami mine; a Bolivian experiment in
              industrial management (draft). Mimeo

US AND LATIN AMERICAN LABOR:

THE DYNAMICS OF IMPERIALIST CONTROL

Hobart A. Spalding, Jr.

Introduction

Latin American labor movements do not evolve within
isolated national frameworks. A host of external factors,
economic and political, affect their development. This
article examines one set of these by looking at relationships between United States and Latin American labor. It
is divided into four parts. The first traces Inter-
American and, where important, Intra-American labor
relations until 1945 to place contemporary trends in
historical perspective. The article concentrates, however,
on events after World War II when external forces impinge
upon Latin American labor in new ways. The rapid growth
of an ever more centralized global economy, dominated
first by the U.S. and later by that nation along with
other advanced capitalist super-powers, initiates a
period of rising interest in Latin American labor by
U.S. business, labor, and government. Set within a Cold
War framework, U.S. agencies and private institutions
develop a variety of mechanisms aimed at controlling
and manipulating Latin American labor. Section two
examines these and shows their workings. It highlights
the American Institute for Free Labor Development
(AIFLD).+ The next section presents case studies
depicting imperialist agencies and institutions working
together in a set geographical locale. The last part
discusses the meaning of imperialist strategy for labor
in Latin America.[1]

Several general themes emerge from the material.
One is U.S. labor's continuing interest in Latin America,
a relationship flowing from its past and present cooperation with U.S. foreign policy and totally consistent
with its domestic practices. Almost from its founding
big labor, represented by the AFL and then AFL-CIO, entered into
collaboration with the government and therefore the ruling
class. In brief, organized labor leadership worked under
the assumption that capitalism constituted the best socio-
economic system and that it could satisfy workers' needs.
It saw labor as a national pressure group like any
other which should seek reform of the system in its favor
but not to change it. Unions existed primarily to acquire
economic benefits for members through collective bargaining

+ A list of all acronyms appears in Appendix I.

whenever possible, only using other tactics when this
recourse failed. A constantly rising material standard
of living for affiliated workers comprised labor's long
range goal. This, in turn, obviously depended upon the
strength of the system, so labor maintained an interest
in seeing it flourish. From this analysis derive the
terms bread and butter or business unionism used to
describe AFL and ALF-CIO politics.

Big labor's past and present foreign policy flows
directly from its domestic positions. It combats any
and all anti-capitalist ideologies. To do this it
aids and encourages unions which espouse a pro-capitalist
line. It attempts to influence existing organizations
and form new ones which will imitate U.S. style unionism.
It also supports all government--dictatorial or otherwise--
which take similar stands. Lastly, where interests
overlap, it works with U.S. companies abroad. Divisions
between business and labor in foreign policy, at home,
stem primarily from tactical questions not from basic
philosophical antagonisms. Labor obtains several direct
and indirect advantages from its alliance with business.
The more U.S. economic power in a foreign country the
less likelihood that opposing ideologies will make headway
in the short run. The larger the sphere of capitalist
influence, the greater the market for U.S. goods and the
profits for U.S. companies, both of which strengthen the
system at home and therefore, indirectly, U.S. labor.
Investment abroad, moreover, assures supplies of strategic
materials needed by the national economy and the U.S. war
machine.

In view of the close relationship between labor
and business, U.S. labor's impact abroad must be studied
in the larger context of imperialism which encompasses
institutions at home like universities, government
agencies such as USAID, and clandestine policy bodies
like the CIA. As part of the "U.S. foreign policy
team", labor's role in Latin America is highly political
despite any contrary claims. Like other imperialist
agencies it operates on several levels. It openly uses
educational programs and financial means to influence
Latin American labor. It also participates in less
visible activities designed either to hide its role or
to disguise U.S. involvement. In short, U.S. labor's
foreign policy can be summed in the phrase: what is good
for U.S. labor (and capitalism) is good for Latin American
labor.

Despite temporary successes in many cases, significant failures mark U.S. labor efforts. In Chile, only
recourse to a fascist government has blunted the
drive of the working class toward socialism. U.S. labor
has concentrated on winning over or controlling workers
in the modernized sectors. They represent, however, a

minority within the working class and thus substantial
numbers remain totally outside the reach of U.S. labor.
Its future in Latin America depends not so much on
unionized workers as upon the yet unorganized mass which
flows into the mainstream of national life in an ever
growing wave. Whether U.S. labor's efforts will prove
successful with this group is highly improbable given the
limits of U.S. style unionism.

1. U.S. and Latin American Labor: The Years to 1945.

        Socialists and anarchists both attempted to form
regional organizations early in this century but the
first full-fledged continental grouping, the Pan-American
Federation of Labor (PAFL), emerged from contacts between
Mexican and U.S. labor groups.[2] Samuel Gompers, head of
the American Federation of Labor (AFL), the leading U.S.
labor body, played a key role in its formation. He
consistently pushed for a joint Mexican-American labor
conference and for hemispheric organization. In 1918 his
idea came to fruition when delegates from the U.S.,
Mexico, and four Caribbean nations created the PAFL.
The founding Congress promptly elected Gompers head of
the group. He, in turn, hailed the event as a labor
supplement to the Monroe Doctrine, clearly indicating
his and the AFL's view that U.S. labor would form the
dominant element in the organization.[3]
        The PAFL's two leading affiliates, the AFL and
the Mexican CROM--that nation's largest labor grouping--
both hoped to profit from their relationship despite
disagreements between them. The Mexicans, for example,
voiced concern over the treatment North American unions
showed their countrymen by either denying them admission
or treating them as second class citizens. They also
urged the AFL to press for the freeing of workers, some
of them Mexican nationals, from U.S. jails. The AFL,
however, could do little to satisfy the first request
in the face of widespread racism particularly strong in
the Southwest where most Mexican and Mexican-Americans
worked, as it lacked power of enforcement over its
locals. The second point also proved thorny because
Gompers had personally encouraged the jailing of many
radical organizers, especially members of the AFL's chief
rival the IWW. For its part, the AFL worried about U.S.
companies using Mexican strikebreakers but this concern
evoked little or no response from CROM.[4]
        Several factors motivated the AFL's interest in
PAFL. Increasing concentration of domestic industry and
its rapid expansion overseas worried the AFL. It needed
all possible strength to counter growing corporate power
and to discourage business from moving abroad to capi-
talize on cheap labor, thus causing unemployment at home.
Support of and influence over a hemispheric labor

confederation could bolster AFL influence in national
affairs and assure it a voice in foreign policy. The
ability to work together with CROM, a pressure group in
Mexico, could make the U.S. government less willing to
alienate the AFL. Cooperation with Latin American
labor, also might avoid criticism that the AFL did not
support internationalist goals and the workers' world
struggle. In truth, the Federation's concern with
foreign affairs stemmed from a desire to enhance its
prestige. Unions organized through PAFL, for example,
would raise wages for their workers. This boosted the
foreign sales potential of U.S. corporations which would
add to their profits and increase domestic employment
by expanding production. In addition, friendly relations
with CROM buttressed the pro-establishment labor forces
in Mexico and helped contain militant groups competing
with CROM. This process, involving ever closer collaboration with the government and the ruling class, reinforced
business' aims and paved the way for increased U.S.
investment by helping to mold a labor movement which
operated within a capitalist framework.

CROM, for its part, through links with the AFL
and other labor movements, hoped to demonstrate its own
ability to mobilize pressure groups, a service which
could ease the conduct of foreign affairs. It did, in
fact, enlist AFL support for the Revolutionary Government
on several specific occasions which may have helped
mitigate the periodic crises that threatened Mexican-
American relations in the turbulent decades after 1910.[5]

When PAFL's first congress met in 1919 the
organization already boasted a newspaper supported by
U.S. government funds raised by Gompers. Nine nations
attended the meeting and passed declarations of mutual
support. They also demanded labor representation at
the Second Pan-American Financial Congress scheduled
for 1920. Gompers eventually won a seat at this gathering
but gained no concessions for labor. Workers from ten
countries attended PAFL's last congress in 1924. It
passed resolutions supporting Dominican, Nicaraguan, and
Venezuelan workers struggling against dictatorial regimes
but accomplished little else. AFL-CROM relations also
continued centering around the issue of discrimination
against Mexicans and problems arising from migration
including the use of Mexican immigrants as strikebreakers.
Gompers' death in 1924 and CROM's fall from government
favor five years later doomed PAFL. Projected congresses
from 1929 and 1931 never met and the AFL's final attempt
in 1938 to resurrect the organization in order to counter
growing radicalism within the ranks of Latin American
labor failed.[6]

Several factors prevented PAFL's becoming a
viable entity. Those important Latin American labor'

organizations which could have lent it weight and prestige
espoused far more radical philosophies than either AFL
or CROM. Central labor groupings did not exist in many
countries and those which supported PAFL in Central
America and some Caribbean nations represented only
small, weak, and often precarious organizations. In
addition, CROM participated only to the degree that it
derived benefits. Lastly, the AFL's desire to extend
its influence and project U.S. unionism did not always
sit well. CROM's newspaper in 1925, for example, reacted
to one joint meeting as follows:

> The delegates of Mexico and the United States
> worked hard and nobly, but for their effort
> to be crowned with definite success, many
> suns and many moons must pass, an
> indispensable interregnum for Anglo-Saxons
> to convince themselves that they are not
> the superior beings they suppose they are.[7]

Two short-lived organizations formed in 1929,
an anarchist one and the Communist, Confederación
Sindical Latinoamericana (CSLA). The latter propounded
an anti-imperialist program with special emphasis on
organizing both industrial and rural proletariats and
claimed 600,000 members from fourteen countries at its
height. It also specifically condemned PAFL as a North
American imperialist organization. Both groups lasted
only briefly and disappeared before 1940.[8] In 1938
yet another regional confederation formed, the Confederación
de Trabajadores de América Latina (CTAL). This body
proved more durable. Under the guidance of the Mexican
leader Vicente Lombardo Toledano, it grew rapidly. By
1944, it boasted 3.3. million members in sixteen countries,
a considerable achievement in view of the labor movement's
embryonic state in most nations.

Unlike PAFL, this organization excluded North
American participation although it maintained close
contact with the Congress of Industrial Organizations
(CIO), the AFL's more progressive rival. This decision
rested on CTAL's position that Latin American workers
must resolve their own problems and that imperialism
formed the most serious obstacle to continental self-
determination. Only revolutionary change could produce
a just society and satisfy Latin American needs. CTAL,
therefore, endorsed class struggle and proletarian
internationalism. It called upon all workers to support
struggles for common economic goals and the world wide
creation of truly democratic and socialist institutions.
Simultaneously, it urged Latin Americans to unite in
the conquest of their own objectives. When war threatened,
CTAL modified its immediate objectives, urging workers
to form an anti-fascist bloc. According to Toledano,

CTAL's task consisted of explaining to workers the nature of fascism's menace to all forms of socialism and thus the importance of supporting the allied cause.[9]

CTAL incorporated various ideologies but Communist organizations predominated. It held regular congresses and sponsored regional conferences. It convened, for example, meetings for petroleum workers in 1948 and agricultural and forest workers as well as transport workers in 1951. The organization lost impetus after 1945 under capitalism's Cold War counter-offensive spearheaded by the AFL. Gradually most of its affiliates either were forced underground by repressive anti-Communist regimes in their home countries or else severely crippled by restrictive legislation and police surveill-ance, which prevented their effective participation in CTAL. By the late 1950's the organization existed mostly on paper and it disbanded officially in 1962. Although the remaining members called for a new leftist Latin American confederation, none has yet successfully formed.[10]

In sum, by 1945 three historical patterns emerged. First, persistent attempts to found regional hemispheric organizations. Second, U.S. labor established a continued interest in Latin America. And third, this interest clearly rested upon the premise that U.S. labor would dominate in any organizations and that it would push for U.S.-style unionism. After 1945, labor, government, and private agencies acting in the name of U.S. and international capitalism accelerated the process and moved rapidly into Latin America.

II. The Cold War and Imperialism: Agencies and
        Organizations.

The onset of war reawakened interest in Latin America on the part of U.S. labor and government. In 1939, the CIO created a standing committee on Latin America. Two years later, Nelson Rockefeller, then Coordinator for Inter-American Affairs heading the Office of Inter-American Affairs in the U.S. Department of State, saw an opportunity to bolster the U.S. image abroad through the AFL and CIO. His office arranged to have those organizations sponsor tours for Latin American labor leaders and agreed to partially fund these. At the same time the U.S. Bureau of Labor Statistics undertook a series of studies on Latin America (which it still does) and several publications aimed at the area, including Inter-American Labor Notes, rolled off government presses. In 1943, the first attaches arrived in U.S. embassies to help insure that local labor unions did not hinder shipments of strategic materials. Four years later, the U.S. Labor Department established a

permanent international labor office which included Latin
America under its jurisdiction.

The AFL, still hoping to take a lead in Inter-
American labor affairs and confront CTAL, proposed a
new regional entity prior to 1944. The U.S. government
frowned upon the plan, however, fearing it might inhibit
cooperation with CTAL's anti-fascist front. At war's
end in 1945 the AFL, now gearing up for an anti-Communist
crusade, again called for the formation of a hemispheric
labor body, this time with government approval. Two
years later it enlisted the ex-OSS functionary Serafino
Romualdi as a full time "labor ambassador" to Latin
America, a post he occupied until 1965.[11]

In the meantime, post-war reconstruction generated
important events for world labor. War time cooperation
between U.S., European, and Soviet trade unions fostered
a desire for continued joint action. Accordingly, at
the initiative of the British Trades Union Congress (TUC)
and Soviet unions, the World Federation of Trade Unions
(WFTU) formed. The CIO joined this body but the AFL
refused on ideological grounds. This burst of friendship,
however, did not last. The capitalist counter-offensive
against the mounting tide of progressivism throughout
Europe and the world soon led to the Cold War confrontation
and the labor arena became a major battleground. In
1949, the major capitalist unions broke with the WFTU
and formed a separate world organization, the International
Confederation of Free Trade Unions (ICFTU) which first
the AFL and then the CIO, once it had purged its more
radical elements in 1949-1950, joined. Even though this
new body pledged itself principally to apolitical,
bread and butter unionism, the AFL showed dissatisfaction.
By 1951 it already began to complain about ICFTU's
softness toward Communists. Although the AFL-CIO (the
two organizations merged in 1957) did not officially
withdraw until 1969, it manifested a desire for an
independent hand in world labor affairs by the early
1950's. It soon accomplished this goal in Latin America
which became by tacit agreement an area virtually conceded
to the AFL-CIO and U.S. government by the world body.[12]

The developing Cold War soon reached Latin America.
The AFL agent Romualdi embarked on a continental tour
in 1946-1947 marshalling support for the proposed AFL-
sponsored regional confederation. In 1948 a congress
in Lima, Peru formed the Confederación Inter-Americana
de Trabajadores (CIT) as a rival to the leftist CTAL
and WFTU (to which CTAL belonged) and to the pro-peronist
Argentine labor confederation, the CGT, typed by the AFL-
CIO as "fascist." The CIT, however, lasted only briefly
due to the shifting international situation. Within
three years it merged into a new body, the Organización

Regional Inter-Americana de Trabajadores (ORIT) which
affiliated with the ICFTU. This first grouping also
fathered by the AFL, adopted ideological positions
similar to its largest affiliate to the North, although
not without internal dissension. The AFL insisted on
excluding the Argentine CGT which prompted the Mexican
labor confederation, also an important member, to withdraw.
That confederation's leader later explained, "This organization has no Latin American head or feet. It is merely
the instrument of the United States State Department, to
be manipulated by...United States labor organizations
and their Cuban satellites."[13] Although the Mexican
entity returned to the fold two years later under
government pressure, its criticism remained valid.

ORIT's ideology and practice closely mirrors that
of the AFL-CIO. Its prime goal is to fight Communism and
to promote "democratic trade unionism." It preaches
reform within the existing capitalist system, denying
the existence of class antagonisms. Rather it sees
Latin American labor as just another interest group
like the military, church, or large landowners. As
such it needs strengthening in order to compete on equal
terms with the others. ORIT points to the U.S. as an
example of the rewards that the system can heap upon
the working class and organized labor. Labor's goals,
aside from fighting Communism, are full employment for
members and ever increasing economic benefits.

ORIT supports only what it calls democratic unions
even if these depend upon political parties or are
government controlled. In reality, ORIT espouses an
all or nothing ideology. Cold War neutrality translates
into a pro-Communist position as does any anti-U.S.
sentiment. Since the U.S. stands for democracy, support
of any non-democratic government, left or right, also
equates with pro-Communism. Behind this rhetoric, as
we shall see, lies a blind anti-Communism which leads
ORIT and the AFL-CIO to support any and all anti-
Communist, pro-U.S. governments or unions. ORIT, in
addition, sidesteps a number of key issues for Latin
American labor. It never examines the question of
capitalism itself or whether workers can achieve equality
under it. It also dodges the issue of U.S. imperialism.
It argues pragmatically that Latin America must accept
the fact that the U.S. will play a major role on the
continent due to its geographical proximity and advanced
stage of economic development.[14]

ORIT's size is hard to estimate. Optimistic
observers claim that the organization includes some 50-
55 national labor organizations and approximately 28-30
million members. Effective membership of course is much

lower as Latin American labor groups grossly overestimate
their size and the percentage of militants compared to
dues payers is small. ORIT receives funds from a number
of known, and probably several unknown, sources, the
principal ones being: AFL-CIO as the largest affiliate,
ICFTU's International Solidarity Fund, and various U.S.
agencies. Its total annual budget is also difficult to
calculate, but one source estimated that in 1961 it
amounted to somewhere between $100-120,000, exclusive of
grants.[15]

ORIT engages in varied activities apart from its
regular congresses where delegates gather to discuss
anti-Communist strategies and general objectives.
Education of Latin American trade unionists constitutes
one activity. In 1951, ORIT began sponsoring candidates
for the trade union leaders school at the University of
Puerto Rico, a project it continued until the U.S.
government took over several years later. In 1962, it
opened a special trade union institute in Cuernavaca,
Mexico on land donated by the State Governor and declared
tax free. At this center ORIT runs regular courses like
those for peasant leaders or women trade unionists as
well as seminars such as the one on peasants and
ideology held in 1971. ORIT also cooperates with several
U.S. government agencies. It set up a special Department
of Economic and Social Affairs, for example, to coordinate
with the Alliance for Progress. In addition it sponsors
periodic Inter-American conferences such as its 1967
seminar on campesinos or a labor education seminar for
70 Latin American labor experts held in conjunction
with UNESCO in 1966.[16]

ORIT maintains that unions should be non-political,
and asserts that it has no political ideology, and does
not partake in purely political actions. Many of its
acts, however, cast serious doubt upon these declarations.
It works closely, for example, with the U.S. State
Department. The U.S. embassy in Mexico printed El Obrero,
an ORIT publication for distribution in Central America
and Mexico. Also, the U.S. Information Agency produced
a documentary film praising ORIT's virtues.[17] Given
this close connection with the fact that over 50% of
its members and at least that amount of its monies come
from North America, it is small wonder that ORIT reflects
its masters voice on other matters. To cite only a few
concrete cases, it took such "non-political" stands as
endorsing the overthrow of the Arbenz government in
Guatemala by a U.S. trained and financed coup in 1954,
the ill-fated Bay of Pigs invasion of Cuba by U.S.
supported exiles in 1961, the ouster of Brazilian
President João Goulart by a reactionary military coup
in 1964, and the 1965 U.S. intervention in the Dominican

Republic. The close relations between the corrupt
leadership of the Cuban CTC headed by Eusebio Mujal and
the AFL-CIO prior to the Revolution seem to have made
Revolutionary Cuba a particular ORIT target. As early
as February, 1959, the ORIT Executive Committee began to
denounce the forthcoming elections in the CTC as unfree,
echoing a position stated earlier by the AFL-CIO. The
fact that Communist candidates actually received a
minority vote in them did not deter ORIT, for apparently
just the ouster of Mujal and his followers justified
condemnation and proof of the CTC's anti-democratic and
therefore pro-Communist nature. In 1962, ORIT called a
work stoppage protesting labor conditions in Cuba and
supporting the U.S. resolution at the Punta del Este
OAS meeting aimed at ousting Cuba from the body. In
1965 it asked for a boycott of all goods moving to Cuba
from any Latin American land or seaport and set up an
Action Committee Against Cuban Communist Tyranny to
publicize the nature of what it termed the "totalitarian
Castro regime."[18] On the other hand, it has taken no
stand against rightist regimes like the current governments
of Brazil or Chile despite the fact that they have
severely curtailed all trade union freedoms. ORIT's
criteria for approval or censure seem to be based on a
particular government's relationship with the U.S. Those
with State Department approval, no matter what their
internal politics, also get ORIT's vote; those without it
do not.

ORIT, in reality, forms only one link in a vast
chain of agencies and organizations that compose the
imperialist network seeking to control and manipulate
Latin American labor. Its methods vary and at times may
even seem to work at cross purposes, but the central
aim remains the stifling of militant, left, working class
movements and the promotion of U.S.-style business
unionism or at best mild Christian or social democratic
forms of it. The network is vast and encompasses a whole
range of national and international bodies. A partial
listing of these includes the Alliance for Progress and
USAID; the Organization of American States (OAS) and the
Inter-American Development Bank (IADB); International
Trade Secretariats (ITS); the AFL-CIO; the labor sections
of every U.S. embassy in the hemisphere; private and state
institutions such as major U.S. universities; private
foundations like the International Development Foundation
(IDF) or Council on Latin America, Inc.; and last but
not least CIA. An examination of any one link sooner or
later leads back to the central nerve center in Washington,
D.C.

Space does not allow more than a quick examination
of these links and their activities. We will, however,

look at one organization, the American Institute for Free
Labor Development (AIFLD), in some depth and then present
several case examples to show how the links work together
to achieve the desired results.

At the right hand of the chain's top, the US government, sits the AFL-CIO and Jay Lovestone, principal archi-
tect of the AFL-CIO's -- and therefore the government's --
labor policies abroad.* The AFL-CIO spends 23% of its
budget on international affairs each year. It is the largest contributor to ORIT and pumps as much as 2 million
dollars annually into a special projects fund to complement
the 1 million flowing into its international activities
accounts. How this money actually gets spent, only the
AFL-CIO top brass know. In addition, the AFL-CIO constantly
sponsors visits for Latin American labor leaders to its
convention or just to see the "American way." It also
undertakes a host of related endeavors in education, social
projects, etc. in Latin America.[19]

The Alliance for Progress and USAID maintain considerable interest in labor matters. The Alliance provides,
among other things, financial assistance. Its first labor
loan, for example, consisted of a $400,000 grant to a
Honduran union for a housing project which one source characterized as an outright "reward for anti-Communist zeal
to a company-controlled union."[20] Universities contribute
their share, too. Cornell University in Ithaca, New York,
for example, cooperates through its School of Industrial
and Labor Relations by training Latin American labor leas-
ers and, under a USAID contract, set up a Department of
Labor Relations at the University of Chile.[21]

International organizations operate in the labor
field at various levels. The OAS recently created two
labor-related commissions in addition to its Inter-American
Advisory Committee designed to work with the Alliance for
Progress and the labor movement. These are the Trade
Union Technical Advisory Committee (COSATE) formed in 1964
and the Permanent Technical Committee on Labor Matters
(COTPAL) dating from a year later. The former gives assistance to OAS members at the trade union level, the latter
at the official ministry level.

International Trade Secretariats also play a role.
These are world groupings of national industrial unions in
a particular industry or related group of industries. During the 1950's many established Latin American offices. In
Peru, no less than five opened branches before 1960. Most
ITS rely heavily on US affiliates for funding but several
receive substantial financing from private foundations.
The State, County, and Municipal Workers and the newspaper-
men's international, for example, got grants from the Gotham
and Granery Funds respectively, both proven CIA conduits.

---

*Lovestone recently retired.

The ITS hold Latin American regional congresses, sponsor educational courses for selected candidates, and provide monetary support to local members for a variety of purposes. The Public Service International, for example, until recently spent about $100,000 annually in Latin America, considerably more than it allotted the rest of the world.[22]

An examination of AIFLD reveals the scope and breadth of US activities in Latin America and shows clearly the degree of cooperation between links in the imperialist chain. We discussed tensions between the AFL-CIO and ICFTU around the anti-Communist issue in the 1950's. These heightened as the world organization increasingly involved itself in the Third World. African nations, for example, held at least nominally to a neutral position regarding the Cold War, and militant AFL-CIO anti-Communism at times proved an embarassment to ICFTU. The AFL-CIO gradually carved out Latin America as an exclusive sphere of interest but did not develop a formal policy until the 1960s. In 1959 Joseph Beirne, head of the Communications Workers of America (and now a top AIFLD officer) inaugurated a training program for Latin American trade unionists. Its success prompted him to suggest to George Meany that the AFL-CIO launch a similar program on a permanent basis. The following year, George Lodge, Secretary of Labor, issued a statement suggesting that bilateral organizations might prove more effective than multi-lateral ones in the labor field. Perhaps in response to these stimuli the AFL-CIO Executive Committee soon endorsed a motion calling for a Latin American education program in which up to 300 non-Communist unionists would receive three months training in the US in the methods and techniques of North American labor and then return home for a nine month period in which to put their knowledge into practice. Thus AIFLD was born.[23]

Inaugurated in 1962 by and under the policy direction of the AFL-CIO, AIFLD's creation came "primarily in response to the threat of Castroite infiltration and eventual control of major labor movements within Latin America." It is dedicated to "strengthening the democratic labor sector in terms of institution building . . . in terms of technical assistance and social projects . . . primarily in the areas of education and training, manpower studies, cooperatives, and housing."[24] In straight terms, AIFLD's central functions consist in combatting non-capitalist influences within the ranks of Latin American labor (it also opposed the CLAT -- formerly CLASC -- of Christian Democratic origin) and to strengthen both US labor influence and business image in order to develop pro-capitalist, reformist unions while maintaining Latin America as a field for investment.

Business, government, and labor provide AIFLD's main
inputs and they share common goals. As Meany said, speaking
as chief of the AFL-CIO, "We believe in the capitalist
system and we are members of the capitalist society. We
are dedicated to the preservation of this system, which
rewards the workers, . . . we are not about to trade in our
system for any other."[25] This sentiment is totally consonant with the words of AIFLD's ex-President and current
Chairman of the Board, J. Peter Grace (head of W. R. Grace,
a company with extensive interests in Latin America) that
AIFLD must "work toward a common goal in Latin America,
namely supporting the democratic form of government, the
capitalistic system and general well being of the individual."
He continued, AIFLD "is an outstanding example of a national
consensus effectively at work for the national interest of
the United States and for the best interests of the people
of Latin America."[26] Just how this works we shall see later.

The US government has provided the bulk of AIFLD's
support. Between 1962-1967, 89% of its funds derived from
USAID; labor contributed 6%, and business, represented by
grants from over 70 corporations, only 5%. This means that
almost 16 million dollars of government money flowed into
AIFLD.[27] Government funding has increased steadily, from
64% in 1962 to 92% in 1967, and by 1971 AIFLD ranked as the
15th largest recipient of USAID contracts with a total of
7.593 millions. At times AIFLD garners support from other
sources. Between 1961 and 1963, one source claims that it
received nearly a million dollars from CIA conduits.[28]
Heavy government funding not only bolsters AIFLD's position
but also means that fewer funds are potentially available
to others, giving it a practical monopoly in determined
areas such as worker housing.

Big business, private institutions, and labor are
amply represented within AIFLD's governing elite. Aside
from Beirne, Grace, and Meany, executives from Anaconda
Copper, Gulf Oil International, Johnson and Johnson International, Merck, Owens-Illinois, and Pan American Airways
as well as members of the Institute of International
Education and the Fund for International Social and Economic
Education, both donees from CIA fronts, hold or have held
AIFLD positions.[29]

Within its overall plan, AIFLD has two central
functions. For one, it trains labor leaders based on the
rationale that Latin American unions tend to form political
ties and that this is undesirable. In a classically arro-
gant and demeaning statement Meany spoke of this function:

We have taken young people that we screen in
their home countries and we bring them to a
center where we put them through a course.

> Some of the courses are short, some of them
> a year, some of them two years, depending on
> the needs. We give them training in basic eco-
> nomics. We let them know something of this
> country's history, something of our back-
> ground. Then we get them into the trade
> union field, and we let them know first,
> for instance, the things that we have got
> to do with South Americans, we have to show
> them the relationship between wages and
> production. This is something that a few
> years ago they were completely ignorant
> about.[30]

Training takes place on both regional and local
levels. Local seminars lasting one week to three months
instruct those attending in history and international
activities of the labor movement, organization, structure
and union finance, collective bargaining, labor legislation, and democracy versus totalitarianism. "The aim of
these local seminars,as well as more advanced AIFLD
courses, is to give basic trade union education to union
members, develop leadership skills, and teach methods of
strengthening their unions against totalitarian infiltration and tactics."[31] Selected students move to regional
and national classes, and then a few ultimately to the
headquarters at Front Royal, Virginia. AIFLD's Centro
de Estudios Laborales del Perú, for example,expended about
$200,000 annually. Opened in Lima during 1962-1963, the
center also ran a branch in Arequipa giving night courses,
two week seminars in various provinces, and ten week
residential programs for the best students from the
shorter sessions. In all, 11,800 Peruvians have received
AIFLD training, including almost all the first and second
line labor leaders of the Confederación de Trabajadores del
Perú, the country's largest labor confederation and an
exponent of AIFLD type unionism.[31A]
By the end of 1974 an AIFLD official could boast
that 259,876 persons had passed through one or another of
the institution's courses. The Front Royal Center graduated 200 persons in 1975 pushing the total number trained
over the 1,800 mark. The composition of the 1972 trainees
shows that school's breadth. Of 140 persons receiving
degrees, -- 100 men and 40 women -- 80 came from Spanish
speaking countries, 20 from Brazil, and another 40 from
English speaking areas.[32]
AIFLD also sponsors courses at Georgetown University
in Washington, D.C. in labor economics, a program formerly
run by Loyola University in New Orleans. In addition, it
underwrites periodic hemispheric educational gatherings

such as its VII Inter-American Labor Economics Course or
the University of Miami seminar on the Caribbean hosted
by the Center for Advanced International Studies there.
On a regional basis, a Central American Institute for
Trade Union Studies founded in 1963, organizes regular
programs for regional labor leaders. Lastly, AIFLD
publishes books and pamphlets, two recent releases
consisting of a primer on democracy and a two volume
history of the world trade union movement in Spanish.[33]

AIFLD's second major function involves numerous
specific projects. These include education for technical
assistance in the field of social service activities;
literacy, vocational, and health and sanitation training
(all of which include the inevitable democracy-versus-
totalitarianism lectures); so-called "Impact Projects"
which encompass donations to backward areas of items like
sewing machines; just plain "union to union" assistance
programs which may involve a simple gift of office
equipment or assistance in a major undertaking.

In Peru, for example, the AIFLD Social Projects
Division helps local organizations apply for loans and
assists in steering these through appropriate bureaucracies:
an Impact Projects Fund and Cooperative Advisory Service
loan money to consumer cooperatives and credit unions as
well as to worker run businesses. Four such projects, a
printing firm, bus line, sewing cooperative, and textile
factory, have been funded. This type of project is based
on the same logic as land reform which distributes small
plots to peasants. First, workers gain a stake in the
system through property ownership and, in theory at least,
become its defenders. Second, it trains people in
capitalist practices and ideology, further deepening
their commitment. Third, in underdeveloped areas where
capital for industrial ventures is scarce, it builds small
industry which does not compete with larger national or
international companies, but often complements them.
Fourth, it ties each endeavor to AIFLD financially.
Lastly, it raises the purchasing power of those involved,
enlarging sales for bigger enterprises.

Still other AIFLD training projects contribute to
its objective. It instructs labor people in organizing
social projects in their communities. Citing the Peruvian
case again, community efforts in the mushrooming shantytowns
(barriadas), a potential hot bed of discontent, receive
financial aid through AIFLD educated residents. This
serves a dual function. It familiarizes participants in
capitalism's way and counters efforts by members of
militant groups to rally support among the poor and
marginal groups.[33A]

Housing developments form another major AIFLD area.
These now exist in over a dozen Latin American countries
and almost invariably are awarded to staunchly anti-Communist

unions facing stiff competition from more progressive
rivals. The unions can then offer cheap housing as an
incentive to potential recruits as well as regular members.
The organization also administers a Regional Revolving
Loan Fund underwritten initially by USAID grants for $625
million. This fund totals some $812.4 millions and has
lent monies in 12 countries for five year terms at little
or no interest. In addition, several Latin American
trade union credit unions have received significant sums
to provide loans for members.[34]
    AIFLD works closely with a host of public and
private US institutions. A recent high level meeting in
Cuernavaca, Mexico for Country Program Directors and
Washington-based AIFLD officers indicates this relationship.
Those present included: Arturo Jáuregui, Secretary-General
of ORIT and an AIFLD Director, the head of the government-
sponsored Mexican labor confederation CTM, directors of
the Asian-American Free Labor Institute and African-
American Labor Center both roughly equivalent to AIFLD
in their respective areas, top level aides from the
Alliance for Progress, the Peace Corps, and USAID, the
Coordinator for Inter-American Affairs for the Secretary
of State, representatives from the Inter-American
Development Bank and Council of the Americas, and the
labor studies director at Florida International University
in Miami. Delegates from seven International Trade
Secretariats also attended.[35]

III. The Cold War and Imperialist Agencies: Case Examples

    This section examines specific actions by
institutions and organizations attempting to shape the
course of Latin American labor in the manner most
favorable for US capitalism. It highlights specific case
examples but the full implications of the combined policies
mentioned are discussed as part of the overall treatment
of imperialist strategy which follows.
    US agents have been active, for example, in both
Brazil and Chile. In the former nation, during João
Goulart's presidency (August 1961 to April 1964) ORIT,
ICFTU, and the US embassy through its labor attaches,
worked hard to support non-Communist labor groups and to
oppose the left-dominated CGT (Confederacão Geral do
Trabalho), the nation's principal national confederation of unio
founded in 1962. At the 3rd National Labor Congress of 1960
at which US labor specialists flown in expressly for the
occasion plotted strategy for so-called "democratic"
trade union leaders. They managed to convince this minority
bloc to pull out of the gathering and thus undermine

attempts to unify labor. The <u>Movimento Democrático
Sindical</u> (<u>MDS</u>), under its adopted motto "God, private
property, and free enterprise," received similar aid and
advice in sponsoring its own meetings and in setting up
trade union courses. In addition, the <u>Instituto Cultural
do Trabalho</u> which had close AIFLD connections and IPES,
partially financed by US business concerns, trained labor
personnel and disseminated pro-capitalist and anti-
Communist labor publicity. AIFLD moved into the rural
Northeast during 1963 in response to growing radical
peasant movements there. After the reactionary 1964
coup against Goulart, it initiated courses and launched
service centers for peasants. As a result in Pernambuco,
for example, rural unions "hold democratic elections to
choose leaders who draw handsome salaries, take courses
from AIFLD, and do very little."[36] In all, some 24,000
unionists and 3,500 campesino leaders from every state
have received AIFLD-related training. In fact, a top
AIFLD official boasted that its graduates had played a
role in the coup and shortly afterwards the AFL-CIO
Inter-American Affairs Director interviewed the military
junta's chief asking for expanded AFL-CIO activity in
Brazil.[37]

In Chile where a strong working class movement has
backed leftist political parties since the 1930s, U.S.
organisms have also been active. In the 1950s ORIT launched
a campaign to strengthen non-leftist unions. In the
1960s, ORIT and AIFLD pursued several attempts to split
the trade union movement by dividing the left-controlled
Central Unica de Trabajadores (CUT -- Chile's leading
labor central) through splitting off the minority
conservative unions. To accomplish this they urged all
entities to join the CUT and paid back dues for those so
inclined in order to allow them voting privileges to make
the staged walk out appear more impressive. The maneuver
failed but AIFLD did create the CNT (Confederación
Nacional de Trabajadores), a conservative body whose
largest affiliate is COMACH, a Valparaíso-based maritime
federation. AIFLD graduates figure prominently among its
leadership and its stated policy, true to U.S.-style
unions, is "to cooperate with owners and the directors of
big business." After the fascist coup of 1973 that
imposed a brutal military dictatorship, the CNT appeared
in a good position to expand its activities. AIFLD
education programs grew particularly rapidly after 1970
when a left coalition, the Unidad Popular, won the
presidential elections and instituted a program designed
to initiate Chile's road to socialism. By that time,
about 10,000 persons had graduated from local AIFLD courses, a
figure equivalent to 3 to 4 percent of Chile's total
trade union membership, and from February 1972 to February
1973, the number of Chileans enrolled at Front Royal
increased almost 400 percent.[38]

U.S. organizations played no lesser role in the
Chilean countryside. By 1967, AIFLD had trained over
3,000 campesino leaders. The International Development
Foundation (IDF), however, proved more important. This
body opened operations in Chile during 1964 as a private
foundation. It emphasized peasant organization and
almost singlehandedly formed the Confederación Nacional
Campesina by supplying legal assistance, technical skills,
and money to create unions willing to join. This peasant
confederation in contrast to similar groups mobilized by
the left, aimed at achieving agrarian reform by establishing
small private holdings rather than through any collective
or cooperative ventures. When it surfaced that IDF
received funds directly from CIA fronts, the organization
retired from Chile and USAID took over its programs. A
number of U.S. sources also supported the Rural Education
Institute. This conservative Catholic institution, backed
by the National Agricultural Society representing large
landholders, conducted classes for peasants and peasant
leaders. Espousing a violently anti-leftist line, the
Institute by 1965 succeeded in creating 23 education centers
in which it trained over 4000 persons. Naturally, both
IDF and USAID quickly became substantial financial
supporters of the Institute.[39]
     In Guatemala, U.S. involvement with labor began
before the conservative coup that ousted the progressive
government of Jacobo Arbenz in 1954. Early that year the
AFL issued a policy statement noting that the government
had allowed Communists to penetrate the ranks of labor
and warning about possible consequences of such tolerance.
After the take-over which it quickly praised, the AFL
sent organizers to regroup Guatemalan unions. Although,
much to big labor's chagrin, the new government crushed
the workers' movement, U.S. influence persisted. As one
observer has written, "United States government and
representative agencies have successfully dominated much
of the organizational framework above the local level"
since 1954.[40] Guatemalan as well as other Central
Americans have trained at San Pedro Sula in Honduras where
AIFLD administers a USAID-funded school. Selected
graduates move on for further training to the University
of Puerto Rico at Río Piedras and to Loyola University in
New Orleans, both recipients of USAID monies. Recently
campesino affairs have received increased attention at
both the Central American school and on the local level.
In 1967, for example, 74 rural leaders including a group
representing unions of United Fruit Company workers
graduated from AIFLD-USAID programs.[41]
     The examples of Jamaica, the Dominican Republic, and
Guyana show that no strategic area is too small to merit
imperialism's attention. The major foreign influence over

the Jamaican trade union movement was the British TUC
until the early 1950s. This situation changed, however,
when the giant international corporations Alcan Aluminum,
Kaiser Aluminum, and Reynolds Metals invested heavily in
the island's bauxite industry after 1949. From then on
U.S. labor and government displayed heightened interest in
the former colony. By 1958 the British TUC officially
abandoned Jamaica and all the West Indies as a special
sphere, leaving the U.S. a free hand with the area's
trade unions.[42]

In 1952 the United Steelworkers of America (USWA)
arrived on the scene and aided the foundation and
growth of the Jamaican National Workers' Union (NWU)
among bauxite workers. After a brief rivalry with the
established union, the NWU emerged triumphant in 1954
aided by USWA funds which paid for local organizers,
strike benefits, and men to train leadership along with
rank and file. The Cuban CTC, which maintained close
connections with the AFL-CIO in these years, also
assisted the fledgling union. Shortly afterwards the
NWU aided by the USWA, the International Mine Worker's
Federation, and CADORIT (the ORIT regional), took the
lead in forging a regional bauxite workers organization
known after 1961 as the Caribbean Bauxite and Mine Workers
Federation. In 1964, under a USAID contract and again
assisted by CADORIT, it began operating a Trade Union
Education Institute at the University of the West Indies.
AIFLD supplied most of the lecturers who naturally
emphasized the importance of AFL-CIO business unionism.
AIFLD also initiated several social projects mostly in
the area of housing.[43]

The British Crown Colony of Guyana became a focal
point for imperialist action in the 1960s. There, under
limited home rule, elections in the early 1950s brought
the People's Progressive Party (PPP) led by Cheddi Jagan
into power. Jagan immediately sought basic reforms but
encountered stiff opposition from entrenched colonial
interests. In 1952 he proposed a labor bill providing
for supervised worker elections in each industry or economic
sector so that the union with majority backing would become
the official bargaining agent in each unit. This measure
threatened established company unions as well as those
controlled by the conservative political parties which
followed the mild reforms espoused by the British TUC.
The sugar industry lay at the center of the controversy.
There, the Man Power Citizens' Association (MPCA) backed
by the Sugar Producers Association, an owners' group, had
secured bargaining rights over the GAWU (Guyana Agricultural
Workers Union) which closely identified with the PPP.
When colonial interests fomented and financed massive
strikes in opposition to the bill, the British authorities

intervened and suspended the Constitution. At the same
time, a violent public anti-Communist campaign financed in
part by the U.S.-based Anti-Communist Crusade succeeded in
splitting off a moderate faction headed by Forbes Burnham
(currently the Prime Minister) of the PPP, isolating the
progressives led by Jagan.[44]

Despite the temporary success of these maneuvers in
weakening the PPP, elections in 1961 again returned Jagan
as Prime Minister. In 1962 he reintroduced the 1952 labor
bill with similar results. Once again the MPCA and its
conservative backers called a general strike and encouraged
rioting. This often took severe racial overtones. The
majority of the East Indian population backed both the GAWU
and Jagan by refusing to strike thus becoming prime targets
for mobs led by paid ruffians. When MPCA worker support
did not materialize to the degree anticipated, the sugar
companies responded with a lock-out but only after issuing
foremen careful instructions to pay workers as long as they
stayed off the job. The ensuing crisis paralyzed the
economy. When an oil shortage threatened to make the
situation intolerable for Jagan, the Revolutionary Cuban
government sent a loaded tanker to Guyana but the shippers
immediately closed the harbor to prevent its landing. This
incident provided additional ammunition for those who accused
Jagan, and by implication the PPP, of being Communist and
even agents of the Kremlin.[45]

The strike dragged on amidst almost constant street
violence. All Jagan's efforts to solve the impasse failed
against his enemies' intransigence. His request that the
ranking British official call a U.N. investigation fell on
deaf ears as did his demand that the colonial authorities
expel foreign labor agitators operating in Guyana. Even
the British mediator eventually sent to resolve the crisis
acknowledged the real aim of the forces manipulating the
strike, saying "The strike was wholly political. Jagan was
giving in to everything the strikers wanted, but as soon as
he did so, they erected new demands."[46] Jagan ultimately
withdrew the labor bill but this did not satisfy his opponents.
They then demanded pay for the days of work lost and Jagan's
guarantee that he would never again submit the bill or a
similar measure. After 80 days the strike ended but Jagan's
position had been irreparably damaged. The British Government
used the crisis as an excuse to mandate that conditions did
allow for the country's independence and thus to re-open
negotiations of the terms under which it would be granted.
The ensuing Constitutional Conference of 1963 resulted in a
new document that instituted a system of proportional
representation in the parliament. This scheme assured
Jagan's nonelection because his supporters lay concentrated
in a set of electoral districts that could not elect a
majority of members to parliament. The following year's

voting brought a conservative coalition into power despite
the fact that the PPP secured more votes than its rivals.[47]
     During and after the crisis Jagan blamed the strike
on imperialist forces. Few outside of his own followers
believed him at the time but he proved to be correct. Slowly
the extent of foreign involvement in the affair leaked out.
Acting on their fervent anti-Communist fears and dread that
the situation could evolve into another Cuba, capitalist
interests marshalled their forces to defeat Jagan. First,
the U.S. had pressured the British into reneging on their
promise for independence until they could guarantee a way
to keep Jagan out of office. Second, Jagan's opponents
received support from several outside sources. The Public
Services International, for example, supplied a portion of
the almost one million dollars paid in strike benefits.
These flowed through its U.S. affiliate, the United States
Federation of State, County, and Municipal Employees. This
latter entity had maintained a full-time Latin American
bureau since 1958, but it really swung into action in 1963.
During the strike it provided money for distress funds for
strikers and the purchase of radio time for anti-Jagan
forces. It also payed travel expenses for opposition union
leaders. One commentator estimated that the total monies
flowing into the effort in Guyana amounted to between
$20,000 and $25,000 weekly and that total expenditures
reached $700-800,000.[48] The New York Times reported that
CIA agents worked in the guise of friendly U.S. labor
unionists and helped to organize the strike and to channel
funds into the "proper places."[49] An ex-union leader later
testified that he knew of the operation and had willingly
accepted it. At this time AIFLD maintained at least half
dozen anti-Jagan trade union leaders on its full-time payroll
under the guise of their being a part of the internship
program.[50] In short, Jagan not only faced the opposition
at home but also the combined forces of imperialism, and
these odds he could not overcome.
     The Dominican Republic became yet another place in
which U.S. imperialism intervened. Before the assassination
of the long-time dictator General Trujillo in 1961, the
AFL-CIO already had trained a number of Dominican exiles
in both Puerto Rico and New York. They quickly returned to
the island and soon formed FOUPSA (the United Workers'
Front for Free Unions), a coalition of anti-Trujillo groups.
Shortly after its founding the AFL-CIO urged a purge of all
"undesirable elements" and when FOUPSA refused even resorted
to bribery. It utilized the same tactic during the 1961-1962
general strike offering FOUPSA's head $30,000 to call off the
movement. When this ploy failed, a defamation campaign
against both the FOUPSA official and the organization
charging that it was really a Communist front achieved the
desired result. FOUPSA split into two factions. One, the

Bloque FOUPSA Libre becoming CONATRAL or National
Confederation of Free Workers under AFL-CIO and ORIT
domination, which used Cuban exiles from the pre-Batista
days to train Dominicans. A closer examination of the
nature of AIFLD course content reveals its central thrust.
One actual curriculum included 18 hours of "Democracy and
Totalitarianism," 5 hours on collective bargaining, and 5
hours on industrial problems, but nothing on standard trade
unionist topics like profit sharing, legislation, or social
security.[51]

CONATRAL's positions reflected U.S. influence. It
opted for bread and butter unionism summed up by the position,
"unions exist to obtain benefits for their members --
period." This attitude clashed with the political
realities of the situation. The Dominican government, as
most in Latin America, could regulate wages, control
strikes, rule over the collective bargaining procedure, and
generally manipulate labor for its own purposes. Nevertheless,
CONATRAL refused support for the populist Juan Bosch in the
presidency even though he allowed labor relative freedom,
advocated profit sharing, and promoted recognition of
majority unions as legitimate bargaining agents in each
sector rather than using government power to give favored
unions that position. CONATRAL justified its action with
the usual declarations of non-involvement in politics but
its stand really flowed from the fact that the U.S. did not
approve of the Bosch government.[52]

Bosch's case merits further attention as it sheds
light on the workings of imperialism. When Trujillo's
regime ended, Bosch emerged as the strongest candidate in
the elections and he duly won them. Although U.S. organizations openly voiced their distrust and later did everything
to assist the military coup that finally ousted him in
1963, other agencies prepared for the contingency that he
would assume power. The International Institute for Labor
Studies, headed by the social democrat Norman Thomas,
funded an Inter-American Center for Social Studies in the
Dominican Republic which trained most of the technicians
and high level government officials who served under Bosch.
Only later it surfaced that the Institute received backing
from the J.M. Kaplan fund, a CIA conduit. Further, the
Institute's vice-president, a man active in Dominican
affairs, had overseen the creation of FENHERCA, a pro-Bosch
peasant federation which mobilized the rural vote. Once
Bosch's term began, however, the federation slowly
disintegrated. This fact, combined with divisions in the
labor movement, left Bosch without any substantial pillars
of organized support and facilitated his overthrow.[53]

Additional actions by CONATRAL and imperialist agencies
deserve mention. Shortly before the military coup that
ousted Bosch, CONATRAL paid for a full page advertisement

in local newspapers calling for the military to save the
country from Communism, a barely disguised invitation for
the action that soon took place. It also played no active
role in the popular uprising against the Cabral government
of April 1965 that led directly to U.S. military intervention.
It did, however, praise the action echoing the AFL-CIO,
State Department, and ORIT line that the intrusion thwarted
Communism and prevented another Cuba. In the 1966 elections,
it almost openly supported the reactionary candidate backed
by the U.S. (and the AFL-CIO, ORIT, etc.) even though he
took an anti-labor position. These stands by CONATRAL's
leadership which rarely if ever consulted rank and file
before issuing the organization's official statements, cost
the organization. After its endorsement of the intervention,
several unions resigned and membership fell from an
estimated 100,000 to around 25,000.[54]

AIFLD also actively operated in the Dominican
Republic. It trained peasant leaders in conjunction with
ORIT and the AFL-CIO and initiated several social projects
among them a housing development for sugar workers in the
town of San Pedro de Macoris. The initial and only
investment for the scheduled 3 million dollar complex
derived 67% from the Inter-American Development Bank and
33% from AFL-CIO, guaranteed by USAID. The project, however,
soon ran into trouble when AIFLD's hidden conditions came
into the open. First, no competitive bidding for
construction contracts took place and AIFLD apparently
assigned them as it chose. Second, AIFLD insisted that
only CONATRAL unions work on the complex. Third, as
AIFLD's custom in similar projects elsewhere, it limited
access to the new housing only to CONATRAL members. The
illegality of these procedures under Dominican law forced
the project to halt.[55]

IV. Imperialist Strategy and Its Implications

The stratagems outlined above are, in reality, only
a small part of an explicit larger design involving a
multiplicity of U.S. and international organizations. Many
of the institutions mentioned in connection with labor
actively partake in other phases of the design. The CIA,
for instance, operates on varied fronts, only one of which
encompasses labor. North American universities do likewise,
training foreign technicians in all areas of the social and
physical sciences, supporting research that actively aids
imperialist domination both in the Third World and at home,
and administering a wide range of programs for that same
end. We have also neglected the vital role of U.S. business
because it falls outside this article's scope. But, no
matter how small the input or how insignificant a particular

piece of the puzzle, it all builds toward the same end: continued domination by the capitalist ruling class over the non-socialist world economy. This is the only and ultimate purpose of U.S. policies toward labor in Latin America and elsewhere.

A further word may be necessary concerning the relationship between imperialism and international as well as domestic institutions. Some of these institutions may appear neutral and many domestic organisms and the individuals that staff them not dedicated to carrying out imperialist policies. Despite this, they all contribute. The OAS, for example, is dominated politically by the United States, which has seldom if ever lost a vote in that body or even encountered significant opposition in it. Further, its programs operate totally within a capitalist framework which only aids U.S. expansion. By the same token, conservative and liberal U.S. academicians also work almost exclusively inside a capitalist framework. Liberal criticism of capitalism only seeks to remedy what it sees as its ills, and rests on the assumption that capitalism can achieve an ideal society. The important point is not an organization's or individual's intent, but the result their efforts produce. The author of the most innocent seeming study that aids imperialism supports that system.

Specifically, U.S. labor strategy aims at fostering by any means counter-revolutionary labor movements and by extension a counter-revolutionary working class. This allows for the continued existence of capitalism on favorable terms and creates a safe business climate for investment. While the greater share of benefits accrue to U.S. big business, North American labor leaders also gain. Having made the accomodation into the capitalist system, labor's bosses have a stake in its continuing strength. Only top officials, however, reap substantial rewards. North American workers may receive some limited temporary economic advantages from super-profits harvested in Third World areas, but the capitalist class exploits them just like any oth workers. Significantly, rank and file are never consulted nor informed about labor's activities abroad but union controlled newspapers feed them standard anti-Communist lines. Labor's commitment in Latin America and elsewhere also strengthen its bargaining position with the government and system in general. By performing needed services it enhances its value to the ruling class. The existence of U.S.-style unions abroad also protects jobs at home in specific instances by assuming continued production through a smooth flow of raw materials. Lastly, labor's leaders have access to patronage through labor posts in U.S. embassies.

What challenges does the U.S. face on the labor front? So far, only two rival organizations have formed in

Latin America: CTAL and the Agrupación de Trabajadores Latino
Americanos Sindicalizados (ATLAS). This latter group
represented the pro-Peronist CGT's attempt to extend its
influence throughout Latin America. U.S. labor had
opposed the CGT almost since the moment it endorsed Perón,
claiming that it was not an independent labor body and
labeling Peronism as akin to fascism. It excluded the CGT
from ORIT and supported the seating of an anti-CGT faction
at ICFTU conferences. ATLAS never became a viable entity,
disappearing shortly after Perón's fall in 1955. Until
recently the AFL-CIO continued to favor non-Peronist unions
in Argentina because Peronists did not unquestioningly
accept U.S. leadership or business unionism. Only when a
right-wing developed inside the Peronist labor movement did
the AFL-CIO and other U.S. agencies move closer to Peronist
organizations.[55a]

At present, the Central Latino Americana de
Trabajadores (CLAT) is the only continental organization
that challenges U.S. hegemony. This entity is the Latin
American affiliate of the former world Christian confederation
of trade unions. It formed in the early 1950s as CLASC,
but adopted its present less partisan name. CLAT takes a
position antagonical to Communism, but the AFL-CIO considers
it dangerous because it condemns capitalism too. CLAT
holds that Latin American unions and workers must develop
their own forms of trade unionism adapted to the area's
particular conditions. It considers that the labor movements
must be democratic, autonomous, seek working class unity,
and strive through political action to promulgate fundamental
changes in Latin American society. George Meany and his
followers, of course, consider this heresy.[56]

Despite the fact that no leftist continental
organization exists, substantial groups of workers do not
agree with the AFL-CIO position and take openly anti-
capitalist stands. In Chile, for example, an organized
and politicized working class helped establish a popular
government in free elections which could only be toppled
by one of the most vicious military coups of recent
history. Despite severe repression, the struggle in Chile
continues and the U.S.-backed "democratic" unions have
made little headway among the working class.[57]

Within the context of a global strategy, concrete
imperialist actions have long and short range implications.
In general, we can see a tendency toward less reliance on
international organizations such as ICFTU and more
reliance on directly controlled entities like AIFLD.
Similarly, ORIT's role appears diminished and more emphasis
placed upon governmental agencies or private, but safe,
institutions. At the same time, labor has pushed the
development of regional sub-groupings like those existing
in the Caribbean or Central America. In conjunction with

the above, regional unions covering workers in the same
industry such as the Caribbean Bauxite and Mine Workers
Federation have also come into vogue. These bodies
facilitate U.S. labor control in a given industry and
provide a means for stabilizing labor conditions in that
industry. Their existence also centralizes training
procedures.

The Jamaican NWU is one example of a union created
with U.S. aid. In fostering this organization, the U.S.
Steelworkers' union gained several advantages. First, by
regulating labor practices in the bauxite industry it
assured an orderly relationship between the aluminum
companies and the Jamaican union. This, in turn,
guaranteed bauxite supplies upon which the jobs of aluminum
workers in the U.S. depended. At the same time the USWA
fulfilled a patriotic duty by promoting anti-Communist
U.S.-style unionism and securing a stable supply of a
strategic material for the U.S. Foreign companies also
backed the formation of the NWU. An aluminum company
executive argued at a Jamaican official hearing in favor
of U.S.-style unionism and indicated that it would
increase the possibilities for future investment in
Jamaica.[58] Once the companies knew that they could count
on a union only interested in economic issues and not
tied to local politics, they then could apply labor
procedures used at home. In other words, they preferred
a safe union to any other union, and even to no union
at all. Further, the tactic has worked. Since the 1950s
no strikes have occurred in the Jamaican bauxite industry
and all disputes settled peaceably. The companies won an
additional bonus because the union screens out those
workers who disagree with its philosophy. A survey of
corporate executives found that they viewed the NWU as
"a useful social institution serving a police function
which is of value to the company."[59] The fact that AIFLD
has trained leaders from unions on the United Fruit
Company properties in Central America must be viewed in
this same light.

Education on all levels, in fact, comprises the
second most important sphere of action after direct
methods. In addition to the obvious value of influencing
trade union leaders, this process meets two other goals.
First, it can create teams of labor personnel who can be
used against unfriendly regimes as happened in Chile and
Guyana. Second, through chain reaction it allows U.S.
influence to spread among those vast unorganized sectors
of the working class. In all only about 15 percent of the
economically active population belongs to a union in Latin
America. More than 80 million agricultural workers, for
example, still have no collective organization.[60] The
potential impact of this as yet unmobilized population is

enormous and it will play a significant role in the future. Given this circumstance it is not surprising that in the 1960s the training of rural leaders received increased emphasis at all levels. Women also constitute another group recently getting more attention. AIFLD now holds a series of special courses for women at Front Royal and in the field.[61] Since increasing numbers of females join the work force annually, this effort, like the one aimed at rural workers, prepares for the future as well as the present.

On a more concrete plane, one consistent tactic used throughout Latin America has been to split labor's ranks as occurred under imperialist tutelage in Brazil, Chile, and the Dominican Republic in recent years. This procedure brings several advantages. First, no united labor front can form to challenge established power. Second, a fragmented movement is always easier to control and when U.S.-supported groups remain in a minority (as in the three cases mentioned), their dependence upon the U.S. grows. Third, a public break highlights disagreements between labor factions and often presents an opportunity for a campaign against the left unions which always "caused the rupture." Lastly, a split also establishes a target upon which to concentrate.

Imperialist policies to this point have proved relatively successful in the area of labor. What accounts for this? First, U.S. agencies can award tangible things to workers such as houses or materially assist unions which are usually poor due to their membership's low dues-paying capacity. Loans and grants or trips to the U.S. also prove attractive to individuals. In a capitalist society such as Latin America these kinds of rewards often effectively buy friends and influence people. Money in the form of strike funds or payoffs to leaders, particularly in situations like that of Brazil where a corrupt bureaucracy has traditionally bought votes in union elections, is another weapon of cooptation. Argument by demonstration also takes a toll. A host of U.S. government agencies and corporations like the United States Information Agency and the major media corporations constantly project the middle-class American image to Latin Americans, reinforcing values already inculcated by the educational system and society in general. This lends credence to labor's U.S. claims that apolitical, bread and butter unionism can lead to economic betterment. The image often proves doubly attractive to Latin Americans who live far below the standards of their North American counterparts.

On the other hand, the official monopoly of information is gradually breaking down. Increasingly progressive Latin American media publish stories, graphics,

and statistics showing "how the other half" actually
lives in the U.S., casting serious doubts on the romanticized
picture peddled by official agencies. At the same time,
growing discontent among U.S. workers over their
deteriorating economic situation due to inflation and the
realization that pure economic advances do not translate
into contentment, raises questions about capitalism's
long range ability to create an ideal society. In turn,
this directly challenges U.S. labor's assumption that
U.S.-style unionism is the best for workers.

Ultimately, of course, imperialism's success in
blunting militant worker action rests not so much on its
ability to bribe, persuade, and brainwash as on its
capacity to muster sufficient force when necessary. In
Brazil, Chile, and Guyana only outright repression could
temporarily check a mobilized labor movement and gathering
popular protest.

What can we conclude then about the future relationships between the U.S. and Latin America in the labor
field? In the final analysis, due to Latin America's
dependent condition and to the nature of capitalism, U.S.
labor policy contains basic contradictions which cannot be
resolved in the long run. Under present conditions it is
not possible to provide a high standard of living for
those who each year join the labor force or who are being
organized. Workers may be entranced by the American
Dream for a period of time, satisfied with meagre gains
at first, or duped by corrupt leaders, but the situation
cannot continue forever as reality will not meet expectations.
Perhaps we can gain some insight into the future from the
Cuban example. There a corrupt, entrenched bureaucracy
controlled the labor movement after 1944. It could not
keep that hold, however, as the forces of change proved
too strong. Substantial sectors of the working class
supported and joined Fidel Castro's 26th of July movement
and workers responded favorably to the Revolution. The
Cuban case shows that the accumulated experience of the
working class in its struggles for self-determination
slowly but surely build into a revolutionary consciousness.[62]

One example, however, does not prove a case and the
historical conditions existing in Cuba do not exist
elsewhere. Yet, with local variations, real contradictions
are found in each Latin American country and in the area
as a whole. In the immediate term, U.S. labor's constant
support of anti-worker governments as in Brazil, Chile,
or the Dominican Republic only alienates workers from its
cause. Nationalism too erodes U.S. labor's position
because Latin American workers increasingly resent taking
orders from foreigners. In the long run, economism in
the Latin American context contains severe internal
limitations. The area's steady de-capitalization places

repeated strains upon national economies. Everywhere,
labor's share of national income has diminished. The
"Brazilian economic miracle" seen by the U.S. as a model
for all the continent, speaks eloquently for the results
of capitalist development. In 1960, 80 percent of the
population received 45.5 percent of total income; by 1970
the figure had fallen to 36.8 percent. Between 1963 and
1970 workers' real salaries declined over 20 percent.[63]
Yet, U.S.-style unionism depends upon increasing material
standards of living. This obviously is not occurring on
a mass scale nor is it likely to in Latin America.
     The U.S. then faces a choice in its labor policies.
It can concentrate upon a small elite group of workers in
the modernizing sector and provide them with more benefits
or it can appeal to all unionized and potentially unionizable
workers. Indications are that the first policy is not
practicable because workers in traditionally unorganized
sectors, like agriculture, show increasing signs of rising
consciousness. Sooner or later economism must front a
wall of its own making. As this happens workers will
come to see social change as the only means to economic
change and actively seek alternatives to the standard
capitalistic economic system imposed upon Latin America.
They did this in Chile and began to in Brazil until the
1964 coup temporarily delayed the process. Ultimately it
means confrontation with the established ruling class.
At this point the Latin American working class is not near
a revolutionary crossroads, but as the historical process
unfolds that moment comes ever closer.[64]

APPENDIX I

Acronyms Appearing More Than Once In Text

A. U.S. Organizations

AFL   American Federation of Labor
AFL-CIO   American Federation of Labor and Congress of
             Industrial Organizations
AIFLD   American Institute for Free Labor Development
CIA   Central Intelligence Agency
CIO   Congress of Industrial Organizations
IDF   International Development Foundation
OSS   Office of Strategic Services (predecessor of the
             CIA)
USAID   U.S. Agency for International Development
USWA   United Steelworkers of America

B. International Organizations

ATLAS	Argrupación de Trabajadores Latino Americanos Sindicalizados
CADORIT	Caribbean Area Division of the Inter-American Regional Organization of Workers (ORIT)
CIT	Confederación Inter-Americana da Trabajadores
CLASC	Confederación Latinoamericana de Sindicatos Cristianos
CLAT	Central Latino Americana de Trabajadores (ex-CLASC)
CTAL	Confederación de Trabajadores de América Latina
IADB	Inter-American Development Bank
ICFTU	International Confederation of Free Trade Unions
ITS	International Trade Secretariats
OAS	Organization of American States
ORIT	Organización Regional Inter-Americana de Trabajadores
PAFL	Pan-American Federation of Labor
WFTU	World Federation of Trade Unions

C. National Organizations

CGT	Confederación General de Trabajo. Argentina.
CNT	Confederación Nacional de Trabajadores. Chile.
CONATRAL	National Confederation of Free Workers. Dominican Republic.
CROM	Confederación Regional Obrera Mexicana. Mexico.
CTC	Confederación de Trabajadores de Cuba. Cuba.
CTM	Confederación de Trabajadores de México. Mexico.
FOUPSA	United Workers' Front for Free Unions. Dominican Republic.
GAWU	Guyana Agricultural Workers' Union. Guyana.
MPCA	Man Power Citizens' Association. Guyana.
NWU	National Workers Union. Jamaica.
PPP	People's Progressive Party. Guyana.
TUC	Trades Union Congress. Great Britain.

FOOTNOTES

1. On Latin American labor in general see the author's
    "The Parameters of Labor in Hispanic America" in
    Science and Society, Vo.. XXXVI, No. 2, Summer
    1972, 202-216, and a forthcoming volume on labor from
    1850 to date by Harper and Row. I would like to
    thank the following persons for comments on earlier
    drafts: Professor David Barkin of Lehman College,
    City University of New York (CUNY), Professor Kenneth
    P. Erickson of Hunter College (CUNY), Mike Locker,
    and Professor Patrick V. Peppe of Lehman College
    (CUNY).

2. F. Pérez Leirós, El movimiento sindical de América
    Latina (Buenos Aires, 1941), 48-54.

3. On early relationships see James D. Cockcroft,
    Intellectual Precursors of the Mexican Revolution,
    1900-1913 (Austin, Texas: 1968), 126-127 and Harvey
    A. Levenstein, Labor Organization in the United
    States and Mexico (Westport, Conn.: 1971), Ch. I and
    II.

4. On PAFL in general see Sinclair Snow, The Pan American
    Federation of Labor (Durham, North Carolina, 1964);
    Levenstein, Ch. 6.

5. Levenstein, Ch. 7.

6. Ibid., Ch. 8, 162.

7. Ibid., p. 121.

8. Brief reviews of AGAT in Moisés Poblete Troncoco and
    Ben G. Burnett, The Rise of the Latin American
    Labor Movement (New Haven, Conn., 1960), 133; Juan
    Arcos, El sindicalismo en América Latina (Bogota,
    Colombia, 1964), 13-14; on CSLA, A. Losovsky, El
    movimiento sindical latino americano (sus virtudes
    y sus defectos) (Montevideo, 1929) which is an
    official report on the founding congress, and Pérez
    Leirós, 50.

9. Pérez Leirós, 48, 54-62; Vicente Lombardo Toledano,
    La Confederación de Trabajadores de América Latina
    ha concluído su misión histórica (Mexico, 1964),
    16-19; 134-137.

10. Toledano, 20-35; Poblete Troncoso and Burnett, 137-139;
    Carroll Hawkins, Two Democratic Labor Leaders in
    Conflict (Lexington, Mass., 1973), 9.

11. Levenstein, 168, 178-183, 187 and Romualdi's rich
    autobiography Presidents and Peons. Recollections
    of a Labor Ambassador in Latin America (New York,
    1968).

12. Henry Landsberger, "International Labor Organization,"
    in Samuel Shapiro, ed., Integration of Man and
    Society in Latin America (South Bend, Indiana,
    1967), 190-110; George Morris, American Labor.
    Which Way? (New York, 1961), 96; Poblete Troncoso
    and Burnett, 140-141; John P. Windmuller, American
    Labor and the International Labor Movement, 1940-
    1953 (Ithaca, New York, 1954), 1691.

13. Quoted in Levenstein, 196.

14. See Poblete Troncoso and Burnett, 142-146 which
    includes ORIT's general program; Hawkins contains
    the best summary of ORIT's ideology.

15. Size estimates from AIFLD Report, Vol. 10, No. 9,
    Sept. 1972, 7 and Hawkins, 1; Budget estimate from
    P. Reiser, L'Organisation Regionale Interamericaine
    des Travailleurs (O.R.I.T.) de la Confederation
    Internationale des Syndicats Libres (C.I.S.L.),
    1951-1961(Geneva, 1962), 156-157.

16. Information on these and other activities in Hawkins,
    23, 117; Hispanic American Report, Sept. 1960,
    468, 491, and Dec. 1961, 944; Windmuller, 187;
    and Arnold Zack, Labor Training in Developing
    Countries (New York, 1964), 31-32.

17. Levenstein, 227.

18. Hawkins, 50-52; Hispanic American Report, March 1962,
    82; Levenstein, 220.

19. On U.S. labor in Latin America see Ronald Radosh,
    American Labor and United States Foreign Policy
    (New York, 1969), Chs. XI-XIII and on Lovestone,
    438-449 in addition to David Langley, "The Colonization
    of the International Trade Union Movement" in
    Burton H. Hall, ed., Autocracy and Insurgency in
    Organized Labor (New Brunswick, N.J., 1972), 297-
    298; financial figures from George Morris, CIA and
    American Labor. The Subversion of the AFL-CIO's
    Foreign Policy (New York, 1967), 79 and Jeffrey
    Harrod, Trade Union Foreign Policy. A Study of
    British and American Trade Union Activities in
    Jamaica (Garden City, N.Y., 1972), 125 .

20. Hispanic American Report, Oct. 1962, 702.

21. P. O'Brian, "AID and Trade Union Development" unpublished ms., 5 and Zack, 33.

22. On the OAS see Hawkins, 58-59; on ITS, Windmuller, 96; on ITS and the CIA, Langley, 303-306; for Peru, William J. McIntire, "U.S. Labor Policy" in Daniel A. Sharp, ed., U.S. Foreign Policy and Peru (Austin, Texas, 1972), 303.

23. On AIFLD's origins see Sidney Lens, "Labor Lieutenants and the Cold War" in Hall, ed., 319; Lodge quotes in Langley, 301; and the AFL-CIO resolution in Hispanic American Report, Oct. 1960, 576.

24. U.S. Senate, Committee on Foreign Relations, Subcommittee on American Republics Affairs, Survey of the Alliance for Progress, Labor Politics and Program, 90th Congress, 2nd Session, July 15, 1968, 9 and 5. This Report details AIFLD's action and organization.

25. Langley, 299 quoting Meany on April 2, 1966 talking to a business group composed of Rockefeller interests.

26. U.S. Senate, 15; on W.R. Grace see fn. 64.

27. Ibid., 11.

28. AID figures from Michael Locker, "AID for the Domestic Economy," in North American Congress on Latin America, Latin America and Empire Report, Vol. VI, No. 2 (Feb. 1972), 20; CIA support from Jim Mellen, "Leaders for Labor -- Made in America," in North American Congress on Latin America, New Chile (Berkeley, Calif., 1972), 55.

29. See Susanne Bodenheimer, "The AFL-CIO in Latin America. The Dominican Republic: A Case Study" in Viet Report, Sept.-Oct. 1967, 19 and AIFLD Report, Vol. 11, No. 5, May 1973, 5.

30. U.S. House Appropriations Committee, Foreign Operations Appropriations for FY 1963, Hearings, 87th Congress, 2nd Session, 1962, Part III, 142.

31. U.S. Senate, 35.

31a. William A. Douglas, "U.S. Labor Policy in Peru -- Past and Future" in Daniel A. Sharp, ed., U.S. Foreign Policy and Peru (Austin, Texas, 1972), 320 and McIntire, 320, 304, 320.

88

32. AIFLD Report, Vol. 8, No. 1, Nov. 1970, 1 and Vol.
    11, No. 1, Jan 1973, 2-3 for figures on graduates,
    Annual Report, 1962-1975, 3   for total trainee
    figures.

33. AIFLD Report, Vol. 10, No. 1, Jan 1972, 3, Vol. 10,
    No. 3, March 1972, 5-6, Vol. 10, No. 9, Sept. 1972,
    1, Vol. 11, No. 2, Feb. 1973, 3, 6, and Vol. 11,
    No. 8, Oct. 1973, 3.

33a. Douglas, 320-321, 324.

34. Details on projects in U.S. Senate, 34ff, Richard K.
    Lorden, "The American Institute for Free Labor
    Development in Action" in Brazilian Business,
    Sept. 1967, Vol. XLVIII, No. 9, 35 and on housing
    especially Susanne Bodenheimer, "U.S. Labor's
    Conservative Role in Latin America," in The
    Progressive, No. 1967, Vol. 31, No. 11, 27;
    Mellen, 55; fund data in AIFLD Report, Vol. 11,
    No. 9, Dec. 1973, 5.

35. AIFLD Report, Vol. 10, No. 1, Jan. 1972, 1-2.

36. Joseph A. Page, The Revolution That Never Was
    (New York, 1972), 232.

37. Timothy F. Harding, "The Political History of
    Organized Labor in Brazil" (unpublished Dissertation,
    Stanford University, March 1973), 330, 415-416,
    425-436, 505, 565-6, 575, 603; trainee figures
    from AIFLD Report, Vol. 10, No. 5, March 1972, 5;
    McIntire, 301.

38. Alan Angell, Politics and the Labour Movement in
    Chile (London, 1972), 265-269; Mellen, 56-58; North
    American Congress on Latin America, Latin America
    and Empire Report, Vol. VIII, No. 2, Feb. 1974,
    31-32; O'Brien, 8, 10.

39. Angell, 252-258; O'Brien, 5-6, 16-19.

40. Brian Murphy, "The Stunted Growth of Campesino
    Organizations" in Richard N. Adams, Crucifixion by
    Power (Austin, Texas, 1970), 457.

41. Morris, CIA, 81-83; Murphy, 459-460; 478.

42. Harrod, 255, 261-262, 273-274, 297.

43. Harrod, 263-268, 276, 285-290, 312,320; on aluminum
    companies in general Philip Reno, "Aluminum Profits
    and Caribbean People" in Robert Rhodes, ed.,
    Imperialism and Underdevelopment (New York, 1970),
    79-88.

44. Background material in Ashton Chase, A History of
    Trade Unionism in Guyana, 1900 to 1961 (Georgetown,
    1968), 206-216 and William H. Knowles, Trade Union
    Development and Industrial Relations in the
    British West Indies (Berkeley, Calif., 1959); on
    the 1950s see Colin V.F. Henfrey, "Foreign
    Influence in Guyana: The Struggle for Independence"
    in Emmanuel de Kadt, ed., Patterns of Foreign
    Influence in the Caribbean (London, 1972), 55-64.

45. Henfrey, 58-62, 65-70; Cheddi Jagan, The West On
    Trial (New York, 1972), 226-234.

46. Quoted in Henfrey, 70.

47. Henfrey, 49, 69-72.

48. Sidney Lens, "Labor and the CIA" in The Progressive,
    Vol. 31, No. 4, April, 1969, 26.

49. Feb. 23, 1967.

50. Henfrey, 70; Jagan, 248-9, 253, 378-382; Lens, 26;
    Morris, CIA, 89-90 says that a dozen AIFLD-
    sponsored agents operated at the time.

51. Susanne Bodenheimer, 17-18.

52. Ibid., 18.

53. Fred Goff and Michael Locker, "The Violence of
    Domination: U.S. Power and the Dominican Republic"
    in Irving L. Horowitz, José de Castro, and John
    Gerassi, eds., Latin American Radicalism (New York,
    1969), 267-272.

54. Bodenheimer, 27-28; Hawkins, 52-53.

55. Bodenheimer, 19, 27; and on other housing projects
    see Susanne Bodenheimer, "U.S. Labor's Conservative
    Role in Latin America" in The Progressive, Vol.
    31, No. 11, Nov. 1967, 27; Mellen, 55.

55a. See Samuel L. Baily, Labor, Nationalism, and Politics
     in Argentina (New Brunswick, N.J., 1967), 121-122;
     on ATLAS see John Deiner, "ATLAS: A Labor Instrument
     of Argentine Expansionism Under Perón" (unpublished
     Ph.D. Dissertation, Rutgers University, 1970) an

unsympathetic treatment; on AIFLD and U.S. labor policy in Argentina see NACLA, "AIFLD Losing Its Grip" in Argentina In The Hour of the Furnaces (NACLA, 1975) Box 57 Cathedral Station, N.Y., N.Y. 10025 and Box 226, Berkeley, CA 94701.

56. See Hawkins, and Emilio Máspero, "Trade Unionism as an Instrument of the Latin American Revolution" in Horowitz, de Castro, and Gerassi, eds., 207-231.

57. Information since the coup in Non-Intervention in Chile, Chile Newsletter (Berkeley, Calif, 1973-).

58. Harrod, 298, 305, 332.

59. Quote from Harrod, 395, see also 389.

60. Figures derived from B. Koval and B. Merin, "El movimiento obrero latinoamericano en la etapa actual" in Panorama Latinoamericano. Boletín Quincenal de la Agencia de Prensa Novosti, No. 100, June 197- (Moscow, USSR), 4, Máspero, 215, and Statistical Abstract of Latin America, G. Paul Roberts, ed., (Los Angeles, Calif., 1968), Table 23, 96-97.

61. See for example, AIFLD Report, Vol. 10, No. 1, Jan. 1972, 5; Vol. 11, No. 7, April 1973, 1; Vol. 12, No. 1, Feb. 1974, 1, two of this year's seven courses at Front Royal are for women.

62. See Evelio Tellería, Los congresos obreros en Cuba (Havana, 1973), 430-560; Hobart A. Spalding, Jr., "The Workers Struggle: 1850-1961" in Cuba Review, Vol. IV, No. 1, July 1974, 3-10, 31.

63. José Serra, El milagro económico brasileño (Buenos Aires, 1972), 28-29, 46.

64. A version of this article including material on Argentina and on the ITS' growing role as AIFLD is forced on the defensive appeared in Latin American Perspectives, Vol. 3, No. 1, Winter 1976, 45-69. In the same issue also see articles on labor and imperialism by Timothy F. Harding and Hobart A. Spalding, Jr., 314, Aníbal Quijano, 15-18 and Kenneth P. Erickson and Patrick V. Peppe, 19-44. Other recent studies are Phillip Agee, Inside the Company: CIA Diary (Harmondsworth, Eng., 1975) on the CIA and labor; and in NACLA's Latin America & Empire Report, Susanne Jonas, "Trade Union Imperialism in the Dominican Republic," Vol. 9, No. 3, Apr. 1975, 13-21, "Labor Coming of Age" in Vol. 9, No. 8, Nov. 1975, 20-24 on Ecuador, and "Amazing Grace: the Story of W.R. Grace & Co.," Vol. 10, No. 3, Mar. 1976, 12-14.

Suggested Readings

The items cited in the footnotes provide additional readings. Several of these make good starting points for the interested student. On U.S. labor see Ronald Radosh, American Labor and United States Foreign Policy. The Cold War in the Unions From Gompers to Lovestone (Random House, N.Y., 1969). On Latin American labor in general Hobart A. Spalding, Jr., "The Parameters of Labor in Hispanic America," Science and Society, Vol. XXXVI, No. 2, Summer 1972, 202-216 and Kenneth P. Erickson, Patrick V. Peppe, and Hobart A. Spalding, Jr., "Research on the Urban Working Class and Organized Labor in Argentina, Brazil, and Chile: What Is Left To Be Done?" Latin American Research Review, Vol. IX, No. 2, Summer 1974, 115-142. On the international aspect in general see Jeffrey Harrod, Trade Union Foreign Policy (Doubleday, Garden City, N.Y. 1972). The AIFLD Report published monthly until recently it became a bi-montly publication is full of detailed information on that organization.

PARLIAMENTARY SOCIALISM AND WORKERS' CONSCIOUSNESS IN CHILE[*]

Patrick V. Peppe

Several recent treatments of Latin American labor, and the Chilean working class in particular, challenge the belief that urban industrial workers are "revolutionary." Some of these studies argue that the proletariat today lacks a revolutionary consciousness, while others go further and strongly imply that important sectors of this class will not develop a revolutionary consciousness in the future.

This article criticizes four hypotheses advanced to support the argument that working-class attitudes and behavior in Chile, like Latin America as a whole, are not revolutionary. The first hypothesis asserts that a predominant concern with economic goals leads the working class to support reformist rather than revolutionary movements. According to a second hypothesis, the benefits which urban industrial workers derive from their location in the "modern" sector of society give them an enduring stake in maintaining exploitative relations with the "internal colony," that is, the peasantry. Third, some authors alleged that industrial workers moderated the ideology of the Chilean Marxist parties because they are "privileged" in comparison to other sectors of the urban lower strata. Fourth, workers in the most modern plants supposedly form an "aristocracy of labor" whose interest in and chances for social mobility make them more conservative than the rest of the working class.

All these hypotheses rely on a common assumption about the causes of revolutionary politics, namely, that the degree of relative economic deprivation experienced by working-class persons will determine their orientation toward revolutionary issues. If this assumption were correct, then a revolutionary ideology within the industrial proletariat would indeed be undermined, deflected or obliterated by the relative advantages this class has won compared to the rest of the urban and rural poor. The first three hypotheses in particular would lead us to believe that the industrial working class forms a more or less undifferentiated and nonrevolutionary mass, while the last suggests that increasing conservatism is the trend of the future.

To analyze these hypotheses, we must first settle on a definition of what is "a revolutionary outlook." I

---

[*] I gratefully acknowledge the assistance provided by a George N. Shuster Fellowship for processing data used in this article. I would also like to thank Hobart A. Spalding, Jr. and John Hammond, Jr. for their helpful comments on an earlier draft of the manuscript.

shall use as a criterion the workers' view of <u>who should own and control the major sources of income and wealth</u>. Thus, a worker can be classified as "revolutionary" if he or she believes that the direct producers (workers or peasants) should own the means of production, or if he or she supports expropriating foreign-owned property and placing it under exclusive national control. This definition enables us to uncover some sources of anti-capitalist and pro-socialist orientations in the working class as these orientations emerge within capitalist societies.

Chile in the late 1960's provided a unique opportunity in Latin America to study the effects of two conditions in the development of a "revolutionary" consciousness in the industrial working class. First, Chile before the civil-military coup of September, 1973, had long maintained a system of formal political democracy. Numerous parties competed on the basis of different and sometimes conflicting ideologies for the people's vote in regular and relatively free elections. The second condition was that Chile's two principal Marxist parties, the Communists and the Socialists, adopted a parliamentary socialist ideology, that is, they participated in political democracy, seeking to bring about socialism through peaceful and electoral means.[1]

To understand how a revolutionary outlook toward property relations can develop under these conditions, we must begin by comparing Chilean workers' attitudes with the public statements of the parties competing for labor's allegiance. The public statements of parties usually represent little more than their leaders' perceptions of, and response to, their social base, as well as to short-term political circumstances. Parties that participate in electoral politics have a strong incentive to stress the most urgent concerns of potential voters and downplay long-term objectives which might raise anxieties and threaten the interests of those who benefit most from the existing system. In Chile, the Communist and Socialist parties advocated "socialism" in the long run, but remained vague about socialism's content. They based immediate policies and strategies on what they thought were the requirements of gaining power through elections. Given this parliamentary socialist ideology we should distinguish (1) the workers' responses to explicit policy alternatives offered by the Marxist parties and by their principal rival, the Christian Democratic Party, (2) their responses to other issues on which the parties differ little, and (3) workers' attitudes toward issues which parties do not address in public, but which are implicit in their general societal aims.

Neither survey findings from the late 1960s nor the subsequent behavior of Chilean industrial workers

lend much support to the four hypotheses we examine below.
The data,however,do support   an alternative hypothesis,
namely, that parliamentary socialism, despite its calculated
tactical ambiguities, played an important role in stimu-
lating and reinforcing revolutionary attitudes toward
property ownership among those workers who identified with
the Communist and Socialist parties before 1970.

We conclude that differential political socialization within a given social, economic and political context
explains revolutionary attitudes better than relative
economic deprivation.

Hypothesis One: Labor's Goals

An important statement concerning the ideological
position of the Latin American working class is contained
in an article by Henry A. Landsberger published in 1966.
He argues that in Chile and in Latin America as a whole,
"labor's goals are economic, not ideological . . . ."[2]
Assessing the extent and causes of revolutionary ideology
in the working class, he concludes:

> Such evidence as we have on the level of expressed
> opinions argues against the existence of a crystal-
> lized extremist ideology either among the labor
> elite or among labor as a whole. Where it does
> exist, it is a direct reaction to economic and
> status deprivation,responsive to relatively mild
> measures and subject to the influence of relatively
> mild reformist ideologies.[3]

This brief statement actually involves four distinct
assertions or assumptions which we can formulate separately
as follows:
(1) The degree of support for revolutionary measures
within the working class as a whole is insignificant. (2)
The support that does exist for revolutionary measures is
not connected with the activities of a particular political
party. Where clear issue alternatives are presented to the work
er by competing parties, he or she will choose the less
radical alternative. (3) Where a revolutionary ideology
gains support within the working class, it is caused by
economic deprivation. (4) If a worker supporting the most
radical party improves his or her economic situation under
a reformist government, he or she will shift support to the
reformist party.

(1) Landsberger's argument in the case of Chile
rests largely on his finding that local blue-collar union
leaders interviewed in 1962 overwhelmingly viewed their
union in economist terms. They thought that union activities
should focus primarily on securing economic benefits for
its members. Only a tiny proportion thought that the
union's three most important goals should include arousing
a political consciousness in the workers. Differences
between Marxist and Christian Democratic sympathizers were
insignificant.

This survey of union leaders unfortunately included
no items on agrarian reform or the nationalization of the
United States-owned copper mines, both of which had just
emerged as political issues in the early 1960s. Neither
did the survey include questions on the ownership and
control of factories -- a matter which, to be sure, no
party had yet raised in public discussions. Thus it was
not possible for Landsberger to determine the degree of
support for revolutionary changes as we have defined them,
or to explore differences between Marxist and Christian
Democratic party supporters on these issues.

However, in a 1968-69 survey of 259 unionized blue-
collar workers in Santiago leather and shoe, textile and
metal industries, we did include questions on these
subjects. In contrast to Landsberger's conclusions about
union leaders, the goals of most workers in our 1968-69
sample went well beyond short-term economic improvements.
(See Table One.) 84.5 percent wanted the copper mines to
be under the exclusive control of the Chilean state. About
a quarter of the sample (27.0 percent) favored transferring
all large land holdings (latifundios), whether well-cultivated
or not, to those who worked them. 35.5 percent believed that
factories should belong to the workers or to the state.
Further analysis showed that about half the sample (49.7
percent) either favored expropriating the factories or all
latifundios. If we define revolutionary goals, then, as
including fundamental changes in property ownership, a
substantial proportion of Chilean industrial workers held a
revolutionary outlook even before the major political
parties publicly and explicitly advocated these goals.

(2) We expected to find significant differences
between Marxist and Christian Democratic workers over the
question of the copper mines, since the key programmatic
conflict between Christian Democrat Eduardo Frei and the
Communist-Socialist candidate, Salvador Allende, during
their 1964 presidential campaigns concerned Allende's call
for full nationalization; Frei proposed a mixed ownership
scheme he labeled "Chileanization." However, only minimal
differences existed between the Christian Democratic and
Marxist parties on agrarian reform during the entire 1960s,

as judged by their official positions: both favored expropriation of large and poorly-cultivated holdings.
Workers' ownership of factories, as we noted, had not been
adopted as a programmatic goal by either party before 1970.
Thus, we could not predict whether party sympathies among
the workers we interviewed would make a difference on these
latter two issues.

Indeed, the positions of workers in our sample did
reflect the programmatic conflict between the Marxist
and Christian Democratic parties on the copper question.
92.8 percent of those who felt that the Marxist parties
had "done more than others to favor the working class"
supported nationalization while 75 percent of Christian
Democrats did. Note, however, that a large majority of
PDC workers adopted the Marxist parties' position on this
nationalist issue. Thus, where a clear and salient issue
conflict between the major political movements received
national publicity during a critical election, even the
supporters of the reformist party in our sample opted for
the most radical solution. This finding would lead us to
reject Landsberger's generalization that the goals of
labor "are not ideological and revolutionary unless the
absence of a reformist alternative drives labor to more
extreme positions."[4]

Differences between PDC and Marxist party supporters
over land and factory ownership were even more striking.
As Table One shows, workers identifying with the Marxist
parties supported such changes in far greater proportions
than did Christian Democratic sympathizers. A majority
(63.1 percent) of Marxist sympathizers favored ownership
by the direct producers of either the large landed properties or the factories.

TABLE 1

SUPPORT FOR REVOLUTIONARY GOALS BY PARTY SYMPATHIES

	Copper mines to state	All _Latifundios_ to those who work them	Factories to workers or state
Marxists	92.8	41.6	47.6
Christian Democrats	75.0	5.0	22.5
All Workers	84.5	27.0	35.5

(3) As for the assumption that economic deprivation
fosters a revolutionary outlook, while relative nondepriva-
tion breeds support for reformist positions, Table Two
shows attitudes toward property ownership by salary level.
Although the highest-paid group does consistently give less
support than the lowest-paid to changes in property ownership, these differences are quite small (ranging from 4
to 6 percent). Furthermore, in no case is there a linear
relationship between salary and attitudes toward property
ownership. Party identification remains by far a better
predictor of attitudes toward ownership than relative
economic deprivation.
(4) Finally, we included a question in our 1968-
1969 survey which enables us indirectly to test Landsberger's
assertion that "a relatively mild improvement in economic
conditions will remove the desire for a total qualitative
institutional change."[5] If this were true, then the reformist alternative presented by Chilean Christian Democracy
should have weakened the attraction of the Marxist parties
among workers whose economic circumstances improved during
the Frei government (1964-1970). However, not one of the
workers in our sample who had voted for Allende in 1964
and who reported that his economic situation subsequently
improved thought that the Christian Democratic party had
done more than others to favor the working class. Although
these workers represented only a small number within our
total sample (n = 16), more than half of them should have
named the Christian Democrats as their prime beneficiaries,
if their political outlook were a function of economic
deprivation.

TABLE 2

SUPPORT FOR REVOLUTIONARY GOALS

BY INCOME (WEEKLY, IN 1968 ESCUDOS)

	Copper Mines to State	All Latifundios to Those Who Work Them	Factories to Workers or State
200 or more	78.0	26.0	28.0
150-199	87.5	25.0	40.6
100-149	87.1	28.0	36.5
Less than 100	84.0	30.0	34.0

To summarize, we find that a substantial proportion
of unionized industrial workers in our sample favored
revolutionary changes in property relations. The level of
support for these changes reflected not only the single specifi
programmatic conflict between the major parties in
1964, but also the general ideological goals of these
parties. Relative economic deprivation turned out to be
a poor predictor of support for revolutionary measures.
Finally, the mild reformist ideology of Christian Democracy
does not seem to have diminished support for the Marxist
parties among those few Allende voters who bettered their
material circumstances during the Frei period. All this
suggests that leadership and political socialization are
more important than relative economic deprivation in
explaining adherence to revolutionary goals within the
working class.[6]

While Landsberger's findings clearly illustrate
the economist orientation of the union leaders toward
their union, they merely reflect the fact that the political parties viewed the function of the union in the same
way. For the Marxist as well as the Christian Democratic
parties, unions served first and foremost to defend the
economic interests of their members. In their view, the
political party, not the union, should assume the tasks of
politicization. Of course, all parties sought to build an
electoral base within the unions -- the Marxists with far
more success than others. Union meetings, local and
national, frequently provided a forum for the discussion
of political issues affecting workers. Yet, the explicit
strategy of the Communists, to which the Socialists
usually acquiesced in practice, aimed at forging maximum
unity within the labor movement. This strategy, they hoped,
would facilitate national electoral alliances with the
multi-class Radical Party and the Christian Democrats.
As a result, they minimized political conflicts within the
unions, even to the point where in 1958 the Marxist parties
eliminated "socialism" as an official objective of the
Central Labor Confederation (CUT) which they dominated, in
the hope that other parties would thus be induced to join
it. Hence we must look to the ideologies of the parties
seeking labor's support to explain union leaders' attitudes
toward their unions.

Our 1968-69 findings suggest that even while the
Marxist parties did not explicitly and consistently gear
their program, their union activities or their political
strategy (beyond the vote) toward achieving definite
revolutionary objectives, they did discuss their ultimate
societal aims and some of their implications among their
supporters in the unions, at the workplace and in working-
class communities. On the broadest ideological level, the

general societal aims of the Marxist parties and the
Christian Democrats remained distinct. The dominant wing
of the PDC, despite growing internal opposition during the
1960's, sought to strengthen and modernize Chilean capitalism, while the Communists and Socialists called for the
establishment of "socialism" by parliamentary means. Working-class supporters of these parties responded appro-
priately to these general ideological differences --
"socialism" v. "reform within capitalism." Revolutionary
goals, once accepted, probably contributed to working-class
support for the Communists and Socialists. Because most
treatments of Chilean working-class politics have ignored
this point, they have consistently underestimated the
revolutionary potential of that class.

Hypothesis Two: Internal Colonialism

A second line of argument, advanced by Rodolfo
Stavenhagen, holds that the working class is "a benefi-
ciary of internal colonialism" and "that is one of the
reasons why a truly revolutionary labor movement does not
exist in Latin America." The economic gains of the working class,
he maintains, come at the cost of agriculture, that is, the peasantry. Hence, "the objective interests of the peasants
and the workers are not identical in the matter of agrarian
reform." Existing social structures in Latin America do
not "naturally" favor an alliance between peasants and
workers.[7]

Nevertheless, in responding to a general question in
our survey, the vast majority of our sample (82.2%)
agreed that "peasants and workers have common interests."
A smaller proportion (66.7 percent), responding to another
question, thought that "workers and office employees have
common interests." Thus, more workers identified their
interests with peasants in the "colonized" sector than
with other groups in the "metropolis."

More concretely, 62.9 percent of the workers in our
sample felt that the poorly-cultivated latifundios should
be turned over to the peasants. Nearly all of the remaining
workers took what we defined as a revolutionary position --
i.e., they favored giving all the latifundios to those who
worked them regardless of how well they were cultivated.
When we asked our sample why an agrarian reform would benefit them, they answered almost invariably that, if properly
carried out, it would yield more and cheaper food. There
is, of course, no technical reason why these expectations
could not be realized, even while improving the traditionally miserable living conditions that prevail in rural
Chile.

The workers' identification of their interests with
those of the peasantry and their near-unanimous support
for some form of agrarian reform probably came in response
to two factors. First, the steady upward trend in food
prices in the 1950's and '60's eroded workers' incomes.
Year after year, governments fixed higher and higher prices
for agricultural goods in an effort to stimulate production
on vastly concentrated and underutilized farm units. The
Marxist parties and many Christian Democrats had long
fixed responsibility for this situation on existing rural
property relations, which enable landlords to exploit both
peasants as producers and workers as consumers. The
Marxist-dominated CUT supported agrarian reform and peasant
unionization, and pressed the Frei government to accelerate
its land distribution program during the late 1960's.[8]
Thus, spiraling food prices and the explanations for them
given by the strongest parties within the labor movement
probably made transparent the connection between latifundio
domination of the countryside and the precarious standard
of living of urban workers.

The internal colonial model remains valuable for
explaining the crucial links between urban and rural
owning classes throughout Latin America, and particularly
in Chile. Yet, it obscures the interests which peasants
and workers have in common. The owners of the means of
production in the "modern" sectors -- industrialists,
bankers and large merchants -- are linked to "traditional"
landowners through family ties and interlocking investments. In Chile, just such a class amalgam first took
shape in the mid-nineteenth century and has endured as a
class down to the present. The political alliances formed
among various fractions of this class have resisted agrarian
reform as well as social and economic benefits for urban
workers. This aspect of class relations in Chile, which
is not unknown in other countries of Latin America, has
given peasants and workers a political interest in forming
alliances against a common enemy.

As peasant organizing proceeded at a rapid pace
during the 1960's, the isolation of the peasantry and their
traditional bonds with landowners began to break down. Here
again, the role of political parties was crucial. For
example, Petras and Zeitlin[9] found that where small property
holders predominated in rural Chile, Frei received a disproportionately high vote in 1958 and 1964. But where
agricultural wage labor predominated, the Marxist parties
were strongest. More important, in rural areas contiguous
to mining municipalities -- the centers of Communist and
Socialist strength -- the Allende vote was high regardless
of the rural social structure. The inability and unwill-
ingness of the Marxist parties to organize peasants on a

significant scale before the 1960s had primarily to do
with official repression and their own electoral priorities,
rather than conflicts of interests between peasants and
workers generated by internal colonialism.

Hypothesis Three: The Industrial Labor Aristocracy

Dependent capitalist industrialization in Latin America
has steadily reduced the proportion of the population employed
in manufacturing and has also stratified the industrial work
force internally. In Chile, and in Latin America as a whole,
industiralization has depended on the importation of "labor-
saving" machinery and production techniques from the more
technologically-advanced countries. As a result, the
proportion of Chile's economically-active population employed
in manufacturing declined from 33 percent in 1925 to 26
percent in 1940 and 1952, falling still further to 23
percent by 1960.[10]
This process undermines the political strength of the
working class simply by limiting its size. Nevertheless,
industrial workers have been able to secure more stable
employment at higher wages than other lower-class groups.
Within the class of industrial wage laborers, the unionized
stratum has won the greatest gains, with those employed in
the modern, technologically-sophisticated plants occupying
the most favorable position.
In this section, we examine the impact of dependent
capitalist industrialization on the industrial working class
as a whole and on the unionized stratum in particular. We
turn to the politics of those employed in the modern plants
in the following section.
In a recent essay, Faletto and Ruiz hold that the
ideology of the Chilean Marxist parties reflected not so
much their leaders' perceptions as the consciousness and
behavior of the industrial workers. They argue that urban
industrial workers are "a privileged group within the popular
classes." These workers' comparatively high and secure
incomes lead them to identify with the middle class. Consequently, their union and political activities are "characterized
by greater acceptance of existing social structures."
Industrial workers, therefore, tend to favor alliances with
the middle class which "permit them to maintain their relative
privileges." Parties representing them follow suit.[11]
Again, data from Chile do not lend support to this
hypothesis. In addition to our earlier discussion on
relative economic deprivation, the salient points are
the following:

(1)   Alejandro Portes, in his study of Santiago slum
dwellers, found higher levels of support for the Marxist
parties and for Leftist radicalism among industrial workers
than among those employed in the service sector.[12]   Thus,
if we classify the urban poor generally as "the popular
classes," the "privileged" industrial workers turned out
to be the most, not the least radical.

(2)   As for class identification, 66.5 percent of
our 1968-69 sample believed that the working class could
"do more" for them than either the middle class or an
alliance between the workers and the middle class.   73.1
percent of Marxist party sympathizers as opposed to 60
percent of Christian Democratic supporters took this
position.   Symbolic as these "subjective class identifi-
cations" might be, the data run counter to the thesis that
industrial working-class identification with the middle
class acted as the intermediate factor leading the Marxist
parties to seek alliances with what they deemed "the
progressive middle class."

Taken together, these data indicate that it was not
the attitudes of the industrial working class that produced parliamentary socialism or that led the Marxist
parties to base so much of their political strategy on
capturing middle-class votes.   In any case, it is doubtful
that industrial workers could have exercised a very direct
or consistent influence over the ideologies of the Marxist
parties.   Such influence would most likely have come through
the unions, the critical institutional link between the
parties and the workers.   Alan Angell,   however, concluded
that the Union Department of the Socialist Party was "relatively unimportant in the overall making of Party policies
or tactics."   Union leaders occupied only one out of thir-
teen seats on the Party's Executive Committee.   Communist
union leaders also played a clearly subordinate role in
their Party's policy-making bodies.[13]

Rather, the parliamentary socialist ideology of
these parties reflected their leaders' assessments of the
strength and consciousness of the various classes in
Chile.   Policies and tactics were accepted or rejected
according to their anticipated contribution to electoral
victory.   The pursuit of alliances with a supposedly progressive national bourgeoisie, i.e., professionals,
technicians, state and private employees, medium and small
industrialists and shopkeepers, emerged as part of the
Communists' and Socialists' attempt to broaden their
electoral support beyond the small industrial working
class.   Accordingly, even after the Marxist parties gained
majority support in the CUT elections of 1972, they still
moderated many of their policies to make them more acceptable
to middle-class voters.

Hypothesis Four: Workers in Modern Factories

The new industrialization has stratified the industrial proletariat into three principal groups:

(1) A small stratum of workers employed in the modern sector (automobiles, steel, metals, petrochemicals). A high proportion of this group is skilled, can command relatively high salaries compared to other workers, along with comparatively good working conditions and chances for promotion within the firm.

(2) Workers in large traditional import-substitution industries, established in the more advanced countries between the 1930's and 1950's. They, like the modern ones, generally operate in a monopoly or oligopolistic market. Machinery and techniques of production in traditional firms generally provide lower salaries, poorer working conditions and fewer opportunities for promotion as compared with the modern enterprises.

(3) The vast majority of workers employed in very small plants. Although barely any research exists on this stratum, the terms and conditions of their employment are widely considered to be worse than those in the larger firms, and highly subject to paternalistic relationships with the owners.

Workers in modern plants, an influential study maintains, respond to their work setting by developing comparatively moderate political and trade union outlooks. Di Tella and his associates found that workers in the modern Huachipato steel plant experienced far more job satisfaction than their counterparts in the nearby coal mining operation at Lota. The authors hypothesized that the "context of satisfaction" at Huachipato induced the steel workers to seek upward mobility within the firm; they were more likely than the coal miners to accept the capitalist system and to use the union as an agency of integration into the existing social system.[14] Although this study remains the leading one on Latin American workers in modern industrial plants it has little or no bearing on the question of whether stratification within the industrial working class generated different political and trade union orientations.

However, in directly comparing the three principal strata of industrial workers, Adolfo Gurrieri[15] found that those in modern industries were more likely than workers in traditional or small plants to seek support from the CUT during contract negotiations. He suggests that the higher wages paid in the modern industries enabled workers there to provide their unions with more financial resources than their counterparts in other firms. Thus, whereas unions in modern industries could hire lawyers and technical staff on their own, workers in lower-paying firms were limited in what they could achieve and hence had a relatively greater need for assistance from the Federation and the CUT. In this sense, then, the new industrialization could weaken class solidarity.

The survey used by Gurrieri contained two questions which should bring out whatever tendencies the new industrialization might have to reduce the revolutionary potential of the working class.[16] A. "Who should organize and direct production?" and B. "What should the worker do? Try only to improve his personal situation; devote a few hours a week to the Union; devote a few hours a week to a revolutionary working-class party." As Table Three shows, workers in modern plants do not differ significantly from those in traditional and small firms in their answers to these questions.

TABLE 3

REVOLUTIONARY ORIENTATION BY TYPE OF PLANT

	Modern	Traditional	Small
A	49.4	48.7	48.3
B	13.3	16.6	13.9

Thus, we find no evidence that the new industrialization has created an "aristocracy of labor" in Chile among workers in modern plants which disproportionately supports capitalist norms of property ownership or the political status quo.

On the contrary, it seems more plausible to argue that the new industrialization puts workers in modern or modernizing plants in a particularly vulnerable position -- one which increases rather than decreases their need for reliance on the rest of the working class. Workers, lacking the political power of industrialists and government officials, rarely participate in decisions about technological change. In Chile, and probably elsewhere in Latin America, those who make such decisions have systematically excluded workers' representatives from such participation. For example, 90 percent of the employers interviewed in a 1966 survey either opposed or gave low priority to suggestions that workers participate in decisions on technological change.[17] A majority also opposed their participation in decisions on training and promotion.

Workers have demonstrated that they know how such technology is likely to affect them. Some of the most

combative strikes in postwar Latin America erupted when
owners or government planners and politicians attempted
to impose new technologies without guarantees of continuing
employment.[18] The scant evidence available on Chilean
workers' attitudes indicates that they too are primarily
concerned with employment. In our survey of Santiago
workers, we asked whether machinery should be installed
if it meant higher wages for some, but unemployment for
others. Two-thirds of the sample responded that the
machinery should not be installed and, strikingly, half
of the minority who believed that they would benefit
personally from its installation also opposed it. Of
course, job security has counted among the traditional
demands of trade unionsim. Yet, in the context of the new
industrialization, such traditional demands take on a new
meaning, since they bring even the most "privileged"
workers into conflict with the needs of modernizing capitalism.

This situation generates a new pattern of action
and reaction between modernizing capitalists and the
industrial working class. When the owners of the Yarur
textile plant in Chile, for example, declared in 1961
that they would "rationalize" production by installing
new machinery, they provoked one of the bitterest strikes
in recent Chilean history. The workers were defeated, a
third of them were fired, and Yarur imposed a modernizing
paternalistic police state in microcosm within the factory
for almost ten years. Nevertheless, even under these
extremely repressive conditions, the Yarur workers became
the first to seize and manage their factory after the
U.P. victory in 1970. Although this action was neither
encouraged or particularly appreciated by the new government, it demonstrates the importance of political leadership
and the broader political context in shaping workers'
attitudes and behavior beyond the walls of the factory.

The contradiction between capitalist modernization
and workers' resistance took another form during the Frei
era. When in late 1967 the government attempted to manipulate inflation compensation so that the state could appropriate and invest part of workers' salaries in automobile,
celusoe and petrochemical plants, workers throughout the
country responded with the most successful general strike
in a decade. Forty-one branch federations, regardless
of the degree of modernization, supported the strike. This
militant reaction to Frei's forced savings plan contributed
significantly to splitting the PDC and bringing its pro-
labor and pro-peasant forces over to the side of Allende
in 1970.*

Conclusions

The degree of support we found for revolutionary
measures among Chilean industrial workers may, of course,
be exceptional in Latin America. Yet, several propositions
emerge from our study which would be worth investigating
in other Latin American countries.

First, adherence to trade-unionist strategies can
co-exist with support for revolutionary goals, where
these goals have little chance to be effectively expressed
within existing political institutions. Industrial unions,
which are independent of the state and in which levels of
participation are substantial, can serve as foci of communication for revolutionary ideas. Second, political
organizations can help create a revolutionary outlook and
attract working-class support on the basis of revolutionary
positions, even when these are not publicly articulated.
Worker or government ownership of industry and thorough-
going agrarian reform in Chile provide cases in point.
Third, given the structural conditions of ownership and
agricultural production in most Latin American countries,
political organizations may attract and consolidate support among urban workers by underscoring their common
interests with peasants in agrarian reform. Last, dependent
capitalist modernization, because it establishes new and
repressive controls over the work force, provides incentives
for class solidarity in response to this repression.

How widespread a revolutionary consciousness of the
kind we have defined has or can become is extraordinarily
difficult to anticipate. Yet, the Chilean case demonstrates
the need for further empirical and theoretical inquiries
into the conditions under which a revolutionary outlook
emerges in Latin America's industrial proletariat.

In Chile, it appears that the parliamentary socialist
leadership of the Marxist parties stimulated and reinforced
revolutionary aspirations in the working class through
public and particularly through informal discussions,
and then channeled these aspirations through the institutions of political democracy. Parliamentary socialism thus
provided a mechanism (Leftist voting) through which potential social conflict could take a "legitimate" form, and
be largely obscured within the existing political order.

Despite the parliamentary socialist leadership's
relative success in creating a positive orientation toward
revolutionary goals in the industrial working class, it
proved unable and unwilling to effectively mobilize that
consciousness. Working under extraordinarily difficult
conditions, its ideology focused narrowly and almost
exclusively on electoral struggles. The leadership thus

deprived itself of the variety of means necessary to
bring about a socialist revolution. In short, while the
Communists and Socialists created some conditions for the
growth of a pre-socialist consciousness, they fell short
of creating sufficient conditions for its realization.

This two-sided character of parliamentary socialism,
largely hidden from view before 1970, took on enormous
significance after the U.P.'s presidential victory. By
all indications, the working class gave widespread support
to the government and its expropriation of the copper
mines, all the latifundios, and a large sector of Chilean
industry. The U.P. received over 70 percent of the total
vote in direct secret elections for CUT officers in
1972, and workers responded overwhelmingly to the government's call for demonstrations or temporary factory occupations when owners threatened to sabotage the economy.
But just as important, many workers went beyond supportive
actions by taking the initiative themselves. Once the
government had promised never to use force against its
base, thousands participated in factory seizures intended
as permanent -- actions which the government neither
authorized nor encouraged. As the Communists reluctantly
recognized in the first year of the U.P., "In the new
conditions created in Chile, it is very easy to carry out
seizures. It is not difficult to mobilize a small group
of workers to take a factory, a rural estate or a few
dwellings."[19] Just as a substantial proportion of Communist-Socialist supporters before 1970 took positions on
property ownership which were more revolutionary than the
programmatic statements of the parties, so an important and
visible sector of the working class later actively sought
revolutionary changes the government felt it could not
risk advocating.

The actual threat which the workers represented to
the owning classes goes far to explain the counter-revolutionary terror instituted, with U.S. aid, by the civil-
military regime. The leading families of the so-called
"oligarchy" formed a cohesive and politically-active owning
class, closely tied to the largest industrial and agricultural properties, as well as to foreign corporations.
On the eve of the U.P. period, class conflict in Chile
had reached the point where, as we saw, about half the
workers in our sample and a majority of the Marxist
parties's base advocated measures which would have expropriated holdings of the entire owning class. Little wonder,
then, that following the U.P. experience, the counter-
revolution has directed its fire principally against the
working class. It remains unclear to what extent the Junta
and its allies can achieve their objective of "exterminating
Marxism" and eradicating support for revolutionary goals in
the working class. If the experience of the political
generation of the 1930's in Cuba[20] is applicable to Chile,

108

then the intense **social** conflicts of the early 1970's are likely to increase, not decrease the receptivity of the Chilean working class to revolutionary movements in the future.

Footnotes

[1] See Patrick V. Peppe, "Forms to Fetters: Parliamentary Socialism in Chile," to appear in the forthcoming volume on ideologies in inter-American politics, edited by Moss Blachman and Ronald Helman.

[2] Henry A. Landsberger, "The Labor Elite: Is it Revolutionary?", Elites in Latin America, Eds., Seymour M. Lipset and Aldo Solari (New York: Oxford University Press, 1966), p. 296.

[3] Ibid., p. 278.

[4] Ibid., p. 285.

[5] Ibid., p. 277.

[6] Three studies of the working class give extensive critiques of the relative deprivation hypothesis and its ramifications. John H. Goldthorpe, et al., The Affluent Worker (3 vols.; London: Cambridge University Press, 1968; Richard F. Hamilton, Affluence and the French Worker: The Fourth Republic Experience (Princeton: Princeton University Press, 1967); Maurice Zeitlin, Revolutionary Politics and the Cuban Working Class (Princeton: Princeton University Press, 1967).

[7] Rodolfo Stavenhagen, "Seven Fallacies about Latin America," Latin America: Reform or Revolution?, Eds., James Petras and Maurice Zeitlin (Greenwich, Conn.: Fawcett Publications, 1968), p. 29.

[8] See Memoria del Consejo Directivo al 5º Congreso Nacional de la CUT, 19-24 de Noviembre de 1968 (Santiago: 1968), pp. 24-25.

[9] James Petras and Maurice Zeitlin, "Miners and Agrarian Radicalism," Latin America: Reform or Revolution?, Eds., James Petras and Maurice Zeitlin (Greenwich, Conn.: Fawcett Publications, 1968), p. 247.

[10]Fernando Henrique Cardoso, Cuestiones de Sociología (Santiago: Editorial Universitaria, 1968), Table 7, p. 80.

[11]Enzo Faletto and Eduardo Ruiz, "Conflicto Político y Estructura Social," Chile Hoy, Ed. Aníbal Pinto (Mexico: Siglo Veintiuno, 1970), pp. 234-36.

[12]Alejandro Portes, "Political Primitivism, Differential Socialization and Lower Class Leftist Radicalism," American Sociological Review, xxxvi, 5 (November, 1971), p. 825.

[13]Alan Angell, Politics and the Labour Movement In Chile (London: Cambridge University Press, 1972), pp. 135, 85 ff.

[14]Torcuato Di Tella et al., Sindicato y Comunidad: Dos Tipos de Estructura Sindical Latinoamericana (Buenos Aires: Editorial del Instituto, 1967), especially p. 108.

[15]Adolfo Gurrieri, "Consideraciones sobre los Sindicatos Chilenos,"Aportes, 8 (June, 1969), p. 111.

[16]I would like to thank Victor Nazar and Adolfo Gurrieri for kindly providing access to this data. The sample included 920 Chilean industrial workers and forms part of a study of workers in five Latin American countries directed by Alain Touraine.

[17]Claudio Fuchs and Luis Santaibañez, Pensamiento, Política y Acción del Ejecutivo Industrial Chileno (Santiago: INSORA, 1967), p. 82.

[18]Landsberger, pp. 281-82.

[19]Roberto Pinto, "The MIR Attack on the Communist Party," The Chilean Road to Socialism, Ed. Dale L. Johnson (New York: Anchor Books, 1973), p. 375.

[20]Zeitlin, Revolutionary Politics, chap. 9.

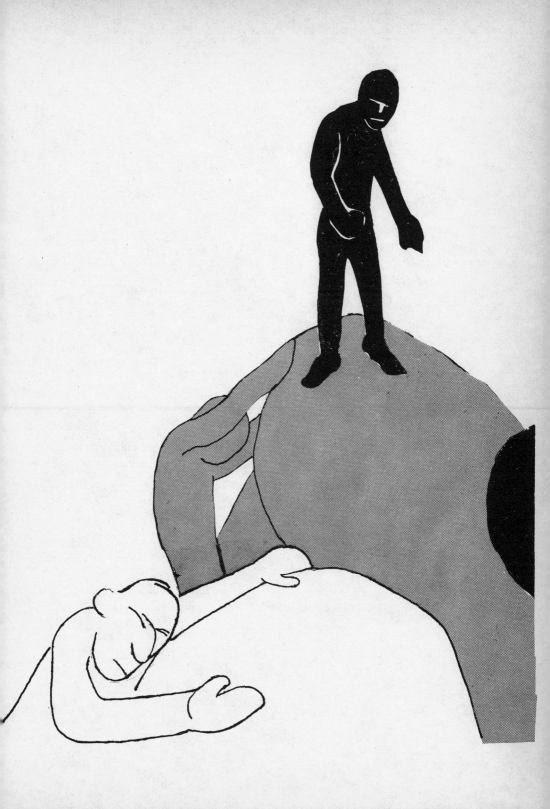

PART II: Ideologies and the Mobilization of Power

PART II: Ideologies and the Mobilization of Power

INTRODUCTION

The study of ideology very seldom comes to rest on
an internal content analysis, important as this might be
as a preliminary step. The sociology of ideology goes on
to place it in the context of the global social structure.
Ideologies are seen as bodies of propositions that are
socially conditioned and politically functional par
excellence. Hence, social scientists are prone to treat
ideologies as manifestations of underlying structural
conflicts and impute them to collective actors. Sometimes social structure is conceived in terms of a model
of class and class conflict. Other times, elite and mass
are the operative concepts. It is only within such frameworks that we can speak of progressive and reactionary
ideologies, that we can perceive the ironies and paradoxes of backward-looking revolutionary movements, or cut
through the populist facade of nationalism to uncover
its stabilizing functions.

The rationalist fantasies of the nineteenth century
looked forward to an age when ideologies would no longer
be necessary, when "isms" would be "wasms" as a Readers
Digest pundit put it. But moving people to undertake
collective action to change their fate, or even convincing
people to support a given status quo requires an interpretation of social conditions that will create unity. While
we reject a view that assumes that all ideologies are
false consciousness (Silva 1971), we distinguish theoretically sound ideologies as those that are generative of
adaptive behavior in response to changed conditions. So
long as reality impinges on patterned responses in such a
way as to reinforce existing propositions, they are considered socially beneficial. Ideologies become obsolete
when they fail to generate such behavior and serve only to
preserve the privileges of a declining minority rather
than responding to the needs of a new reality.

Hobsbawm (this volume) makes explicit a distinction
that has existed in the usage of ideology by anthropologists and to a lesser degree the other social sciences.
He uses the term ideology both as "a formulated and generally recognized system of beliefs about society (often
with a recognized brand-name, such as liberalism,
nationalism, communism, etc.) from which programmes of
social and political action can be or are derived;" and as
"a similar system of beliefs, which is not formulated as
such or consciously held, but which nevertheless forms the
basis of social and political action of a given group of
men." Ideology used in the first sense requires a consistent, shared perception of reality in order to sustain

111

a common course of social action. In the second sense,
members of a society can, and often do, entertain incon-
gruous world views without endangering social interaction
or indicating social disintegration. Wallace (1970: 25)
has also pointed to the fact of heterogeneous perspectives
in rejecting those "culturologists" who maintain that
social unity rests on homogeneity.

This argument can be pushed one step further to
indicate that heterogeneous perspectives can be enter-
tained not only by the same people but by the same person
without feeling any discomfort of "cognitive dissonance"
(Festinger 1957) unless he or she is required to make
choices between alternatives. Pre-conquest myths, the
rituals that reenact them, and modern political ideologies
not only can coexist but can give strength to the self-
determination of indigenous people entering the modern
market nexus as proletarians or traders, as Nash and the
Buechlers show in their articles. Mass media and control
institutions of the dominant sector of society are among
the avenues for channeling and controlling the responses
of various sectors of the population to changes, as the
Melvilles demonstrate in their article.

The reader may treat the following essays as
attempts to bridge the gap between theories of cognition
and historical descriptions of events by analyzing the
motivations to think and act in the context of the events
that evoked theory and practice.

Myth provides a bridge between the past and the
future as indigenous people enter into modern social
movements. June Nash considers the way myth and ideology,
as a specific socio-political philosophy, are products
of group consciousness, and serve to interpret change and
provide motivation and meaning to mobilize social action.
She analyzes three transitional phases for the Andean
Indians: the Spanish conquest, independence and national
corporatism. She concludes that myth, far from being an
outmoded expression of irrational fantasy, is the first
stage in explaining a changed reality and continuously
emerges in liminal stages as people seek to reinterpret
their life conditions.

Eric Hobsbawm analyzes ideology both as a socio-
political theory and as a system of action in Colombia,
asking the questions: how far does the rise of ideological anti-elites reflect a consciousness of new problems
requiring new solutions and how far are the changes
effected by these ideological groups the result of their
theories? The paradox of tradition-oriented entrepreneurs
as harbingers of modernization, raised by Fals Borda, is
posed in reference to peasant movements and social action
systems tied to liberalism and communism. Hobsbawm shows
how Colombian communism seeks to establish, or reestablish,
the traditional norms and values of peasant society.

Jorge Dandler studies ideology and political organization in the Department of Cochabamba, Bolivia, during the fifteen months between the April Revolution of 1952 and the agrarian reform of August 1953, Dandler explores the intersection of mobilized peasants with governmental and political organization. He finds that, while in certain contexts leaders manipulated relationships in a clientelist fashion, the campesino movement in Cochabamba had a dynamic and ideological self-assertiveness of its own. Ideology and clientelist politics may therefore complement rather than exclude each other. Dandler's essay converges in this sense with the problematic outlined by Erickson in his study of Brazilian workers.

Judith-Maria and Hans Buechler reveal another aspect of ideology in symbolic communication, "a code which expresses both similarities and differences between alternate modes of behavior." The new market syndicate in La Paz mediated between city government and market vendors, as well as serving as intermediaries between the federation leaders and their cadre. In the many celebrations carried out by the syndicates, informal channels of communication are maintained with government leaders and vendors and their representatives. The rapid changes which have affected Bolivians in the past few decades are vested with meaning in the ritual and symbolic exchanges that occur in the context of these market celebrations.

Erickson maintains that populism is at base an elite phenomenon. The ideological function of populism consists in obscuring continued elite domination through tactical and symbolic concessions to workers. Control of populist movements does not rest in the hands of workers or peasants. The Brazilian data analyzed by Erickson point up the following characteristic of populism: governments and elites turned to populism for tactical rather than strategic reasons. They did not consciously seek to increase real power or economic benefits for the working class. Rather, they aimed at shifting the base of support for the government once the economic resources on which it had formerly relied began to contract. Populism, Erickson concludes, does not alter the class base of participation in political decision making, but represents instead an attempt to strengthen the mass base of support for established elites.

Bertram Silverman gives us a view of the link between economic organization and social conscience in the context of Cuban socialism. Cuba's rejection, after 1966, of an economic organization based on the money motive reflects strong commitment to revolutionary principles and socialist ethics. Silverman argues that Cuba's revolutionary ethics does not mean an end to ideoloby in the Marxian sense. He attempts to show how Cuban economic organization and developmental strategy have been closely tied to Cuban praxis, and ideology has frequently served to rationalize practice and policy goals. While ideology has played an important role in mobilizing mass commitment to social and economic goals, it has also had the effect of obscuring underlying forces. Silverman proposes to unravel those underlying forces in terms of the real and serious dilemmas confronting Cuban socialism (e.g., the dilemma of "primitive accumulation" without coercion). Such analysis may help to "demystify" revolutionary ideology. Social scientific "demystification" of ideology, Silverman suggests, is as necessary vis-a-vis socialist societies as it is pertinent to the critical analysis of capitalism. Its ultimate goal is to bring socialist theory and practice into a more conscious and harmonious correspondence.

Guatemala is a kind of epitaph for United States liberal involvement in Latin America, and so we have reserved the Melville's analysis of it for the end. They show how the verbal symbols of "sovereignty," "constitutinality," "anti-communism," "democracy," "freedom," and "private property" link the three major power domains in Guatemalan society: the army, the church and the large landowning aristocracy. As peasants become aware of the sources of their poverty, they are less inclined to give credence to this ideology that maintains their obedience to repressive institutions.

REFERENCES

Festinger, Leon
  1957 -- A Theory of Cognitive Dissonance.   Evanston,
        Ill.: Row, Peterson.

Silva, Ludovico
  1971 -- Teoria y Practica de la Ideologia.   Mexico:
        Editorial Nuestro Tiempo.

Wallace, Anthony
  1970 -- Culture and Personality.

MYTH AND IDEOLOGY IN THE ANDEAN HIGHLANDS

June Nash

Myth is the first attempt people make to explain the world and their place in it. Ideology grows out of myths but relies on them to gain acceptance. As a product of collective consciousness, myths sustain group identity. The spiritual conquest of a people comes when the defeated adopt the myths and ideology of the conqueror. The Spanish never completed this process in the Andean area, nor have the nationalists after independence. Indians still draw on their own myths to interpret their life conditions. In their emerging identity as rural or urban proletarians, they merge new ideologies spread by the labor movement with the parables provided by old myths.

The problem I shall consider here is the way myth and ideology serve to interpret changing life conditions. Both myth and ideology, used in the sense of a specific socio-political philosophy, are a product of group consciousness, but they differ in their form and in their effect on action. Myths provide the parables for adjusting to given conditions. Ideologies are the distillation of concrete reality yielding slogans to motivate political action. The parables contained in myth provide a strategy for action and a morality implicit in the distribution of rewards and punishments. Ideology makes explicit the rationale for behavior and identifies moral forces with socially defined groups. Both myth and ideology are often joined in the same discourse. Mythic symbols are part of the rhetorical devices used by the ideologues in swaying opinion. Ideological appeals of the past are often called myths that sustain the interest groups that benefited from them. This perjorative use of myth is based on the affectations of rationality opposed to primordial sentiment expressed in myth that laid the basis for racist dichotomies of the gente de razón, or the rational man, and the indigenous people in the expansion of the West.

Both myth and ideology have been discredited as the product of irrational man. The question of how ideology distorts perception was first raised by Comte in his critique of the French ideologists (Lichtheim 1967: 11). But as each social philosopher exposed the irrationality of past ideas and ideals supporting the status quo, he forged the ideology of the future. Hegel recognized the transitory character of ideologies, but went on to create an ideology of the nation state. Marx and Engels (1947) located "False consciousness" of the German middle class in ideologies of dominance designed to validate the position of power of this sector and proceeded to

create an opposing ideology of the proletariat. Both
relied on myth to give substance to their utopias, in
Hegel's case the myth of the super nation, and in the case
of Marx and Engels the myth of the proletariat in the role
of redeemer (Eliade 1960: 26).

The critique of past ideologies by these social
philosophers paved the way for successively more pene-
trating analyses of contemporary consciousness. Hegel's
recognition of the relativity of truth to historical conditions contributed to the Marxist analysis of the German
ideology. Marx's critique of distortion in the German
ideology as derived from the conditions of dominance and
subordination is a starting point for contemporary Latin
American analysts' critique of the ideology of the bourgeoisie. Economic dependency has led to an ideological
dependency, as Corradi (this volume), Ianni (1971), Salazar
Bondy and others (1968) have pointed out.

The mystification in the analysis of contemporary
Latin American reality stems from a social class that
denies access to positions of self-realization to large
sectors of the society. The contributors to Peru Problema
(Salazar Bondy et al 1968) have shown how the economic
stagnation and political lability of the Andean area are
rooted in archaic systems for dominating Indian and mestizo populations coupled with dependency on external powers
for preserving the political position of the elites who
benefit from the system. Indians have been falsely cari-
catured in myths promoted in the interest of subordinating
them first as tribute payers to the Inca elite, then as
forced labor for the Spaniards, and finally as a powerless
proletariat in a nationalized bureaucracy. The danger for
the dominant group lies in their becoming consumers of
their own false myths and as a consequence losing their
ability to respond adaptively to change. In the Andean
case, the myth of the apathy and backwardness of the Indian
population has led to a faulty analysis of development
which blames that segment for the failure of schemes for
modernization and change. This serves to reinforce a
systematic discrimination against primary producers and a
reinforcement of the power and privilege of the non-pro-
ductive export-import sector of the economy as Huizer
(1970) demonstrates. Whyte (1970) has indicated how this
"myth of the passive campesino" has distorted public
policy in Peru.

The attack on myth and ideology because of their
abuse by dominant groups should not discredit these modes
of thought. Societies need these "symbolic templates" as
Geertz (1966: 62) has called them, in order to organize
sentiments and attitudes in changing conditions. The paradigms expressed in myth and made explicit in ideology are

as necessary for political beings to understanding their
life conditions and responding to them as the paradigms
expressed in models are to scientists, enabling them to
experiment and draw valid rules and general laws.[1] The
problem in the social sciences is that we are still saddled with the Weberian dichotomy of "purposeful-rational"
and "traditional" conduct which, as Mannheim points out
(1936: 303-4) "expresses the situation of a generation in
which one group had discovered and given an evaluative
emphasis to the rationalistic tendencies in capitalism
while another, demonstrably impelled by political motives,
discovered the significance of tradition and emphasized
it as over against the former." This kind of thinking
left anything labeled traditional to the fascist ideologues who exploited this capital of accumulated sentiment
and ritual of the past to underwrite the wars of conquest
in the twentieth century predicated on nationalist sentiment and primary group identification hypostatized in
racial allegiance.

Saddled with this Western dichotomy, myth was
considered to be the mode of thought of archaic man and
ideology that of modern man.[2] Recent anthropological
investigation suggests that myth and ideology are not
historically separated stages of thought, but are cognitive developments generated by the trauma of change.
Turner (1968: 576) has called such periods of change
"liminal stages" or "periods of structural impoverishment
and symbolic enrichment." The generative factor, he
says, "comes from being outside of a particularized
social position, to cease to have a specific perspective
...in a sense to become (at least potentially) aware of
all positions and arrangements and to have a total
perspective."

I shall analyze three such transitional stages for
miners in the highland plateau of Bolivia. The first
began with the Spanish conquest when the culture shock was
worked out in myths and oral traditions. The second came
with independence and the century of developing a national
consciousness that culminated in the Revolution of 1952.
The third stage is now in the making with the failure of
"national corporatism"[3] and its solutions for incorporating
the peasants and workers in state administered bureaucracies that has led to a confrontation of nationalistic and
socialistic ideologies. In these stages myth and history
are intertwined in the consciousness of the past and the
potential role of the proletariat in the future.

I

The mines of Oruro where I have been making a study
of changing ideology[4] have been exploited since the Spanish

colonial period and possibly earlier by Inca invaders.
The preconquest culture of the Uru Uru is described in the
following legend:

The community of Uru Uru was one of fishermen
and pastoralists devoted to the worship of the
Sun. Every day Huari was awakened by the first-
born daughter of the Sun, Ñusta. He fell in love
with her and pursued her with arms of smoke and
volcanic fire. The father came to her aid and
hid her in the caves. Huari swore that he would
bring vengeance against the town by turning it
against the true religion. He became the apostle
of a new religion and preached against Pachacamac
and his religious and social work. He thundered
against Inti, the Sun God, and the old social
hierarchy. He exalted the superiority of material goods over spiritual, and of the labor of the
mines over that of the field. The Urus resisted,
but when Huari showed them gold and silver, they
rebelled against their old beliefs and sacred
authorities. Desirous of riches, they abandoned
the daily hard but healthy work in their fields.
They stopped praying to Inti and turned to wild
drinking and midnight revels with chicha, a
liquor unknown before then. In their drunken
state there came forth toads, snakes, reptiles
and ants who, in the acts of the witches sabbath,
overwhelmed them. The inhabitants of the neighboring towns and even their friends and parents,
appropriated their goods. The people, abject
with vice, were transformed into apathy, silent
and loveless beings.
The town would have disappeared because of
internal fights had not Ñusta appeared on a rain-
bow one day after a heavy storm. Accompanying
her were the chiefs and priests who had been exiled from the town when the people were diverted
from their old ways. Little by little, men returned to what they had been. They revived their
traditions, customs, religion and social order.
They imposed Quechua on the Uru dialect. The
fields would have recovered and even surpassed
their fertility if Huari, in vengeance, had not
sent four plagues on the repentant town: a serpent, a toad, a lizard and ants. The monstrous
serpent moved from the mountains of the South and
devoured their fields and cattle. As the Urus
fled in terror, someone shouted for Ñusta and she
cleft the monster in two with a sword. The other
three plagues, advancing from the other compass

points, were also killed by the intervention of
the Nusta who overwhelmed the vengeful Huari.
Today a church stands on the hill where the giant
serpent was killed, and there is a chapel at the
lake where the lizard's rocky profile is reflected in waters that turn red in the noon light
from the blood he shed (Translated from Beltran,
1962).

The mythic time encompassed in this legend can be
related to the Inca invasion and merging into the Spanish
conquest. The first of these invasions brought to an end
the Garden of Eden when the Uru Uru were pastoralists and
agriculturalists, as the people turned from agriculture to
work in the Mines for the Inca. They were delivered from
the plagues brought upon them by the Quechua virgin, Ñusta.
The return of the four plagues can be related to the Spanish
conquest. This threat was overcome by the introduction of
the Christian faith, when the Ñusta was transmuted to the
Virgin Mary and Catholic churches and shrines were built at
the sites of the slain monsters. The myth cannot be simply
dismissed as unreflective, uncritical thought in contrast
with rational, analytical modes of thought. The kernel of
the Marxist understanding that new modes of production en-
gender new relations to production and unleash unforseen
powers is implicit in the central drama. The resolution of
the conflict, or syntehsis of the dialectic in mythic
thought lies in supernatural powers that must be propitia-
ted--first Ñusta, the daughter of the Inca Sun God Inti and
then the Virgin Mary who symbolized submission to the
Christian conquest in the New World. The uncertainty and
anxiety brought about by the economic transformation are
overcome by rituals of propitiation.
During Carnival, the myths of Huari and the monsters
are enacted in dance and drama. The first written record
of these pageants date from 1789 (Beltran 1962: 8). In one
of these enactments the protagonist, called Nena Nena, is
an unemployed miner who lives by theft. He is admired for
his exploits in making a joke of the police. He despaired
of marrying his beloved, the daughter of a middle-class
merchant, when her father heard of his banditry. He intended to flee with the girl on the night of the carnival celebration. As they were leaving the store, the girl cried,
"My father!" and her lover was wounded by the father as he
pursued them. Nena Nena was led by the Virgin to the hos-
pital where he died in bed. Another version shows the hero,
called Chiru Chiru, as a petty thief who stole from the
rich and sold at reasonable prices in the barrios of the
poor. He always carried a small print of the Virgin Can-
dalaria, and when he returned from a successful theft, he
burned a candle for her. One night he was knifed while

stealing. He ran home in the night and died before the eyes of the Virgin of his constant veneration. Her print was transformed into a genuine wooden image, which still stands before the entrance of what was the richest silver mine in Oruro and is now closed. She is called the Virgin of the Socavón, or Mine Shaft, and the miners used to give an offering to her each day that they came safely out of the mine. Those who venerate her and dance for her during Carnival feel that she protects them and enables them to amass wealth and not waste their wages in petty vices.[5]

Both Chiru Chiru and Nena Nena are identified with Huari or Supaya, the spirit of the mountains. The Spaniards applied the term Devil to this power, but this distorts the concept of this force as potentially benevolent and the source of riches. Supaya lives on in most of the hills and mines of the area. Traces of the monsters with which he threatened Oruro are still present in the barren hills and plains surrounding the city: the serpent, cleft in two, can be seen in a rocky craig encircling one of the hills. Nearby is the church of Chiripujyo where the serpent is venerated on the first Friday of August and of Carnival. The patron of the church, the Saviour of Chiripujyo, a crucified Christ image, is worshipped on May 3. After the people make offerings to him, they go the head of the serpent and perform the ch'alla, an offering of liquor and burned k'oa, combining the foetus of a llama, sweets, colored wool and confetti. Formerly this ceremony was communal. Townspeople arrived in a group with older married couples accompanying young couples about to be married. The elder couples presented the young people to the serpent asking for fertility of crops, animals and those who were about to be married. They then gave advice to the young on how to live with a partner and raise a family. Communal aspects of this ritual, like those of most rituals in Oruro, have been lost and people perform individual rites for their own welfare and that of their family.

The stone effigy of the toad, which can still be seen at the foot of the hill of San Pedro, has been dynamited, but a metal effigy accompanies it to remind people of where it is located. His potentially destructive power is still respected, as the following story of his destruction attests:

> In 1935 an army colonel forbade the people to worship the stone image of the toad. When they persisted, he ordered his soldiers to blast the image with dynamite. Some people said the colonel was afraid that when people came to ch'alla the toad, they would remember their ancestors and what they were and would rebel against conditions as they are now. When the

colonel blasted the toad, people said that he
would be destroyed just as the image was, and
that he alone would bear the punishment. Three
months later, the colonel had a stroke and became paralyzed, and a year from the date that
he destroyed the toad, he died. And to this
day, the people go to ch'alla the remains of
the toad.

The special day for venerating the toad is Tuesday of the
week of Carnival. Hundreds of people gathered at his remains in the year 1970 when I observed the ceremony. Each
family group made their separate offering of liquor, confetti, paper streamers and burned the foetus of the llama
with other objects. They then built a miniature house
nearby to remind the toad of what they wanted in life,
drank, chewed coca and smoked. It was essentially the same
ritual as that performed for the serpent.
      The blood of the lizard still glows at noon in Lake
Poopo. In a church nearby is the patron Savior of Kala
Kala, considered to be brother of the Savior of Chiripujyo.
Miners as well as campesinos ensure the growth of their
children by taking a length of colored wool measured to
the child's height to the savior with offerings of candles
and flowers in order to ensure future growth.
      The mountains of sand at the eastern margins of town
are silent evidence of the legions of ants that threatened
to devour the inhabitants of Oruru. These sand dunes are
the habitat of small lizards which people say are the kill-
ers of Christ, or Jews. On Friday of Holy Week children
and even some adults go to catch these "Jews" and kill them
as penance for their own sins.
      Supaya is venerated inside the mines in the form of
the Tío, or uncle. Llama pastoralists say they have seen
him accumulating mineral which is carried on the backs of
vicuñas and llamas to the mines at night so that the riches
of the mine will not be exhausted. Miners say the Tío
controls the veins of ore and determines which of them will
find it. He is represented in the mines by images found
at each level of the mine in places which will not be disturbed by dynamiting. He has horns, and his hands are out-
stretched, ready to grasp the offerings of liquor and coca.
He is sometimes clothed in a stiff canvas vest and wears
high boots and a cape. Bright pieces of lead or silver are
inserted in the eye orbs. His teeth, made of glass or
metal, are sharpened "like nails," as one miner said, and
his face is sometimes painted "an ugly red." Sometimes he
is accompanied by the figure of a bull which helps him get
out the ore with his horns. In other mines he is accompanied by a harem of "Chinas," temptresses who intercede with
the Tío if he is angry and wants to "eat the blood" of
the miners.

The ceremony of offering to the Tío, in the ch'alla,
is basically the same as that made to the other monsters.
It is performed on Tuesdays and Fridays, especially the
first Friday of each month and a special ch'alla, called
Karaku, or in Spanish convida (invitation to drink) is performed with music and dancing on the first Friday of August, the month of the devil, and on the first Friday of
Carnival. In addition to the offerings of liquor, coca
and cigarettes given in the ordinary ch'alla, the miners
buy white llamas or sheep, kill them and save the blood.
They wrap the bones in white and red wool and bury them
intact in the mine where no one will disturb them. The
blood is splashed at the entrance of the mine and in the
work areas as an offering to the Tío. The flesh is cooked
and eaten without salt. In return for their offerings,
the men ask the Tío for richer veins of mineral, and they
plead for their own life and security.

These myths reenact strategies of restoration and
appeasement by which natural and human forces are kept in
balance. Animal sacrifices replenish the forces of productivity, restoring the equilibrium upset by mining, and
the offering of blood to the Tío keeps him from unleashing
destructive forces. When mining was intruduced, the
ch'alla gave miners a sense of their position in the new
economy and helped them avoid the alienation typical of
industrial workers by tying them to their agricultural
past and to their relatives and neighbors who remain in
agriculture.

A basic theme in the legends of the colonial period
is that of the disinheritance of the Indians by the Spaniards. There are many versions of the following tale, told
by a miner who had heard it from a very old working com-
panion:

A llamero (llama pastoralist) named Wallpa
was looking for one of his flock when night fell
and he became very cold. He made a fire and
fell asleep. With the heat of the fire, the
ground warmed up and a silvery stream flowed
out. The Indian grew afraid looking at it.
"What is this stream?" he asked. He went to the
city to advise the authorities. They went to
the hill with the Indian and discovered the riches. As they were looking, a voice said, "This
richness is not for you. This is for men who
will come from far away." In the city, the man
announced what he had heard. Afterward, the men
from far away arrived. The town authorities put
the Indian who had found the silver in jail. The
strangers, who were Spaniards, began to work the
mine. It was the Cerro Rico of Potosi.

The historical version recounted by Padre Bartolome
Martinez y Vela in La Villa Imperial de Potosi differs in
that the discoverers of the mine were Inca on their way to
Chile. According to this version, the Inca heard the voice
say in Quechua, "This richness is not for you; it is for
the white man who will come from far." After the conquest
by the Spaniards, an Indian named Wallpa, who was the serf
of a Spaniard, discovered the silver in the manner recounted above and worked it with his compadre (ritual co-parent,
a relationship sanctioned in the baptism, confirmation or
other religious ceremony involving the child of one) until
one day they fought and Wallpa told his master about the
mine. Then the master took over the mine and exploited it.
This "official" version does more to sanction the exploitation of the mines by the Spaniards, while the miner's version focuses on the Indian's own culpability in permitting
it. He drew this moral from the tale he told:

> The Bolivian authorities should never have
> put the Bolivian in jail. But that is the way
> they are. To this moment the Indians have not
> taken advantage of their riches. If they had,
> Bolivia would have had industries and factories
> of all kinds. Those who rule are to blame.

The concomitant of a sense of disinheritance is the feeling
that the exercise of authority by those in power is ille-
gitimate. The mythic projections of a people deeply conscious of oppression and disinheritance remain part of the
workers' understanding of their place in history.

II

The strategies reenacted in the ch'alla are those
of propitiation and appeasement. A new strategy, that of
confrontation and militant action, emerged out of the labor
struggles of the twenties and culminated in the labor union
organization of the forties. These labor movements made it
possible for workers to become a decisive force in the
Movimiento Nacional Revolucionario (MNR), the populist
front that overthrew the governing military clique that
represented the tin mine owners, in 1952. In the rhetoric
of the union leaders in the decades before the revolution,
the morality play was the force of good, represented by
the rosca, or tin barons. The solution posed by the ideology of nationalism was the seizure of the mines and establishment of state corporations. In this drama the monsters
were the army guerrillas who were the instruments of the
rosca, and the heroes were the labor leaders.

In the massacres of the miners prior to the revolution, the martyrs proved the basic postulates of the class

struggle. One of these was the martyr of the 1942 massacre, María Barzola. The workers had decided to present
a petition for increased wages when the price of tin rose
during World War II. On the 21st of December the men and
women who worked in the mine and on the slagpile went to
the owners, as described to me below by a labor leader:

> At 10 in the morning the workers of Cancavi,
> Socavón and Miraflores united. We were going
> to see the administrators, 6000 of us, peace-
> fully, without any weapons. We arrived about
> 400 meters from the office and they (the sol-
> diers called in by the administrators) began to
> fire at us. We were a mixed lot, women, child-
> ren, men. María Barzola was a delegate for the
> pallires (women who work on the concentration
> of metal). When she approached the soldiers,
> they shot her. We couldn't advance, and so we
> escaped. We were asking 40 percent increase in
> wages. We were surprised by the attack on us.

Every miner knows the story of the massacre. It is always
stated simply. María Barzola symbolized the just demands
of the workers. Her death and the slaughter of innocent
children gives the workers a fundamental sense of the meaning of class warfare. Her words as she seized the flag of
Bolivia when the men fell back as the soldiers aimed their
guns "are engraved in the hearts of all miners," another
miner told me. They were:

> It is not only the men who can fight. We
> women, too, can act. If the men hide below their
> beds, we shall go out and meet those who kill
> people. It is we women who have to face the
> children and tell them there is nothing to eat.
> Come all of you! Hurry!

As with all archetypal figures, there are many versions of María Barzola's life. Even in Siglo XX where she
lived, people disagree as to what she was like when she was
alive. Some say she was an older woman, addicted to coca
and alcohol who worked occasionally on the slag heap to get
money for her vices. Others say she was a regularly employed pallire (pre-concentrator of mineral) who had organized her co-workers. Nestor Taboada, in his documentary
novel, El Precio de Estaña (1960), chose the version of
her as a prostitute and alcoholic who left the arms of her
lover, an administrator of the company, to join with the
workers on the morning she was killed. There is not even
agreement as to her progeny. Some say she has one daughter,
another a son who survived her and who was voted to a seat

in the town government of Llallagua, the commercial center
adjacent to Siglo XX, in memory of her heroism.

The memory of María Barzola has been discredited by
an alliance of women calling themselves Barzolenas, who
supported the MNR government's disruption of worker organizations in the late fifties and early sixties. They broke
up union meetings when workers voiced opposition to the
stabilization plan freezing of wages, and they invaded senate meetings to shout down opponents of the government.
But the workers claim her as their own and reject the
transmogrification of the myth. Like the Ñusta, she symbolizes the compassionate awareness of their needs. But
unlike the Virgin Ñusta, she was one of them, her heroism
stemmed from her immediate experience in the mines, and
she called men to action rather than to passive appeasement.

The ideological outcome of the dominance by the
rosca in the first four decades of the twentieth century
was to define a common enemy for workers, professionals and
the middle-class of commercial entrepreneurs. This was
crystallized in the MNR fight against the rosca and imperialism. The victory of the MNR in 1952 led to a glorifica-
tion of the themes of Revolution, Nationalism and Anti-
imperialism. Each of the interest groups that contributed
to the overthrow of the rosca claimed to be the true in-
heritors of the Revolution. The process by which these
antagonisms became factionalized is explored in the following section.

III

After the victory of revolutionary forces, labor
was for a short period the driving force for structural
change. Unified under the Central Obrera Boliviana (COB)
they presented a new image of workers armed with machine-
guns seized from the army, a bandaged head bloody but
unbowed. This image appears in the first issue of Rebel-
ion, organ of the COB (10 de Mayo, 1952), in the mural
hung in the union hall of Siglo XX and in the statues
raised in the mining centers of Catavi-Siglo XX, Colquiri
and San José.

The revolutionary attitude of labor persisted after
the fighting was over. In the inaugural issue of Rebelión,
their position is put forth as follows:

> Our class and revolutionary position has kept
> us on the margin of all foreign influence in
> our historic interests and we are intransigent
> in our irreconcilable and antagonistic atti-
> tude. Because a natural or historic right helps
> us and because the future is ours, because we
> are the only revolutionary force capable of

> ensuring that the human society will be saved
> from the destruction of capitalist powers. We
> are enemies of the collaboration of classes and
> we are disposed to defend our political inde-
> pendence with arms in hand.

Two years later, when the mines were nationalized
and the land reform passed, this intransigent position was
relaxed. In the phase of co-government, Mario Torres Calleja, then Secretary General of the Federación Sindical de
Trabajadores Mineros de Bolivia (FSTMB) proclaimed (1955):

> The nationalization of the mines makes possible
> our liberation from dependency that for 50 years
> we have maintained with foreign capital, and
> makes possible not only the reversion to the
> country of the natural riches that the governing
> rosca had alienated at a base price, but that
> permits us to use the dollars derived from its
> exploitation in diversifying,economically and
> industrially,the country, the first step in rais-
> ing in an effective form the welfare of the
> working classes of the country.

Bolivia as a nation had gained little in the four centuries
of exploitation of the mines. Communication and transportation facilities were underdeveloped. The wealth of gold
and silver benefited the Spanish cities and left the country impoverished. Nationalization of resources and industry was seen as a panacea for economic problems.
    The Bolivian ideology of nationalism, as in the
case of most primary producers in Latin America, is a
defensive reaction to a position of economic dependency.
Nationalism is seen as a prime means of welding together
conflicting class interests within the country to resist
the encroachment of the metropolitan centers. In this
sense, it contrasts with the aggressive nationalism of
Europe in the nineteenth century by means of which centralized governments were able to extend economic power
around the world. It is in this framework that one can
appreciate the threat to Bolivian nationalism posed by
programs of aid through the Alliance for Progress and AID
after the MNR government was recognized in 1956 by the
United States State Department. Aid was contingent on acceptance of the stabilization plan which provided for the
freezing of wages and contracts at a low level. This was
the noose that eventually hung the MNR government by alien-
ating labor support. President Siles said in 1957 that
the United States "has given me just enough rope to hang
myself" (quoted in Patch 1960: 174). Lechin, (1962: 60),
leader of the Central Obrera Boliviana (COB) claimed that

the Alliance had not resulted in progress for Bolivia but for the United States.

The workers' growing awareness of the increasing discrepancy in their share of the national products came to a peak in Siles term of office in 1959 when the FSTMB called a strike against COMIBOL. Bedregal, President of COMIBOL (1962: 14) called upon workers to support national interests and reject "outmoded sindicalism" that threatened the state by challenging COMIBOL:

> It isn't just a continuation of Patiño, Hochschild and Aramayo, but a system of economy with out proposals of private profit and whose only owner is the pueblo of Bolivia. One ought to insist on the concept that the nationalization of the mine does not have as an object only the betterment of the conditions of work and of the life of the miner, but also the entire transformation of the economic and social conditions of the Bolivian nation. Also one must remember that the mines of COMIBOL are administered by a directory in which the FSTMB behind the worker controls the company...However...the FSTMB and its union act as if they were not part of it.

Although Bedregal and the presidents, both Siles and Paz who succeeded him in office in 1960, continued to use the rhetoric of nationalistic self-interest, the alienation of workers with the MNR government deepened and became acute in the strikes of the sixties. On the tenth anniversary of the Revolution of 1952, Bedregal appealed to unity in the name of Revolution:

> ...the Revolution, comrade textile workers, is a collective task of flesh and bone, vital, dynamic, where the masses participate as actors in every transformation and through it form the inspiration of the masses and even of the politicians, the cowards, and the apolitical.

Paz Estenssoro (1964: 17) tried the same tactic of legitimizing his government by claiming to be the inheritor of the revolution, but class opposition increased and the rising antagonisms could no longer be mediated within the MNR. The Triangular Plan negotiated between COMIBOL and the Bank for Interamerican Development, West Germany and the United States which stipulated greater labor discipline in response to capital investments terminated miners' support of the MNR government. Lechín broke with the MNR and formed the Left National Revolutionary Party (PRIN) and Paz responded by reinforcing the army, using it to occupy the

mines. Among other union leaders, the government arrested
Federico Escobar and Irineo Pimentel. Escobar's death in
a clinic that he entered for a minor operation led to accusations by miners that he was killed by his enemies. In
the April 1970 meeting of the FSTMB he was enshrined as a
martyr to the labor movement and a gold plated statue was
dedicated to his memory and that of the other victims of
the repression of the labor movement in the sixties by
the very political leaders who had been their allies in
the fifties.

Barrientos took advantage of the growing civil dis-
order in 1964 as strikes were called to counter Paz Estenssoro's increasingly repressive actions to declare
himself in rebellion. He was able to mobilize some of the
dissident groups by his claim to bring the country back to
the "sacred values of the April 9 revolt" (Barrientos 1965).
He referred to his coup as the "Revolution within the Revolution," but out of his actions to "save" the revolution
came the worst massacres in Bolivian history. In the military actions of occupying the mines by the military in
1965, scores of workers were killed in San José, Catavi,
Siglo XX, Huanuni and other mining centers. Radio trans-
mitters operated by the unions were seized and union halls
taken over by the administrators of COMIBOL. An unparal-
leled slaughter of workers occurred on the night of San
Juan, June 24, 1967 when without provocation workers were
killed in their homes and in the streets of the mining encampment as they were celebrating the warming of the earth
ceremony.

The despair resulting from the massacres deepened
in the interim government of Siles Salinas who took office
after the accidental death of Barrientos in the spring of
1969 and remained in office until the military coup of
Ovando on September 26, 1969. The mood of the workers was
expressed by one of the miners I interviewed in that period:

> Everywhere the working masses are discontented,
> without any faith in the proposals of the lead-
> ers...Just when we need a united force, we are
> disunited. I would not want a river of blood,
> but sometimes it is necessary.

Another worker who had lived through the massacre of December 21, 1942 in Siglo XX and who was fired as an agitator
in 1949 and then rehired in San José, gave the following
account of the workers' growing disillusionment with the
government:

> From 1952 to 1955 we miners were doing well. We
> were making $b1000, $b2000 and even $b3000 (about
> $85 to $250 in United States currency). Stabili-
> zation didn't affect my pay check until 1962. I

was earning $b1500 to $b2000 until 1964.
Since then, I have hardly been able to eat...
In 1965, the army came at night. I was sleep-
ing at 9 in the evening. My wife woke me and
told me they had come. They took the office of
the sindicatos. They took our radio and killed
some of the guards. On the following day we
couldn't do anything; we had to work. Since
that time we have been controlled. The yellow
union has taken over. We haven't had a united
assembly since that time. The working class is
reorganizing. When Siles came in after Barrientos' death, he promised us guarantees, but these
have not been carried out. We continue the same.

The workers, reflecting on the decade of the sixties
have lost faith in most of their leaders. They rejected
the leaders of the "yellow unions," the company controlled
unions in the Barrientos Siles interim, and the old leaders who were in hiding and in exile could not mobilize any
action. Some sought a compromise with the government, especially under Ovando who was organizing a campaign for the
presidential elections which were to have taken place in
May, 1970. One former union leader reflected as follows
on the union struggles of the fifties:

In principle, ideological doctrines are too
rigid. They do not see human necessities nor
values. They just put ideological principle
ahead of everything and they do not look at
reality...After the revolution everyone had his
ideological doctrine linked to personal ambi-
tion. Arce wanted to be president of the republic. And there were many others who wanted
to be president of the republic. As for we
workers, they sold us, they deceived us, they
betrayed us. As for the Partido Comunista de
Bolivia (PCB), it is a left that is completely
nationalized. We need a new left. Comunistas
Criollas have a left ideology, but never act
on their principles.

When Paz Estenssoro again took power in 1960 the
MNR was completely fragmented. Paz had alienated sectors
of the middle class who supported Walter Guevara Arce's
right to succeed to the presidency in this period as his
reward for action in the revolution of April 1952. He
had lost most of labor's support because of their opposition to the stabilization plan initiated by Siles Zuazo.
Although Juan Lechín Oquendo was his running mate, this
did not appease labor. Paz countered Lechin's opposition

to the increasing reliance on the military and the anti-
labor decrees implicit in the Triangular plan developed
for the reorganization of the mines by the Bank for Inter-
american Development, West Germany and the United States,
by sending him to Rome as ambassador. Labor leaders in
the mines were forced to carry on the fight without their
"maximal leader" at a time of crisis when the gains in the
fifties were being systematically wiped out. Federico
Escobar and Cesar Lora led the strike in 1963 that was
labor's major organized move to resist the trend to state
nationalism that now rejected labor's role in decision-
making. By 1964 Paz had no political capital left. In a
series of strikes supported by teachers and students as
well as mine workers and other sectors of labor, Paz's
government was toppled and General Rene Barrientos seized
power. Proclaiming his government to be the inheritor of
the revolution, he called his program the "Revolution of
the Reconstruction." Labor soon realized that his promises to support the working class were false when he cut
wages and the work force in accord with the Triangular
plan. In May, 1965, he ordered the military to enter the
mines and four years of the most restrictive period in
labor history since the time of the rosca ensued. When he
died in an airplane crash in 1969 he had even lost the
support of large segments of the peasantry who were dissatisfied with the limited payoffs they were getting in
his government. His Vice President, Siles, a half-brother
of the former president, was unable to reverse the anti-
government forces. Finally General Alfredo Ovando, who
had supported Barrientos in the coup of 1964, decided not
to risk an election planned for May, 1970, and seized power in Spetember 1969. He forestalled a general strike
threatened by the Federation of Bolivian Workers by nation-
alizing the Gulf oil holdings and further confused his
opponents by giving amnesty to some of the former labor
exiles and to jailed leaders. These concessions gave a
limited freedom for labor to reorganize its ranks and re-
asses its position vis-a-vis the nationalist military
regimes with which it had been saddled.
        Ovando tried to attain legitimacy by stressing in
his rhetoric continuity with the revolutionary movement,
calling it the Acción Nacional Revolucionaria (ANR).   He
tried unsuccessfully to identify the interests of the
people with those of the army (1969: 6):

                The Bolivian revolution is not the patrimony of
                determined persons. The Bolivian revolution is
                the patrimony of a people, a people of which the
                Armed Forces are a constituent part and from
                which they cannot be divorced.

The miners were not impressed. For them, the army is a
parasitical force that lives off their backs and whose
only justification for existence is to fire on them when
they go out on strike. At the first meeting of the Federación Sindical de Trabajadores in April 1970 the workers expressed their political appointees in COMIBOL. The Catavi
delegation and the Congress spoke out as follows:

> The constant and unending fights of the mine
> workers in all historic periods and against the
> different governments of turn to secure better
> conditions of living for their families, who
> know better than the miners what they have suf-
> fered in their own flesh, the brutal repression
> of the oppressive organizations and the assas-
> sinator's machine gun to silence the voice of
> protest against the economic and social injus-
> tice that they were submitted, the most pro-
> ductive class, are well known to the rest of
> you. We can hardly forget the massacres of the
> field of María Barzola, Villa Victoria, Uncia,
> Potosi, Llallagua and other centers of work by
> the feudal mining oligarchy, nor for this forget
> the persecution and torture of the governments
> that lent our natural riches to foreign compan-
> ies making of the workers simple machines of
> production. The fight of the workers in gener-
> al, and in particular of the miners, has been a
> fight without limit for survival without any
> hope. The worker not only receives salaries that
> are below his productivity but maintains himself
> on salaries of hunger, of misery and of low nu-
> trition, threatening him with sickness that
> could end his life. Half of the workers of the
> mines must retire from work and live the life of
> an invalid and be a burden on society that does
> not know how to understand him and remunerate him
> as a human being when they reach the age of
> thirty-five years. The statistics and the daily
> reality of the mines teach us that the index of
> mortality is frightening beyond any calculus.
> It is necessary that we defend our natural
> riches because they represent the natural reserve
> with which our children can build a new society
> and a country, owner of its destiny. In short,
> as workers, we are persecuted and separated from
> the source of our income. Our wages were lower-
> ed in order to raise the salaries of the hier-
> archies that are maintained in the bureaucratic
> posts of COMIBOL for political favoritism and a
> government without social sensibility. We have

not invented these reasons nor are they the
product of false accusations. They are born
from the reality in which the miner lives.
There are those of us who leave our lungs in
the mine shafts and others their energies in the
shops of the company, giving life to the country
(Tape recording of Social and Cultural Commission).

Given the reality of their life conditions, so well expressed by the miners, they could no longer accept the unfulfilled promises of the national revolution. The conclusions reached by the miners were summarized in their report of the political commission (FSTMB April, 1970,
mimeograph report).

The "national revolution" as a means to confront the problems of independent and semi-
colonial countries, for its lack of capacity to
confront the pressures of imperialism in its
multiple connotations, has failed as a system;
the numerous attempts in Latin America, in other
regions and particularly in Bolivia have been
strangled and always have ended in frustration.
The progressive measures[7] realized by the
Ovando government can triumph only on condition
that the present process passes into the hands
of the proletariat. Only by this road can
nationalist tasks be transformed into socialism
and our method of arriving at that stated historic end is the social revolution that will
permit us to transform the nationalist process
into a socialist one.

The experiment of national corporatism in COMIBOL proved
to the workers, in the statement of the thesis, that "state
capitalism served only to consolidate our backwardness and
dependency."
After days of speeches denouncing the "bourgeois nationalist regime" at the Congress, Ovando finally responded
anti-climactically in a press interview (El Diario, May 9,
1970):

The socialist thesis adopted by the Fourth
National Congress of Workers (COB, whose meeting
was called after that of the FSTMB, and who also
adopted the thesis of the FSTMB) is anti-national
and does not respond to the historic moment that
the Bolivians live. Therefore, as the head of
the government, I ought to say emphatically that
I will be opposed to it.

The call for an armed combat by workers to bring socialism
was, in the words of General Juan José Torres, then chief
of the armed forces and later to become president in the
October 1970 coup, "provocative" and he asserted (Presencia May 22, 1970):

> In these circumstances, nationalism is obliged
> and indebted to defend itself, and therefore we
> will reiterate what for some time we have said
> in emphatic form, that the armed forces consti-
> tuted as the iron arm of the Revolution, will
> fulfill its debt and will ensure a peaceful
> future for the rise of the Revolution.

Ovando's response to the "provocation" of the federation was to purge the cabinet of civilian ministers who
criticized the growing military control in the government
such as Quiroga Santa Cruz and Bailley in July, 1970. His
moves were renounced by the COB as a "golpe militar fas-
cista" (fascist military blow). Despite labor's denunciation of the Ovando government, they did not respond to the
guerrilla movement launched by students in Teoponte, the
site of an American owned gold mine in the Yungas region
of the department of La Paz. It wasn't until the movement
was crushed by the army that the COB recognized the guer-
rilleros as heroes of the anti-imperialist struggle and
joined students in a symbolic funeral of the dead on
September 21. Five days later, Ovando's government quiet-
ly celebrated the first anniversary of the coup which gave
him the presidency, but his regime was already discredited
in most politically mobilized sectors of the country.
The other side of the nationalist coin that was the
official ideological currenty of the post-MNR military
governments was the ideology of anti-imperialism. Rolon
Anayo (1966) and other commentators on political changes
in the sixties saw imperialism as the universal scapegoat
for all of Bolivia's problems -- for changes in the price
of tin on the world market, for defeat of local industries
in stabilization, for the unproductivity of the mines and
for the imbalance in trade. It became more and more apparent to organized labor that the "governments of turn"
could not counter imperialism and in fact were increasingly
depending on aid from the United States. The first break
with the MNR had come with the indemnization of the mine
owners shortly after nationalization and the final split
came when the Triangular Plan went into effect. Looking
back on the Triangular Plan from the perspective of 1970,
the delegates at the XIV Congress pointed to its denation-
alizing effect in yielding control of the state mines to
foreign capital interests that financed it. Later, when
Ovando agreed to indemnify Gulf Oil for the nationalization

of their holdings and to sell crude oil to Gulf-owned re-
fineries in Spain, labor was again disillusioned with the
progressive moves he made when he took office. By the end
of his year in power, there was no credibility left in his
pose of anti-imperialism. Five days after the anniversary
celebration, Rogelio Miranda took advantage of Ovando's
absence from the Burned Palace, as the government headquarters in La Paz are called, and declared a rebellion of
the generals. In the following seven days, called "The
Week of the Generals," six presidents entered and left the
Burned Palace. The contest became something like a soccer
game between sectors of the armed forces, with the people
standing by, watching with consternation, dismay and a
wild sense of the absurd as generals kicked the football
of power from one to the other of the contestants. General
Juan José Torres caught the ball of power and was forced
to run with it for the next nine months. His promise to
"maintain the Nationalist process" was his pledge to
restore wages to the pre-1965 level.

The "nationalist revolution" that Torres promised
to maintain sought financial backing from the socialist
regimes rather than relying exclusively on United States
backing. There was little difference in the public rhetoric that characterized his administration, but there was
a profound difference in the latitude given to labor and
students. By giving free play to the political parties
and organized labor groups, the scene appeared anarchic.
While not promoting socialism, Torres did not use any police or military force to counter the moves made in the
name of socialism as some small mines and haciendas were
seized by workers and peasants. With labor threatening to
make a reality of co-participation in the administration
of the nationalized mines, with the peasants organizing
under Pekin-oriented Communist Party leadership, with the
non-commissioned officers working out a petition against
the privileges of the superior officers and expressing
loyalty with labor, and with Russia buying up some of the
best real estate in La Paz's main thoroughfare, the remaining sector of export capital interests and the army
decided to back the rebel Col. Hugo Banzer who, along with
Rogelio Miranda had made an attempt earlier in the year to
remove Torres. In August, with the support from United
States promises to underwrite the government once they
gained power, they entered Santa Cruz where there were the
strongest pro-American forces and then began their northern
push. Torres succumbed on August 22, within ten months of
the abortive coup of Rogelio Miranda that threw him into
power. In one of the many paradoxes that characterizes
Bolivian politics, Miranda later supported his successor,
Banzer, and as a reward   was made chief administrator
of COMIBOL.

IV

For the militarist governments that have kicked the
presidency from hand to hand in the last decade, the rhetoric of revolution, of nationalism and of anti-imperialism
was a product of an interpretation of history in which the
class struggle was seen as an anachronism and survival was
predicated on the advance of national interest which was
supposed to overarch class and regional conflicts. The
failure of nationalist solutions has defeated the populist
front ideology and forced labor into a confrontation with
the middle class. The incompatibility of nationalism and
socialism was proven three decades ago in Europe when
Nazism and Fascism were defeated in the wars of conquest
they started. As Merleau-Ponty pointed out in countering
the nationalist-socialist arguments of Thierry Maulnier in
1946 (1964: 101), "if a socialism is 'national,' it ceases
to be a socialism; the bourgeois of all countries have
understood very well that the addition of this prefix
eliminates all that is disturbing about socialism."

In Bolivia the nationalist ideology is sustained
only by military repression exercised by a leader without
legitimacy in the popular sectors. Labor leaders and the
rank and file have denounced their policy of economic dependency in a world market controlled by monopoly capitalism and exposed the sham of political independence. In
their own rhetoric, they have sharpened the dialectical
struggle, now defined as one between workers and a bureaucratic state autocracy supported by the army.

The big question for future political action in
Bolivia is whether the rank and file workers will support
the program their leaders call for in the Thesis of the
XIV Congress. In the few months of relative freedom
allowed by the Torres regime they did not have enough time
to consolidate the gains made in the reconstruction of the
FSTMB to consolidate their ranks. Furthermore they had
not succeeded in overcoming the distrust in the leadership
of the unions that was a product both of the populist period when trade union leaders were coopted by the MNR as
well as of the militarist period of repression under Barrientos. In the current repression brought in by the
Banzer coup in August 1971 union leaders are in jail or
exile and there is no chance for recuperation of labor's
force short of a revolution.

In the mood of despair and disillusionment with political solutions, workers have turned to their cultural
origins to find the strength to survive. After the unpro-
voked massacre of mining families in Catavi and Siglo XX
on the eve of San Juan, June 24, 1967, when workers were
celebrating the "warming of the earth" ceremony for the
Pachamama, workers have increased their celebration in

defiance of military oppression and in an assertion of their will to survive. When I visited the encampment on the night of San Juan, on June 23, 1970, people told me that they had doubled their efforts to honor the Pacha-mama in memory of the dead. The FSTMB, recognizing the importance of that occasion in the history and sentiment of the working class, set that night as the date for beginning the courses for the development of new union leaders.

For the miners, there can be no return to the self-image projected in Chiru Chiru or Nena Nena. These mythic Robin Hoods, who tried to correct the imbalance of an unjust world through chicanery and thefts, never disturbed the underlying structure of inequality. The miners have exercised power and they will not be content to return to the past. They have experienced demagoguery in their unions and in the governments that they brought to power.

"The Tio is still the real owner of the mine," one miner said to me during a ch'alla. He did not mean this literally; his remark was a satirical denunciation of the bureaucrats who subverted the hopes of workers in nation-alization of the mines and development of the country. The main issue is that the alienation from the political and economic system that exploits them has not yet alien-ated them from the social and cultural roots of conscious-ness that gives them the strength to resist.

The new myths of the working class are constructed around the martyrs of the class struggle. María Barzola, as a victim of one of the massacres carried out by the rosca, symbolizes the invincible spirit of the mining com-munity and the necessity for fighting foreign capitalism. Other myths are in the making as Federico Escobar, Cesar Lora and other leaders who were the martyrs of the strug-gles against the administrative and state bureaucracies in the national corporatist period of the sixties are honored in the mining centers. Che Guevara is the leading mythic figure of the student movement in their mobilization against imperialism, but for the workers their own martyred workers are the only ones invoked in union meetings. María Barzola has a soccer field dedicated to her memory, Feder-ico Escobar is remembered in the gold leaf statue rendering his image in front of the theatre dedicated to him in Siglo XX and Cesar Lora's name is still scrawled on the walls in the memory of his heroic life and death. But most of the leaders who survived the past two military coups have been discredited by the rank and file and it is an open question as to how those who have been exiled or jail-ed in the recent coup will fare. In the interim between the death of Barrientos and the military coup of Banzer only the dead were heroes. Memorials to them have acquired mythic dimensions as new leaders invoke their names as they try to carry on the truncated revolution.

Myth is a mode of understanding that recurs in
periods of traumatic change. In myth, as Cassirer points
out (1946), "one can trace directly how humanity really
attains its insights into objective reality only through
the medium of its own activity and the progressive dif-
ferentation of that activity; before man thinks in terms
of logical concepts he holds his experience by means of
clear, separate mythical images." Cassirer thought of
this as a stage in pre-history, but one can see that in
recurrent liminal stages such as those I have traced for
Bolivia, myth is a way of responding to current changes.
As the expression of that connection between action and
consciousness that Marx and Engels called "the direct
efflux of their material behavior," (1947) myths are the
first stage in explaining reality and projecting these
understandings in a common idiom. Ideology, cut off from
this primary consciousness expressed in myth, lacks the
power to mobilize men and women to action.

FOOTNOTES

1. Kuhn's (1962) analysis of the thought processes in
    scientific communities reveals the same basic organ-
    izing principles discussed here.

2. Halpern (1961: 135) points out that while myth is the
    characteristic form of belief of primitive man and
    ideology that of modern man, myth is also at times a
    significant category of modern man's thought. Turner
    (1963: 576) carries this analysis one step further in
    showing that mythmaking is generated when people break
    with the past.

3. Malloy and Burke (n. d.) spell out the process by which
    the popularity of the early MNR became transformed into
    the nationalism corporatism that characterized the
    latter decade in Bolivia.

4. My first field trip in the summer of 1969 was supported
    by the Social Science Research Council and continued
    aid for a return trip in the year 1970 was provided by
    the Fulbright-Hayes Title IV National Defense and Edu-
    cation Fund. I am grateful to both granting agencies
    for making field work possible, and to the Guggenheim
    Foundation for providing me with a fellowship that
    gave me free time to write up the material.

5. "Correvolando" is a culture hero even more akin to the Robin Hood model in the folk tales of the Cochabamba Valley (Ugarte 1968).

6. The "progressive measures" referred to were the nationalization of Gulf and the rehiring of union activists in the mines.

7. These progressive measures include the nationalization of Gulf and the recall of the exiled labor leaders.

REFERENCES

Barrientos, Ortuño, René
    1965 -- Proceso historico de la Revolución Nacional: Mensaje a la Nación. La Paz.

Bedregal, Guillermo G.
    1962 -- La Revolución Boliviana, sus realidades y perspectivas dentro del ciclo de liberación de los pueblos latino-americanos. La Paz: Dirección Nacional de Informaciones de la Presidencia de la Republica.

Beltrán Heredia, B. Augusto
    1962 -- Proceso ideological historia del carnaval de Oruro. Oruro.

Cassirer, Ernst
    1946 -- Language and Myth. New York: Dover Publications.

Eliade, Mircea
    1960 -- Myths, Dreams and Mysteries. New York: Harper Torchbooks.

Geertz, Clifford
    1966 -- "Ideology as a cultural system," in Ideology and Discontent, ed. David Apter. New York: The Free Press.

Halpern, Ben
    1961 -- "'Myth' and 'Ideology' in modern usage," History and Theory I, 2: 129-149.

Ianni, Octavio
    1971 -- Sociología da sociología Latino-Americana. Rio de Janeiro, Civilizacão brasileira.

Kuhn, Thomas S.
  1962 -- The Structure of Scientific Revolutions. Chicago:
         The University of Chicago Press.

Lechin Oquendo, Juan
  1962 -- "La industria azucarera en 1961." Boletin Economia.
         2. La Paz: Ministerior de Economia.

Lichtheim, George L.
  1967 -- The Concept of Ideology and Other Essays. New
         York: Random House.

Malloy, James M. and Melvin Burke
  n.d. -- "From national populism to national corporatism:
         the case of Bolivia 1952-1970."

Mannheim, Karl
  1936 -- Ideology and Utopia. New York: Harcourt Brace
         and World.

Marx, Karl and Frederick Engels
  1947 -- The German Ideology. New York: International
         Publishers.

Ovando, Alfredo
  1969 -- El Pensamiento de la Revolucion. La Paz:
         Ministerio de Informaciones No. 6.

Patch, Richard
  1960 -- "Bolivia: U.S. assistance in a revolutionary
         setting," in Social Change in Latin America.

Paz Estenssoro, Octavio
  1964 -- La Revolucion Bolivna.a Direccion Nacional de
         Informaciones. La Paz.

Ponti, Maurice Merleau
  1964 -- Sense and Nonsense. Evanston, Illinois: Northwestern
         University Press.

Presencia
  May 22, 1970

Rebellion
  May 1, 1952

Rolon Anayo, Mario
         Sociedad y Desarrollo. La Paz: Editorial
         Universitaria.

Salazar Bondy, Augusto Jose Matos Mar, Alberto Escobar
Jorge Bravo Bresani and Julio Cotler
  1968 -- Peru Problema. Lima: Francisco Moncloa, ed. S.A.

Taboada, Nestor
   1960 -- El Precio de Estaña. La Paz: Escuela Grafica
          Salesiana "Don Bosco".

Torres Calleja, Mario
   1955 -- A dos Años de la Nacionalización de las Minas.
          Pblc. FSTMB.

Turner, Victor
   1968 -- "Myth and Symbol," International Encyclopedia of
          the Social Sciences. New York: Crowell Collier
          and Macmillan, Inc.

Ugarte R., Miguel Angel de
   1968 -- "El 'Correvolando'" In Antología de Tradiciones y
          Leyendas Bolivianas, Antonio Paredes-Candia, ed.
          La Paz: Collección Popular.

Whyte, William
   1970 -- "The myth of the passive Indian," Estudios
          Andinos 1.

"LOW CLASSNESS" OR WAVERING POPULISM?

A PEASANT MOVEMENT IN BOLIVIA (1952-1953)

Jorge Dandler

During the last decade, a number of studies have advanced our knowledge about peasant movements and in general, about the role of peasants in the revolutionary struggles of the Third World.[1] In an outstanding work on this subject, Wolf demonstrates that the most important revolubions of the twentieth century to date (Mexico, Russia, China, Viet Nam, Algeria and Cuba) were the outcome of the peasantry's active participation within the alliance of revolutionary forces, but adds, significantly, that the results of these revolutions were in the long run different from the expectations of the peasants who made them possible, although achieving one of their fundamental aims--recovery of the land (Wolf 1971).[2]

Although these studies have contributed to a better comparative understanding of peasant movements, controversy concerning the degree of the peasantry's revolutionary role continues, especially within Marxism.[3] Are peasants revolutionary or not? Do they not always depend on the more advanced leadership of the proletariat? Basically, there are two traditions of interpretation within Marxism concerning peasants and their revolutionary role (Shaning, 1972: 22-24). One tradition takes the proletariat as the vanguard capable of producing a revolution. This view is primarily derived from an analysis of the class struggles and contradictions in European capitalist societies. The other tradition takes into account the peasantry as an essential factor in the revolutionary struggle. According to this view, conditions for a socialist revolution are ripe in countries of the Third World and although in these cases peasants do not necessarily replace the proletariat, they form a majority sector in the alliance of revolutionary forces (China, Viet Nam).[4]

In the present essay, we shall attempt to analyze the active role that peasants have played within a revolutionary process and as part of a coalition of forces where the organizations of the mining proletariat nevertheless were the vanguard forces. Specifically, we shall examine the development of peasant mobilization in the Department Cochabamba, Bolivia, during the fifteen months between the

Revolution of April 1952 and the signing of the Agrarian
Reform Decree in August 1953, Bolivia being one of the
countries in Latin America where a profound process of social change occurred. We do not intend to analyze the
background of the Revolution, its achievements or the
limitations of the Agrarian Reform. We shall examine how
peasants took part as a political force in the process of
transformation, focusing our attention on a strategic region and social mobilization. An analysis of a particularly crucial period after the MNR (Movimiento Nacionalista
Revolucionario or Nationalist Revolutionary Movement) came
into power may contribute to a better understanding of the
Bolivian Revolution and its long-term consequences. Our
main interest is to present a specific case, contributing
to the comparative theoretical analysis of peasant movements. Although the Bolivian peasantry was not the passive
element of the rural France described by Marx (Marx 1973,
orig. 1852), neither was it the active force of the Chinese
revolution or of the Indochina War. Our case represents
a transition period during which the peasantry played a
dynamic role, but the movement itself differs from other
cases since Bolivian peasants participated in an alliance
with other social sectors through a populist movement only
capable of carrying out an incomplete revolution. Such a
phenomenon within a populist framework may contribute to a
better understanding of peasant movements in Latin America.

The Study of Peasants as a Class

Analysis of the peasantry from a social perspective
and with respect to political strategy has frequently received only secondary importance within Marxism, except, of
course, China, Southeast Asia and Eastern Europe. As
Alavi (1973: 27-28) points out, Marx himself developed much
of his analysis of the peasantry from an economic standpoint; it was primarily in relationship with his interest
in the development of capitalism that he wrote about pre-
capitalist economic formations. On social and political
aspects, Marx emphasized the problems of European capitalist countries and the role of the proletariat. However,
in his brilliant historical essay, The Eighteenth Brumaire
of Louis Bonaparte, Marx presented a clear and detailed
picture of the French peasantry in mid-ninteenth century,
showing how this social sector constituted the base of
political support for an authoritarian and beaurocratic
regime. His classic definition of the peasantry[5] has
been frequently used as universally applicable, but close
reading of the essay shows such a generalization to be
false. His definition of the peasantry was specific to
France within a historical context. It could also be
taken to encomapss a peasantry of small landed propietors,
politically disaggregated as a class. The same essay

contains a conceptual distinction between a <u>class in
itself</u> and a <u>class for itself</u> which will allow us to pose
certain questions concerning peasants as a class and their
participation as a class in the Bolivian mobilization
process:

> In so far as millions of families live under
> economic conditions of existence that separate
> their mode of life, their interests and their
> cultural formation from those of the other
> classes and bring them into conflict with those
> classes, they form a class. Insofar as these
> small peasant proprietors are merely connected
> on a local basis, and the identity of their
> interest fails to produce a feeling of com-
> munity, national links, or a political organi-
> zation, they do not form a class. They are
> therefore incapable of asserting their class
> interest in their own name (1973: 239).

For Marx, a class for itself was not something im-
mutable or abstract, but a concrete, historical realization, nor was it merely an economic substratum. As Mezaros
writes, it refers "to the 'being' of the class: i.e., he
indicates the line of solution in terms of the complex
determinants of a social ontology as contrasted with some
economic mechanism."[6]
Nor is class consciousness posed as a merely subjective phenomenon but instead, is intimately related to
<u>political organization</u>. In other words, this historical
realization refers not only to the <u>subjective</u> state wherein
a class possesses an awareness of itself, its problems and
the world it lives in, but above all, to <u>objective</u> forms
of organization created by such a situation and self-image,
assigning goals, forms of struggle and their organizational
expression. This approach requires to identify different
degrees of class cohesion as specific cases are analyzed.
Exploring this important relationship between class
consciousness and organization, Shanin uses the concept of
"low classness" to contrast the peasant class consciousness
and its political organization with respect to the proletariat. According to Shanin, this in part is due to the
more immediate nature of peasant demands as well as the
peasantry's socio-political weakness:

> Peasants in their political struggles tend
> to fight for land rather than for broader
> political aims, have an eye on the local day-
> to-day concerns rather than to care for general
> long-term concepts and ideologies...The vertical
> segmentation of peasants into local communities,

class and groups and the differentiation of
interest within these communities themselves
has made for difficulties in crystallizing
nationwide aims and symbols and developing
national leadership and organization...(Shanin
1971: 255-6).

Similarly, Hobsbawm argues that the proletariat
tends to assume a more solidary, persistent and militant
stance in the long run than do peasants; at the most, he
continues, a peasant movement has a regional scope or may
have a national impact when the movement develops in one
or two strategic regions or produces highly mobile armed
groups (1973b: 10). According to this view, peasants generally depend on outside leadership and direction in order
to exercise influence at the national level.[7]
     In summary, a definition of peasants as a class for
itself implies: a) a consideration of their socio-economic
context; b) an evaluation of their subjective views as a
product of their historical experience and embodied in a
plan of action;[8] and c) forms of organization, concrete
expressions of class consciousness and identification of
allies and enemies. In the present essay we are especailly
interested in studying the latter aspect: how the Cochabamba peasants organized and expressed themselves concretely as a class in a specific historical context.
     So far we have emphasized the need to analyze the
specific historical context of peasant mobilization.
Within Marxism itself, there are four classic studies of
the peasantry showing the relationship of this sector to
the social process (Marx 1973, Engels 1969, Lenin 1950,
Mao Tse-Tung 1965). In recent years, Shanin and Sweezy,
among others, have stressed the need to carry out specific
or "contextual" studies of proletarian and peasant movements within a process of social and political change
(Sweezy 1968: 33, also cited by Shanin 1972: 22-24). According to Shanin, a revolution is fundamentally an interaction, a "relational event," characterized not solely by
the acts of one class but by the dynamic interplay of the
following facets: 1) A major structural crisis of the
society, 2) A major crisis in the ruling elite and its
legitimacy to govern, 3) A "cristallization of classes expressed in an at least temporary increase in class self-
identification and to militancy along class lines, and
4) "Operation of revolutionary elites capable of providing
leadership in a revolutionary struggle" (1972: 26).[9]
     We shall not study each of the above factors in
detail as we consider the Bolivian case, but they should
be kept in mind as we study: a) the role of peasants as
an active force within a broader populist movement, b)
peasants as a class for itself, how they become organized
and express their common objectives, and c) peasants as

they relate to a process of social change, following concrete political strategies.

In considering a historical period of intense social
and political mobilization, we shall focus our analysis on
organization, leadership and ideology at an intermediate
level. It is at this level and with this three-fold approach that the relationship between mass mobilization and
national decision-making powers may best be studied. The
role that peasants have played in this process of political
mobilization, as well as the limitations involved, become
clearer as we gain a better insight as to the characteristics and structure of this intermediate level, in the
final analysis, embodied in the populist nature of the
Bolivian revolutionary process of 1952.

With respect to the three aspects mentioned (organization, leadership and ideology) we seek to determine
those elements contributing to the peasantry's cohesion as
a class as well as those which restrain such a process.
In an essay with a title suggestive of the problem (Peasant
Classes and Primordial Loyalties"), Alavi analyzes the
mechanisms that contribute to or limit the peasantry's
class solidarity; to study the "cleavages that cut across
class lines" are as important as to study those aspects
that contribute to the solidarity of peasants as a class.[10]

With respect to organization, we are interested in
its horizontal as well as vertical features. Let us take
an example. The peasant sindicatos in Bolivia becomes a
strategic social and political innovation. The campesino
converts the sindicato into an instrument of power with
which he identifies himself and considers as his own. At
the local level, the sindicato operates as a local government and is affiliated to sindicato organizations at the
district, provincial, regional, departmental and national
levels. The sindicato also becomes an extension of the
MNR party and the state. We note that in certain contexts,
sindicatos act as a body, with their own leadership, political militancy and armed militia, as well as alliances
with urban and mineworkers' organizations. On the other
hand, we also find "clientelist" relationships. The sindicato in certain contexts operates on the basis of close
inter-personal bonds between a leader and his followers.

The leader who has built a network of relationships
outside the locality or region can channel resources and
favors to his followers in return for political support
and personal loyalty. At the same time, this political
intermediary maintains close relationships as a "client"
with individuals in higher positions.[11] After the 1952
Revolution, an important asset of a leader was a loyal
following with armed backing or the votes to support a
political patron at a higher level.

Concerning leadership, we are interested in the background and strategies of peasants in Cochabamba who become leaders, and how and what type of peasant followers become rapidly involved in the mobilization. To what extent do governmental authorities and political organizations intervene and provide differential access to resources, expertise and legitimacy, with the result that some campesino leaders and organizations prevail over others? Consequently, to what extent can we precisely identify or find examples of relative independence and self-organization vis-à-vis the revolutionary regime? And finally, what is the role of ideology among peasants? We are here interested in detecting the content of peasant demands and more specifically, how peasant leaders process an explicit sense of exploitation shared by campesinos as a class into an awareness of their political capacity to act as a unified force. In other words, how do peasant leaders develop a blueprint for action and an organization with power capability? Just as we have been unable to isolate peasant organizations or leadership from the broader societal context, we shall find that their ideology, of course, includes symbols and important elements of urban and mine-workers' class consciousness, political parties as well as of the diffuse populist ideology and MNR rhetoric. On the other hand, we should also take into account values, attitudes, demands and relationships which may limit or inhibit class ideology.

I. The Bolivian Revolution of 1952

At the closing of the 1920's and beginning of the 1930's, Bolivia experienced a profound crisis that shook the very foundations of its traditional economic and political system. Within a period of six years, Bolivia suffered the consequences of the Great Depression and the Chaco War with Paraguay (Klein 1969 and Malloy, 1970). From the defeat of the war, a young generation of military and civillian leaders emerged to search for alternatives to transform Bolivian society. This ideological and revolutionary ferment was also evident among miners and other workers, whose struggles during the decade after the war marked by such historical incidents as the Massacre of Catavi in 1942, the founding of the Bolivian Federation of Mineworkers in 1946 and the launching of their famous Tésis de Pulacava during the same year (Barcelli, 1956: 127-239). On the other hand, campesinos did not remain bystanders to these political currents. They have a rich history of organizational groundwork, rebellions and other attempts to seek their liberation during the 1930's and 1940's.[12] This general effervescence in the society culminated in the Revolution of 1952. The MNR emerged

victorious as a result of the critical participation of
miners, workers, a rebellious police and other forces in
the armed uprising of April 9-12 against the army. It was
particularly through this event that the MNR became a vig-
orous, popular-based revolutionary party in command of a
social and political movement which had begun to take form
since the Chaco War. As soon as the MNR leaders assumed
power, they reaffirmed the commitment to nationalize the
mines, implement an agrarian reform and broaden the parti-
cipatory role of the people in the political process.

Although campesinos did not participate in the
immediate events of April, as soon as the MNR assumed
power, signals spread that a new era was to begin for them.
One slogan called forth as follows: "compañero y hermano
campesino, ha llegado la hora de tu liberación, ya serás
libre, dueño de la tierra que trabajas."[13] The extent of
this message was not clear, probably not even to the top
MNR leaders themselves. Nevertheless, the revolutionary
situation opened a growing opportunity structure for a
variety of political agitators and organizers to make contact with campesinos, mobilize and arm them, and search
for leaders among them to proselytize about the Revolution
and the rights of the campesino. Certain rural areas soon
became critical foci of agitation and mobilization which
influenced the scope and impact of the agrarian reform.

The MNR in Power[14]

As a result of the April uprising, the MNR faced a
certain diffusion of power due to the disorganization of
the army and the armed mobilization of civilian forces.
The MNR proceeded to consolidate its power base through
the reinforcement of civilian militia, party cells (comandos) and an administrative reorganization of the governmental apparatus. The Bolivian Labor Central (COB, Central
Obrera Boliviana) and a Ministry of Campesino Affairs (MAC)
were important innovations. The COB became the most important mobilization instrument of armed labor and civil
militia. Also, this organization provided a crucial power
base for workers and the MNR left, reinforced by a principle which granted the COB co-government status with the
MNR (co-gobierno) and a powerful role in the management of
the nationalized mines (control obrero).[15] The COB was
led by Juan Lechín, head of the Bolivian Mineworkers'
Federation, and Minister of Mines. An important core of
the COB leadership consisted of former members of the
Trotskyite POR (Partido Obrero Revolucianario) who collaborated with the MNR with the objective of radicalizing
the Revolution from within and through mass mobilization.
The Ministry of Campesino Affairs was headed by Nuflo
Chavez Ortiz, spokesman for agrarian reform and rural mobilization through sindicatos and prominent leader of the

MNR left.[16] The COB, MAC and the Miners' Federation considered themselves vanguard of the proletariat and leaders
of a peasant-proletarian alliance.

Meanwhile, the MNR as a party proceeded to strength-
en its own cells (comandos) in the cities, provinces and
mines, as well as to organize civilian militia directly
under their control. Since many cells were headed by
regular MNR leaders, COB leaders and others associated with
the left were distrusted as intruders and extremists who
bypassed departmental and MNR comandos in the mobilization
effort.

The MNR was a populist movement; its power rested
on mass mobilization, an alliance of classes and a diffuse
ideology of reforms and social change.[17] The MNR Revolution provided a symbolic and rhetorical repertoire of
positive and negative symbols which were shared by a broad
spectrum of its leaders and supporters, including the POR
(see Chart). When specific policies had to be decided and
implemented, conflicting groups elaborated further symbols
under this basic "umbrella," to capture support and influence policy decisions. In many respects, the controversy
over agrarian reform created more dissension within the
MNR than nationalization of the mines, reorganization of
the army, control obrero or universal suffrage (Malloy
1970: 188-89). Concerning the agrarian reform, there were
those in the moderate right and traditional MNR party
hierarchy who agreed that the campesino should be incorporated through suffrage, education, and above all, an agrarian reform which was to be carefully studied and implemented in an orderly manner. Within this wing, some argued
to limit the latifundio in size and eliminate free service
obligations. In this moderate view, the sindicato was conceived as a labor union to act as a bargaining agent and
only secondarily as a political instrument. Their motto
was "order and work."

In contrast to this moderate view, many leaders of
the MNR left, such as Lechín and Chávez Ortiz, were inclined to model campesino sindicatos after labor and mining
unions, primarily as political instruments, armed and organized to support and radicalize the Revolution. Distribution of land, of course, was a key goal. But there were
disagreements concerning how agrarian reform was to be implemented. While the Minister of Campesino Affairs supported a commission to study agrarian problems and prepare
a decree, Minister Lechín, skeptical of "expert" commissions, argued that "mass action" and "consciousness" were
more important. An effective motto introduced by the MNR
left was, "land for the one who works" (tierra para el que
trabaja). Others took a more radical stance which was in
agreement with the POR: agrarian revolution, labor-campesino government, total distribution of land, the establishment of collectives and a people's army.

The countryside became a vast arena of political mobilization. The most dynamic organizers and agitators were associated with various leftist groups, some escaping the control of the Ministry of Campesino Affairs.

We shall now examine the rise of peasant leaders and organizations in the Cochabamba valleys, how these relate to the multiple pressures within the revolutionary movement and how some leaders manage most effectively to develop and transmit an ideology that was most directly appealing to campesinos as a class.

II. The Campesino Movement of Cochabamba

During the early months after the April uprising, there was an intense flurry of activities in the Cochabamba Valleys and Serranías (highlands), becoming a rather strategic center of political mobilization in Bolivia.[18] There were two striking features about this phenomenon in Cochabamba: 1) a bewildering array of individuals and organizations at various levels took upon themselves the task of reaching the countryside and tapping rural leadership, and 2) there was a significant potential leadership pool among campesinos, many of whom already prior to 1952 had demonstrated leadership, developed political connections with the MNR and other parties or participated in the mining labor union movement.

Many of these men visualized opportunities and made themselves available for the new and still largely undefined dask for which the Revolution's leaders began to call. Therefore, the strategy of potential peasant leaders to develop power capabilities and legitimacy was to obtain some form of recognition by a formal authority which assured them a position of other resources, and at the same time, to prove the strength of the followings which they could muster in the countryside. Although both of these aspects were important, some first chose to obtain some form of legitimacy conferred from higher authorities, while others attempted rather to obtain their strength directly through mass mobilization.

Within a broad movement such as the MNR, and particularly due to the diffusion of power during the early months, legitimating authorities were multiple and frequently conflicted over priorities, disposition of resources or promotion of leaders. Inevitably, leadership rivalries developed because of the very nature of clientelist relationships between a peasant leader and followers or between a governmental authority and peasant leaders.

During the immediate months after April 1952, an early network of rural agents was established in Cochabamba by the departmental Prefect. As former chief of the Cochabamba party organization, the Prefect was intimately

acquainted with MNR membership in the provinces and he
personally selected the individuals. These rural agents
were vallunos (rural "valley people," not highland campesinos), effectively bilingual and able to communicate in
the social and cultural idiom of valley or highland people,
as well as urban or town politicians:

> We needed these men. For example, I had one
> organize public rallies in the countryside
> and accompany me in order to convey the Revo-
> lution's message much more effectively than
> I could, even though I also addressed campe-
> sinos in Quechua. He was more genuine --
> he spoke to campesinos from his heart,
> having himself been a campesino once.[19]

Although these agents managed to establish sindicatos in various areas, few of them amassed any powerful
followings in the countryside now did this network coal-
esce into a formal organization, in part due to the relatively moderate orientation of departmental and provincial
authorities. The latter were bypassed by leaders of the
MNR left, such as Ministers Lechín and Chavez Ortiz, who
had greater flexibility to innovate, channel resources and
provide expertise through the COB, the Ministry of Campesino Affairs or the Mineworkers' Federation. Two campesino leaders (Sinforoso Rivas and José Rojas), soon
eclipsed the men of the first network and developed relatively exclusive rival domains with stronger personal followings and cohesive organizations. Rivas established a
Departmental Campesino Federation with headquarters in the
Lower Valley, actively supported by the COB and the Ministry of Campesino Affairs. In contrast, Rojas built his
leadership and organization into a militant regional following in the Upper Valley on the basis of personal charisma, a core of subordinates and the historical experience
of Ucurena as the country's first rural sindicato.[20] Once
backed by a strong following, Rojas projected himself to
higher authorities and campesinos as a more genuine campesino leader than Rivas or the MNR rural agents.

a) A Departmental Federation

The establishment of linkages between peasants,
politicians, party and governmental organizations at various levels is best seen through a description of various
activities which took place in Sipe Sipe, subcapital of
the Quillacollo province in the Lower Valley. This town
had served for more than a decade prior to 1952 as a focus
of contact and agitation among peasant leaders of the lower
Valley and neighboring highland provinces of Ayopaya and
Tapacari which culminated in a large-scale rebellion in the
latter two provinces in 1947 (Dandler 1971: Chapter 3).

When a new mayor was installed in Sipe Sipe shortly
after the April Revolution, he established contact with
campesinos and some of the pre-1952 leaders in the region.
As assistant mayor, he named Sinforoso Rivas, who is described by campesinos as a sharp, cunning valluno, very
capable as a business and political operator, literate,
and equally fluent in Spanish and Quechua. Son of an
hacienda tenant (colono), he worked in the mines in his
early twenties, where he rapidly rose through various positions beyond what most men of his social background
achieved (employee in the company store and payroll office). There he became involved in the mining labor union
movement and closely acquainted with Lechin and other mine
leaders. Because of political involvement, Rivas and many
others were fired en masse in 1946 after the overthrow of
the Villaroel regime. He returned to the Lower Valley,
started a prosperous business which involved influential
contacts in the mines and the Lower Valley, and also
became a provincial representative of the judiciary
(corregidor).

As soon as Rivas became assistant mayor in April
1952, he promoted himself to higher authorities. In an
interview with Minister Lechín in La Paz, Rivas discussed
the agrarian problems of his area, stressed the necessity
to organize campesinos and offered his services. The
Minister promptly replied that the best place Rivas could
serve the revolution was in the lower Valley and promised
him full personal and official backing. After these critical negotiations, Sipe Sipe became an intense center of
rural mobilization. The rapid establishment of an effective network which included the neighboring highlands was
considerably facilitated by the organizational groundwork
there which had developed a decade earlier and the availability of campesinos with considerable expense.[21]

These organizational efforts achieved formal recognition through the founding of the Departmental Campesino
Federation on August 6, 1952, in Sipe Sipe. Headed by
Rivas, the Federation was formally associated with the COB
and designed to have formal jurisdiction over all campesino organizations in the Department. This association
offered campesinos an important mechanism to articulate
their demands. On the other hand, to the Ministry of
Campesino Affairs and other governmental organizations,
the Federation became an important nexus to channel resources, organize the countryside and delegate formal
authority. Nevertheless, the Federation did not control
all rural agents, leaders or followings in the Department
nor was Rivas accepted by all as their highest leader.
Simultaneously, a rival domain was emerging in the Upper
Valley under the leadership of José Rojas.

b) A Rival Domain
     Political contacts and organizational efforts
developed rapidly in the Ucurena area after the April
uprising:

> when the Revolution occurred many of us
> were already prepared, we knew that we had
> fought very early to achieve freedom from
> the patrón and had organized Bolivia's first
> rural sindicato...but only a few obtained
> land and the rest of us remained colonos...
> that was only the beginning.

     Several men in the Ucurena area projected themselves
as leaders. They all sought to re-establish the earlier
sindicato and demand expropriation of the remaining hacienda lands. Simon Aguilar and Froilan Escobar were strongly favoured by the provincial MNR cell in Cliza because of
their pre-1952 association with the party. Aguilar, a
tenant from the local Monastery of Santa Clara hacienda
lands, was appointed by the Prefect as rural MNR agent.
Escobar was the nominal leader of small plot owners (piqueros) in Ucurena who had bought land during the early
1940's through the original sindicato.
     José Rojas was another leader; he was born in
Ucurena, lost his father at an early age, and with his
young brother and mother worked on the Convent lands to
retain the family's usufruct plot. At the age of sixteen,
he joined the Army and fought in the Chaco War. After the
war, he interacted with leaders of the original sindicato
and followed their struggle from the beginning. During
the 1940's he became closely associated with the school
director, a provincial PIR leader who assisted the sindicato through some of its most difficult years. Rojas
assumed the leadership of the sindicato in 1946 and expanded the organization to include other Convert colonos
who remained dependent on the hacienda. In the 1947
elections, the PIR carried out an active political campaign in the Cochabamba valleys. The sindicato of
Ucurena supported the PIR legislative candidate and through
a well-organized registration of literate campesino votes,
the PIR assured its victory in the province. The PIR candidate had promised that his party would press for the
expropriation of the Convent lands and a national agrarian
reform. But promises remained unfulfilled. In 1950 the
government legalized a former fraudulent sale of Convent
lands to non-campesinos in order to avoid a direct transaction with its own tenants (Dandler 1969: 110-111).
Nevertheless, such an adverse government decision, as well
as the attempts by peasants to articulate their demands
through an electoral campaign, contributed to their determination and persistent search for new strategies.[22]

Because of his previous political association,
Rojas did not count with the support of provincial MNR
leaders during his attempts to reorganize the sindacato in
1952. But he shrewdly promoted himself as leader closer
to the masses, by identifying himself with local colonos
or the landless. Applying a strategy with which he won
the sindicato leadership in 1946, he contrasted the class
consciousness of landless campesinos with the lack of commitment among small plot owners (piqueros) who had failed
to maintain the sindicato alive once they had obtained land
in the early 1940's. Indeed, the landless peasants who
held usufruct plots on the hacienda (colonos) became the
most mobilizeable force in rural Bolivia during the agrarian reform process, confirming a significant distinction
made by Marx about class consciousness among landless
peasants, in contrast to those who had land, and validated
by other historical examples elsewhere.[23]

Rojas emerged as a seasoned politician among peasants, able to project a charisma and sense of loyalty
among his followers. According to a lieutenant:

> Rojas above all was a sharp opportunist
> (hombre muy vivo) who also felt and knew
> how to present demands which were closest
> to our hearts. He personified our wishes,
> while other leaders outside Ucurena were
> not as campesino as he was.

He allied himself with trusted subordinates to consolidate
local support within the area and later in the Upper Valley. One lieutenant was a colono who had built a following
in Ucurena within several weeks after the April Revolution
(Crisostomo Inturias). Another was a young law student
from Ucurena, son of a small-plot owner and member of the
Trotskyte POR party, who left the University to join the
campesino movement (Encarnacion Colque).

Rojas attended various meetings of the POR in
Cochabamba, where he listened to their arguments for an
agrarian revolution rather than a gradual reform (total distribution of land, collectivization and a labor-campesino
government). According to several witnesses, Rojas was
skeptical of collectivization, presented the point of view
of campesinos and discussed their immediate aims. His own
recollection to the author clarifies his position:

> The only lasting thing for a campesino was to
> be free of the gamonales (landowners and other
> exploiters) and become full owners of our lands
> ...We realized this through our own painful
> experience of Ucurena...Some of our compañeros
> achieved their freedom as a united body in the

form of a sindicato before 1952. But even
our little school was thought to be a menace
to patrones...We tried to unite again with
the help of a party (PIR), willing to press
total expropriation of the hacienda, but the
gamonales, oppressors and the Rosca (elite)
again conspired against us...We knew they
could not go on with such a farce.

Initially suspicious of the MNR, Rojas was not politically impressed by the labor decrees drawn by the MNR
during the Villarroel regime (1943-1946), which were not
enforced long. The explicit goal of many peasants prior
to 1952 certainly went beyond the mere limitations of labor
obligations, as many of the rebellions during the late
1940's indicate (Dandler 1971: Chapter 4). Understandably,
Ucurenos found among their readiest non-peasant allies
those who were associated with parties that were most ideologically committed to an agrarian reform and active in
the countryside prior to the 1952 Revolution (PIR and POR).
     The roots of Ucurena's militant stance was not so
much based on a sudden ideological conversion of a few men
or Rojas in particular. Ucurenos had a deep historical
awareness of their struggle for land ownership and freedom
from landowners. They were convinced that they could settle for nothing less than a total distribution of the
latifundio. To Ucurenos a latifundio qualitatively included all the haciendas. This undifferentiated view of
the hacienda system is crucial to understand the militancy
of Ucurena and the ability of Rojas to win numerous campesino adherents far beyond his locality after the April
Revolution. Furthermore, this is an important reason why
Rojas antagonized many moderate authorities within the MNR
regime and campesino leaders such as Rivas, who were more
inclined to differentiate properties according to various
legal subtleties. When the regime called for campesino
support, Ucerenos were too impatient to accept further
promises, studies and legalities. In short, they were
ready to organize themselves and act. The task to lead
them fell on Rojas, who was regarded as the best to articulate these simple but commonly held demands.
     Once Rojas build a following within Ucurena, he
applied the following strategy, which in this instance reveals the complementarity of clientelist and class relationships.
     (1) He proceeded to ingratiate himself with the
Prefect as compadre, to gain his favor away from rivals
that were promoted by provincial and departmental authorities; (2) Insisted that the founding of the Sindicato
Agrario de Cliza should take place in Ucurena, location of
the first agrarian sindicato in Bolivia (1936) rather than

in the "mestizo" town of Cliza; (3) Accepted a subordinate
leadership post of this sindicato through a compromise
with Aguilar (Dandler 1971: 168-179); (4) Having a properly
legitimated organization, the sindicato began to confront
landowners and administrators one-by-one with commands to
be immediately implemented (labor agreements, replacement
of administrators and others); (5) During this time the
sindicato leaders presented to the President a formal petition to expropriate haciendas in the Ucurena area, re-
iterating an old goal. Campesinos obviously felt that they
had an extraordinary opportunity and a good bargaining
position to present concrete demands in exchange for
political loyalty to the government.

The sindicato soon split because of personal rivalries and intense localism. Rojas consolidated his local
following while Aguilar, having minimal influence in Ucurena, proceeded to organize other sindicatos in the Upper
Valley as NMR and Federation representative. This early
instance of leadership rivalry and sindicato fission reveals characteristics which became increasingly common as
mobilization of peasants assumed an important dimension in
Bolivian politics after 1952. Even within a small locality
such as the Convent hacienda, campesino leaders strongly
competed for a following and vital support from higher
authorities. Nevertheless, since the rural political arena
was covered, leadership struggles developed at higher
levels for the control of a provincial organization and
eventually the departmental Federation itself, as will be
shown subsequently.

Once Rojas consolidated firm local support in Ucurena, he established a powerful center of sindicatos in
the Upper Valley (Central Sindical Campesina del Valle),
in early November 1952. This was a tactical move to control a regional domain where rivals were also busily organizing sindicatos and to obtain governmental backing.
In reaction to this initiative, Aguilar and other leaders,
backed by Rivas, organized a parallel central in the province at the end of 1952. The style and political acumen
of Rojas and his lieutenants is well demonstrated by their
visit to an Upper Valley hacienda to organize a sindicato:

> When we arrived there was a large mass of
> campesinos waiting for us...the patrón had
> left afraid of us. We made sure to announce
> that we were a comission with the proper cre-
> dentials. Some seemed afraid and did not know
> what to expect. We had good preparation since
> Rojas planned the presentations very well.
> First I (Colque) spoke, since I was qualified
> to speak about laws. I spoke about labor regu-
> lations and how they should be clearly under-
> stood by everyone and enforced on the hacienda...

and if the patrón did not cooperate, to let
Ucurena and other authorities know in order
to have the law properly implemented. Then
Inturias spoke how campesinos should organize themselves. He also told them about
Ucurena's history of struggle against patrones.
Afterwards, Rojas began a fulminating speech
which went much further than the previous
speeches. He talked about the coming of an
agrarian revolution which would make campesinos owners of the land and free them from
the gamonales, and in order to accomplish this,
campesinos had to become a solid mass ("como
una masa de pan" - like bread dough), organized
into sindicatos. These organizations must be
made up of "real Indians" wearing sandals, not
shoes nor using hair fixer (Indios netos con
abarcas, no con zapatos ni peinados con gomina
...) He was criticizing Rivas and other leaders who were not campesinos...The motto was
Agrarian Revolution...that the campesinos should
carry their rifles on their shoulder to defend
their rights. Then Rojas would take off his
old campesino hat shouting that those campesinos who were for the Agrarian Revolution used
such hats to symbolize their poverty, while
those who talked of legalities, promises and a
peaceful Agrarian Reform showed their bourgeois and high living tendency (tendencia
burguesa y acomodada)...After all these speeches
we proceeded to organize the sindicato by
first electing the officials, signing a founding charter (acta de fundación), with the signa-
tures of all associated campesinos. The officers and members took an oath to defend the MNR
Revolution and Agrarian Reform. We explained
each official's role... We then walked away with
another hacienda behind us... and became their
advisors in many matters: how to run a sindicato, deal with the patron, request help from
authorities for a school and other projects...
when the Agrarian Reform decree was signed, we
helped them in their litigations and contacted
officials to help them (personal interview).

Through this description, we can discern how a campesino
leadership and organization was welded together. Rojas
drew upon the symbols and rhetoric of the Revolution, re-
worked them with other culturally relevant symbols and effectively exploited the historical experience and notoriety
of Ucurena, with the result that he presented a plan for
action and all the while, promoted himself as the leader

closest to campesinos. In other words, an ideological
program was generated which expressed a sentiment of class
consciousness. On the other hand, the relationship of
leader-follower or leader-urban politician also involved
an idiom which tended to structure clienteles vertically.
The ideological and clientelist aspects of political
strategy have also been illustrated in our previous analysis of Rivas. The roles which leaders assumed with respect to their followers and authorities at different
levels were multiple. They brought the message of the
Revolution, built a <u>conciencia</u> (consciousness) and presented themselves as legitimators of campesino solidarity
and representatives to lead men, channel resources and
articulate goals.

c) Competition For Political Domains
        The impact of rural mobilization and agitation on
Cochabamba had grown to widespread effervescence by late
1952. The collective enthusiasm of the Revolution had now
taken roots in the countryside. The organization of sindicatos, beginnings of armed campesino militia and the general atmosphere of rising expectations, generated pressures
which the government itself found difficult to control.
Unrest in the countryside and policy conflicts at the
nation's capital were exacerbated by leadership struggles
for the control of the Cochabamba Peasant Federation, conflicts among campesino leaders concerning the agrarian
reform issue, and land take-overs by campesinos.
        By the end of 1952, Rivas made efforts to affirm the
Federation as the sole legitimating agency and spokesman
for campesinos in the Department. Encouraged by the Government, the Federation moved its headquarters to the city
of Cochabamba to centralize activities. Furthermore, it
presented a petition to the Government with the following
main points: (1) A national decree to establish the juridical status of agrarian sindicatos and their Federation;
(2) creation of a commission to prepare an Agrarian Reform
decree with the participation of campesino delegates; (3)
immediate expropriation of several haciendas in the Ucurena
area; (4) replacement of most provincial authorities prior
approval by the Federation, and; (5) provision of arms to
strengthen agrarian militia (Dandler 1971: 197-8). Since
these requests were accepted, bhey offer a measure of the
considerable resources which were extended to campesinos
for their support.
        While the Federation attempted to work through
formal channels, Rojas translated his demands into effective action in the countryside. He organized a massive
rally in the town of Cliza and announced that campesinos
would no longer tolerate abuses by landowners. Challenging
the government to take immediate measures, he affirmed that
if necessary, campesinos would take matters into their own

hands. Various authorities hastily intervened to prevent
an armed attack on Cliza and haciendas. A compromise was
reached to enforce labor obligations uniformly and dismiss
hacienda authorities. Shortly thereafter, the Government
announced that it was preparing a special expropriation
decree to benefit peasants in the Ucurena area (Los Tiempos,
November 13, 1952; interviews).

Indicents such as the threat against Cliza demonstrated the capacity of peasants to assert their power in
a context when it had become clear to them that landowners
no longer had authority or governmental backing. No longer willing to wait for further legalities and time-consum-
ing negotiations, they assumed de facto control of the land
in Ucurena:

> we became very strong during the Cliza threat
> and realized that authorities were on our side
> but that they were too slow...the patrones were
> scared because now they had little power...we
> did not take over the lands (on a specific date)
> ...we did it without violence because we had
> power and nobody wanted to listen to the pa-
> trones or further government promises...besides,
> the patrones and administrators were scared,
> many did not come back...they did not get their
> products after the harvest (beginning of March)
> (interview).

On April 30 (1953) the government signed a special expropriation decree which de facto recognized these developments in Ucurena, four months prior to the signing of the
national agrarian reform decree.[24]

While the process to assume control of the land had
begun in Ucurena, a massive public gathering in the city of
Cochabamba was organized by the Federation at the end of
1952. The rally was an impressive mobilization of several
thousand campesinos representing several hundred sindicatos.
There was considerable expectation that the Government was
to announce more specifically its agrarian policy. Yet,
the contradictions and conflicting pressures within the MNR
at this crucial juncture were implicitly revealed in speeches of three Ministers who attended the rally.[25] No one announced a specific policy except that the Government needed
time to consider the agrarian reform and that a commission
would soon be established. Not all the Ministers seemed in
agreement with this announcement. A campesino leader who
attended this meeting revealed an awareness of these contradictions and that campesinos expected more:

> there were few proposals except general
> speeches which we could carry back to our
> compañeros in the countryside...and there

> were differences of opinion. In a way,
> Lechin and Chaves Ortiz were saying that it
> was up to us now. When a POR leader spoke
> to the masses at the stadium he said things
> which were very direct and closest to us...
> he was offering a plan (interview).

Indeed, the POR speaker openly criticized the MNR for the
landowners and "reactionaries" in its ranks, argued for
more arms to campesinos and workers, and urged the masses
to "directly nationalize the land, distribute the latifundio and organize collectives" (Los Tiempos, December
23, 1952).

This public meeting in Cochabamba underlined the
fact that the agrarian reform issue involved greater conflicts of interest and policy disagreements within the
regime than previous measures. At the beginning of 1953,
the agrarian question was being debated at various cabinet
sessions and within the COB. On January 6 (1953), an
abortive plot of the MNR right occurred, clearly related
to the growing influence of the COB and the MNR left within the government, as well as the peasant mobilization in
the countryside. Discussion of principles and strategies
continued during the party's convention in February. The
MNR left demanded a massive purge of rightists within the
party and a clearer revolutionary stance with respect to
agrarian reform and other issues, while moderates denounced
that the party was already too infiltrated by leftists.
In many respects, the man still in command of the situation was President Paz Estenssoro himself, who represented
a pragmatic-center line, attempting to maintain the unity
of the party along its populist course (Malloy 1970: 232).

At the departmental level, a leadership crisis
developed within the Campesino Federation concerning the
agrarian reform issue and relations with the government.
In order to control growing unrest in Cochabamba, the
government sent a "coordinator of campesino affairs" there
with broad authority to act as an ideological and political
arbiter.[26]

Shortly after he began to assume these responsi-
bilities, a "coup" (golpe) occurred within the Federation
which allegedly had been engineered by the POR and radical
labor leaders with the support of Rojas and other campesino leaders (January 1, 1953). Rivas and his lieutenants
were ousted from the leadership of the Federation and replaced by other campesino leaders which indluded Rojas as
subordinate official. From the beginning, the new Federation leadership displayed a considerably more radical ideology. Its slogans were Agrarian Revolution, nationalization of the land, general armed mobilization and an effective labor-peasant government. The crisis of the Federation

further alarmed the MNR hierarchy that the campesino movement in Cochabamba was dominated by "leftists" who "agi-
tated" the countryside.

The Federation crisis lingered for several weeks.
Two competing groups claimed the authority to speak for
campesinos in the Department. By the end of January 1953,
Rivas and his followers occupied the Federation headquarters and reinstalled themselves with official support. But
the leadership conflict had not been resolved. Summing up
the situation several years later to the author, the
former coordinator stated as follows:

> it was clear to us that there were too many
> men in the Cochabamba countryside who wanted
> to become top leaders. In addition, there were
> some who were not genuine campesinos and who
> worked with the POR. We had to select and help
> those leaders who would support the Government
> and could not be easily swayed by the extremist
> POR. We reached an agreement with Rojas and
> Inturias of Ucurena. Both had important follow-
> ings and were among the most genuine campesinos
> of all top leaders in Cochabamba. We promised
> resources and support to them, as well as posi-
> tions in the Federation, as long as they no
> longer would become involved with extremists.

This was an important political transaction, since
up to this time Rojas had not fully identified himself with
the MNR: Rojas felt that he had a great deal more to win
through an understanding with the Government than by risk-
ing further confrontations, especially since POR men were
not able to deliver comparable resources and support from
the power structure (interview). Furthermore, the agrarian
reform issue was still sufficiently fluid for the Government to accept less moderate views and leaders such as Rojas, because of their sizeable following in the countryside.

Once the Federation crisis had been provisionally
resolved, the primary organizational impetus fell on Rivas
and Rojas. Rivas had an expertise which the Government
needed to lead a departmental organization in the process
of institutionalization. He agreed with a policy of controlled mobilization and an orderly implementation of an
agrarian reform, a stance which was in tune with pragmatic-
center leaders within the regime. On the other hand, Rojas
soon proved more effective in building a rural following
for himself and the Government encompassing a larger area
than Rivas. He continued to articulate a considerably more
militant viewpoint concerning the Agrarian Reform. Rojas
effectively maneuvered to establish campesino power and
displaced hacendados and their administrators within his

area of influence. Many of the latter abandoned their
properties in the presence of armed sindicatos that refused to work or negotiate with them. The influence of
Rojas also extended itself to provincial governments;
authorities that were partial to landowners were replaced
by others who accepted the new realignments of power.
Moreover, the government's recognition of Ucurena's de-
facto land takeovers through a special decree signed four
months before the Agrarian Reform further enhanced the vanguard image of Rojas and his followers.

The consequence of backing two rival leaders resulted in their consolidation of power in two territorial
domains.[27] The location of their headquarters (centrales)
was an important factor. Ucurena and Quillacollo were
within easy reach of the city of Cochabamba for immediate
communication and massive mobilization of armed militia.
Both were situated in separate, densely populated valleys
with adjacent highlands. Although formally affiliated to
the Federation, provincial organizations and local sindicatos frequently operated as clienteles directly linked to
one of the centers. Elected officials of the numerous
satellite sindicatos were generally loyal local campesinos
promoted by Rojas or Rivas. At the same time, many of
their close lieutenants, acting as Federation inspectors,
initially exercised considerable authority over the pre-
dominantly monolingual (Quechua) population of neighboring
highland provinces.

Certain rules concomitantly developed to maintain
boundaries and prevent the encroachment of the rival con-
tender into the other's sphere of influence. Once provincial and sub-provincial organizations had been established, it was not infrequent for an armed group associated
with one of the two leaders to carry out a golpe or coup
and install a loyal local leadership. Such practices became a common feature of politics in Bolivia, particularly
during presidential and legislative election campaigns,
when personal rivalries among national leaders intensified
struggles for positions and followers among leaders at
various levels of rural, labor or urban organizations.

Although campesino mobilization on Cochabamba had
been streamlined into a regionalization of clienteles under
two powerful leaders, from the point of view of the Government or the leaders themselves, it was important to formally demonstrate greater unity within the movement before
the signing of the Agrarian Reform decree (August 2, 1953).
The government called for a departmental campesino congress
for mid-June 1953. Nevertheless, "unification" was only a
tentative proposition. In later years, as internecine
strife within the MNR deepened or as the Armed Forces later
displaced the MNR, campesino congresses became parodies of
"unification," actually serving sectarian interests or
forming part of a political cooptation process.

d) Resolution of the Agrarian Reform Issue

The decree was signed, symbolically, in Ucurena on August 2, 1953, the Day of the Indian. Nearly a hundred thousand campesinos from most regions of Bolivia, armed and organized into sindicatos, came to witness this important event. As the implementation of the decree began in the countryside, campesino organizations assumed a most important role. Sindicatos became an effective instrument in the legal expropiation and land distribution procedures. In those areas where campesinos exercised considerable power, such as in the Upper Valley, haciendas were totally expropriated, regardless of subtleties in the agrarian reform law. Consequently, a fundamental dilemma had been resolved: how much land should be left for the hacendado? How far should the campesino be mobilized?

III. Conclusion

We have considered a particular case within a given historical context of mobilization and the extent to which peasants played an active role. Our analysis dealt with an apparently revolutionary political situation in which peasants began to act as a class-for-itself through the following process:

a) In view of their own experience and adopting some of the positive and negative symbols of the National Revolution, peasants synthesized their own ideology, permitting relatively independent and previously unchartered actions;

b) They developed their own forms of organizations and struggle, acting not only politically but also as armed militia: the sindicatos became an instrument of local government, asserted political control in the provinces and became the principal link between the peasantry and the national government;

c) On the basis of their ideology and political organization, peasants made demands and asserted their influence in ways which constituted a power capability to be reconed with.

Nevertheless, closer analysis reveals that this mobilization gradually lost momentum, as political partners were sought within a context of shifting alliances, internecine strife within the MNR, and the vague overall ideology guiding the entire evolutionary process. The ideological force of national and peasant symbols appeared to cede at times to a concern on the part of leaders to strengthen their personal clienteles, to assure their legitimacy from above. Leadership to address peasant demands toward aims beyond the agrarian reform appeared fleeting indeed. Our focus on relationships at an intermediate level revealed a gradual identification of leaders and organizations with the shifting goals of conflicting sectors characterizing the national populist coalition. Such institutional weakness and ideological ambiguity characterizing populist movements prevent them from assuming a sustained revolutionary leadership and establishing a new order.

As we have attempted to show, peasants of the Cochabamba Valleys were certainly not passive bystanders to the revolutionary movement. But we have also found that the peasantry's revolutionary role was limited by the populist movement itself and the very nature of the national revolution. Indeed, a paradox of peasant movements in countries of the Third World is that peasants begin to act as a class-for-itself in the marxist sense only when they find forms of organization and ideology adequate to satisfy their demands and when they mobilize within a revolutionary struggle; however, this struggle can be sustained and revolutionary goals reached only when peasants are allied to a national revolutionary movement. The peculiarities of the Bolivian revolution - and not of the Bolivian peasants - have led us to conceptually distinguish the first as an unfinished revolution and the latter as a social sector which ascended to a certain level of class-consciousness and organization ("low classness"). That this should have been the outcome not only for peasants but for the Bolivian proletariat, confirms that the Bolivian revolution, as a populist phenomenon, is a significant case to ponder as we consider the nature of social classes and revolutionary movements in Latin America. We have sought a definition of peasants as a class-for-itself within a particular historical context and at a level of analysis which permitted a grasp of the relationship between locality and region with the broader national milieu. On the other hand, the absence of sustained ideological and organizational leadership within populist movements demonstrates not only that they are harbingers of future disappointments but also that it is impossible to adequately deal with the problems of the peasantry and the dynamics of social classes, without simultaneously considering the possibilities and outcome of a social revolution.

FOOTNOTES

1. Wolf (1969), Alavi (1965), Stavenhagen (1970), Landsberger (1969), Huizer (1973), Quijano (1967), Moore (1966); some outstanding recent works within specific Latin American countries: Alberti (1973), Firoavanti (1974), Gilly (1971) and Womack (1968).

2. See also Hobsbawm (1973a: 21).

3. We do not consider very useful for our purposes, to dwell on the controversy concerning peasants and the "limited good" image that continues to fascinate some cultural anthropologists in the United States. For a critique, see Huizer (1970).

4. Part of the problem is that frequently a "hypothetical proletariat" (not analyzed in a specific historical context) is contrasted to an "empirical" peasantry (an actual historical example), but not sufficiently analyzed within a revolutionary process. (Shanin 1972: 22-23).

5. "The small peasant proprietors form an immense mass, the members of which live in the same situation but do not enter into manifold relationships with each other. Their mode of operation isolates them instead of bringing them into mutual intercourse. This isolation is strengthened by the wretched state of France's means of communication and by the poverty of the peasants. Their place of operation, the small-holding, permits no division of labor in its cultivation, no application of science and therefore no diversity of development, variety of talent, or wealth of social relationships. Each individual peasant family is almost self-sufficient; it directly produces the greater part of its own consumption and therefore obtains its means of life more through exchange with nature than through intercourse with society. The smallholding, the peasant, and the family; next door, another smallholding, another peasant, and another family. A bunch of these makes up a village, and a bunch of villages makes up a department. Thus the great mass of the French nation is formed by the simple addition of isomorphous magnitudes, much as potatoes in a sack form a sack of potatoes... (Marx 1973: 238-239).

6. Meszaros (1971: 86), cited by Alavi; see his discussion of this point (1973: 29).

7. From a more theoretical point of view, Lukacs (1971) contrasts the proletariat with all other classes for its special position in society and history. The proletariat's struggle for its class interests is to be identified with the historical progress of all the society. All other classes, in contrast, seek goals which do not go beyond their own limited interests.

8. According to Geertz (1966: 66), ideologies provide a blueprint for action, they are "maps of problematic social reality and matrices for the creation of collective conscience."

9. Lenin posed a similar scheme (1970, orig. 1918).

10. "The complex mediation of the processes by which class solidarity is established and manifested, escapes the attention of those Marxists who focus exclusively on dramatic demonstrations of class solidarity of peasants in revolutionary action" (Alavi 1973: 29).

11. See Galjert (1964) and Powell (1972). The "horizontal" and "vertical" aspects are not to be interpreted as mutually exclusive but complementary. In certain contexts, local solidarity and "vertical" alliances may reinforce "horizontal" solidarity. In a controversy concerning the peasant movement led by Juliao in Northeastern Brazil, Galjart (1964) emphasized the clientelist features, while Huizer (1964) those aspects which contributed to. class movement. Each rejects the other's approach. Alavi (1973) and the present essay attempt to identify both tendencies.

12. Antezana and Romero (1969), Dandler (1969, 1971), Pearse (1972) and Iriarte (1975).

13. "Fellow and brother campesino, the hour of your liberation has come, you will be free and owner of the land you work." La Nacion 10-VI 1952.

14. For some studies on the MNR, see Malloy (1970), Whitehead (1969), Zavaleta (1974b) and Lora (1964).

15. On the limitations of co-gobierno, see Zavaleta (1974a, 1974b) and Lora (1964).

16. Nuflo Chavez Ortiz was one of the authors of a pact between the MNR left and some leaders of the PIR (Partido de la Izquierda Revolucionaria) that was signed in Chile (1950) and which emphatically included agrarian reform as an objective (Canelas, 1966: 124-126).

17. According to DiTella, the sources of populist strength
    are (1) an elite placed at the middle or upper-middle
    levels of stratification, impregnated with an anti-
    status quo motivation; (2) a mobilized mass formed as
    a result of the "revolution of rising expectations";
    and (3) an ideology or a wide-spread emotional state
    to help communication between leaders and followers
    and to create collective enthusiasm (1965: 53, also
    cited by Malloy 1970: 58).

18. Other areas, such as Achacachi in the Northern High-
    lands, also may have played a strategic role in the
    early mobilization of campesinos. Unfortunately, we
    do not have comparable information for the period
    covered in the present paper. See Patch (1956, 1960),
    Carballo (1963), Dandler (1969, 1971) and Albo (1968)
    for background discussion on the Cochabamba Valleys
    and the agrarian issue.

19. Interview with Dr. German Vera Tapis, Minister of Agri-
    culture and later Prefect of the Department of Cocha-
    bamba during the period covered by the present paper.

20. Ucurena had achieved notoriety as the first rural
    sindicato in Bolivia (1936-1940's). Assisted by sym-
    pathetic townsmen and other allies, the sindicato
    obtained preferential rental rights to some of the
    Monastery of Santa Clara's lands through a special
    presidential decree in 1936. The rental contract was
    soon annulled by a succeeding president and repressive
    measures were taken by landlords and departmental and
    provincial authorities. Thanks to a determined campe-
    sino leadership which demanded nothing short of owner-
    ship of the land, and a continuous, multilevel network
    with non-campesino allies, including teachers at the
    recently established school, the sindicato remained
    active for more than a decade in spite of intermittent
    repression. Partial successes, such as a limited pur-
    chase which freed some campesinos from the hacienda
    and a Supreme Court decision in their favor, only
    strengthened their conviction as the exploited (Dandler
    1969).

21. The present analysis of the Lower Valley is based on
    fieldwork. See also Carballo (1963).

22. In the national elections of 1947, the PIR and MNR had
    begun to cultivate political support among a potential-
    ly vast population of peasant voters. In the 1951
    elections, the MNR made a much more concerted effort to
    win peasant votes in a number of provinces, a factor
    which undoubtedly contributed to its victory at the polls.

23. For an analysis of social differentiation in the
    Cochabamba Valleys and Highlands, see Dandler (1971:
    Chapter 2).

24. For a text of the special decree of April 30, 1952,
    see Dandler (1969: 186-193).

25. The Ministers who attended the mass meeting were Lechin,
    Chavez Ortiz and Guevara Arze (Mines, Campesino Affairs
    and Foreign Relations). Significantly, President Paz
    Estenssoro had cancelled his visit.

26. Victor Zannier was well prepared to assume such a
    strategic position. Fluent in Quechua, a Cochabambino,
    he had been a university leader; strongly identified
    with the PIR, he later supported the MNR in the 1949
    revolt and the 1951 elections.

27. Rivas had virtual control of the provinces of Tapa-
    cari, Quillacollo, Cercado, Ayopaya and to some extent
    Arque. On the other hand, Rojas encompassed a larger
    domain of provinces in the Upper Valley, adjacent high-
    lands and southern areas (Cliza, Tarata, Arani, Punata,
    Tiraque, Anzaldo, Totora, Sacabamba, Mizque and Ai-
    quille). Nevertheless, Rojas was never able to control
    a number of sindicatos in Cliza and neighboring provin-
    ces. A dissident central was established in Cliza as
    early as December 1952, at first supported by Rivas in
    order to undermine the hegemony of Rojas in the Upper
    Valley region. On the basis of this split, Cliza and
    Ucurena later became centers of competing domains led
    by Miguel Veizage and Jose Rojas, respectively. A
    violent, protracted "war" erupted in the region from
    1959 to 1964, as these caciques struggled for the
    hegemony of peasant organizations in Cochabamba. This
    conflict was intimately related to the internecine
    strife within the MNR over presidential succession.
    The process of political segmentation in Cochabamba
    and the military's "pacification" of the valley, even-
    tually served as the basis for the "military-peasant"
    pact and General Parrientos' overthrow of the MNR in
    November 1964. The pact has been subsequently used as
    a banner by all military governments in Bolivia, until
    it was recently shattered during the 1974 massacre of
    Cochabamba peasants who rebelled against the govern-
    ment's economic policies. On this recent event, see
    Comisión "Justicia y Paz" (1975).

REFERENCES

Alavi, Hamza
  1965 -- "Peasants and Revolution," The Socialist Register
         London: Merlin Press.
  1973 -- "Peasant Classes and Primordial Loyalties," Jour
         nal of Peasant Studies, I: 1, 23-62.

Alberti, Giorgio
  1973 -- "The Breakdown of a Provincial Power Structure:
         The Peasant Movement of Yanamarca Valley, Peru,"
         Sociologia Ruralis, XXI: 3/4. Spanish revised
         version in Alberti G. and R. Sanchez, Poder y
         Conflicto Social en el valle del Mantaro, Lima:
         Instituto de Estudios Peruanos (1974).

Albo, Javier
  1968 -- "Ucurena en el contexto de la Revolución Nacional
         Boliviana (1935-1967)," paper presented to the
         Seminar on Peasant Movements at Cornell Univer-
         sity, Ithaca (mimeographed).

Antezana, Luis y Hugo Romero Bedregal
  1968 -- Origen, desarrollo y situación actual del sindi-
         calismo campesino en Bolivia, I-IV, La Paz,
         Estudio de la Estructura Agraria en Bolivia,
         CIDA/Universidad de Wisconsin (mimeographed).

Barcelli, Agustin
  1956 -- Medio siglo de luchas sindicales revolucionarias
         en Bolivia (1905-1955), La Paz: Editorial del
         Estado.

Barta, Roger, Eckart Boege et al.
  1975 -- Caciquismo y Poder Politico en Mexico, Instituto
         de Investigaciones Sociales, UNAM, Mexico:
         Siglo XXI.

Barta, Roger
  1974 -- Estructura Agraria y Clases Sociales en Mexico,
         Mexico: Editorial Era.

Canelas, Amado
  1966 -- Mito y realidad de la reforma agraria, Cochabamba:
         Editorial Amigos del Libro.

Carballo, Manuel
  1963 -- "Agrarian Reform in Bolivia," B. A. Thesis,
         Princeton University, unpublished.

170

Cockcroft, James D. and Bo Anderson
  1966 -- "Control and Cooptation in Mexican Politics,"
     International Journal of Comparative Sociology,
     Vii: 1, March.

Comision de "Justicia y Paz"
  1974 -- La Masacre del Valle (Cochabamba-Enero 1974),
     Cochabamba, La Paz, Febrero 1974 (mimeographed).

Dandler, Jorge
  1969 -- El sindicalismo campesino en Bolivia: Cambios
     estructurales en Ucurena (1935-52), Mexico:
     Instituto Indigenista Interamericano.
  1971 -- "Politics of Brokerage, Leadership and Patronage
     in the Campesino Movement of Cochabamba, Bolivia
     (1935-52)," Ph.D. dissertation, University of
     Wisconsin, Ann Arbor: University Microfilms Inc.

Di Tella, Torcuato
  1965 -- "Populism and Reform in Latin America," in
     Claudio Veliz, ed., Obstacles to Change in Latin
     America, Oxford: Oxford University Press.

Engels, Frederick
  1969 -- The Peasant War in Germany, London: Lawrence and
     Wishart.

Fioravanti, Eduardo
  1974 -- Latifundismo y sindicalismo agrario en el Peru.
     El caso de los valles de la Convención y Lares
     (1958-1964), Lima: Instituto de Estudios Peruanos.

Galjart, Benno
  1964 -- "Class and 'Following' in Rural Brazil," America
     Latina 7: 3-24.

Geertz, Clifford
  1966 -- "Ideology as a Cultural System," in David Apter,
     ed., Ideology and Discontent, New York: The
     Free Press.

Gilly, Adolfo
  1971 -- La revolución interrumpida: Mexico, 1910-1920,
     una guerra campesina por la tierra y el poder.
     Mexico: El Caballito.

Gutelman, Michel
  1971 -- Reforme et mystification agraires en Amérique
     Latine, Le cas du Mexique, Paris: Francois Maspero.

Hobsbawm, Eric
  1973a-- "Class Consciousness in History," in Istvan
          Meszaros, ed., Aspects of History and Class Con-
          sciousness, London: Routledge and Kegan Paul
  1973b-- "Peasant and Politics," Journal of Peasant
          Studies, I: 1, 3-22.

Huizer, Gerrit
  1973 -- Peasant Unrest in Latin America, London: Penguin.
  1970 -- "Resistencia al cambio como una potencial para
          la acción radical campesina: Foster y Erasmus
          reconsiderados," América Indígena, XXX: 2, 321-44.
  1964 -- "Some Notes on Community Development and Rural
          Social Research," América Latina, VII: 4, 128-44.

Iriarte, Gregorio
  1974 -- Sindicalismo campesino, La Paz: Centro de In-
          vestigación y Promoción del Campesinado (mimeo-
          graphed).

Klein, Herbert S.
  1969 -- Parties and Political Change in Bolivia 1880-
          1952, Cambridge: Cambridge University Press

Landsberger, Henry, (ed.)
  1969 -- Latin American Peasant Movements, Ithaca:
          Cornell University Press.

Lenin, V. I.
  1950 -- The Development of Capitalism in Russia, Moscow:
          Foreign Languages Publishing House.
  1970 -- "El infantilismo izquierdista y el espíritu
          pequeno-burgues," Obras Completas, II, Moscu:
          Editorial Progreso.

Lora, Guillermo
  1964 -- La Revolución Boliviana, La Paz.

Lukacs, Georg
  1971 -- History and Class Consciousness, London: Merlin
          Press.

Malloy, James M.
  1970 -- Bolivia: The Uncompleted Revolution, Pittsburgh:
          University Press.

Mao Tse-Tung
  1965 -- "Report on an Investigation of the Peasant Move-
          ment in Hunan" (orig. 1927), Selected Works, I,
          Peking: Foreign Language Editions.

Marx, Karl
  1973 -- "The Eighteenth Brumaire of Louis Bonaparte,"
         Surveys from Exile, London: Penguin, pp. 143-249.

Meszaros, Istvan
  1971 -- "Contingent and necessary class consciousness,"
         in I. Meszaros, ed., Aspects of History and Class
         Consciousness, London: Routledge and Kegan Paul.

Moore, Barrington, Jr.
  1966 -- Social Origins of Dictatorship and Democracy,
         Lord and Peasant in the Making of the Modern
         World, Boston: Beacon Press.

Patch, Richard W.
  1956 -- "Social Implications of the Bolivian Agrarian
         Reform,: Ph.D. dissertation, Cornell University,
         Ithaca. Ann Arbor, Michigan: University Micro-
         films, Inc.
  1960 -- "Bolivia: U.S. Assistance in a Revolutionary
         Setting," in Richard N. Adams, ed., Social Change
         in Latin America Today, New York: Vintage Press.

Pearse, Andrew
  1972 -- "Peasants and Revolution: the Case of Bolivia,"
         Economy and Society, I: 4.

Powell, John D.
  1972 -- "Peasant Society and Clientelist Politics,"
         American Political Science Review, LXIV, 411-425.

Quijano, Anibal
  1967 -- "Contemporary Peasant Movements," in Elites in
         Latin America, S.M. Lipset and A. Solari, eds.,
         Oxford: Oxford University Press.

Shanin, Teodor
  1971 -- "The Peasantry as a Political Factor," in Peasants
         and Peasant Societies, T. Shanin, ed., London:
         Penguin.
  1972 -- "Class and Revolution," Journal of Contemporary
         Asia, I: 2, 22-35.

Stavenhagen, Rodolfo (ed.)
  1970 -- Agrarian Problems and Peasant Movements in Latin
         America, New York: Doubleday Anchor.

Sweezy, Paul M.
  1968 -- "The Proletariat in Today's World," Tricontin-
         ental 9.

Wolf, Eric R.
  1969 -- Peasant Wars of the Twentieth Century, New York:
         Harper and Row.
  1974 -- Review of Teodor Shanin, The Awkward Class:
         Political Sociology of Peasants in a Developing
         Society: Russia 1910-1925 (Oxford: Clarendon
         Press, 1972) in Journal of Peasant Studies, I:
         3, 401-404.

Womack, John Jr.
  1968 -- Zapata and the Mexican Revolution, New York:
         Random House.

Zavaleta, Rene
  1974a-- El poder dual en América Latina, Mexico: Siglo
         XXI.
  1974b-- "La Revolución Democrática de 1952 y las tenden-
         cias sociológicas emergentes," UNAM, Centro de
         Estudios Latinoamericanos, Facultad de Ciencias
         Políticas y Sociales, Mexico, D.F. (mimeographed).

CONDUCT AND CODE: AN ANALYSIS OF MARKET SYNDICATES

AND SOCIAL REVOLUTION IN LA PAZ, BOLIVIA

Hans C. Buechler

and

Judith-Maria Buechler

The development of new institutions in rapidly changing societies has become one of the major focuses of anthropology in recent years. A problem posed by such studies concerns the ways in which previously established social patterns determine the direction of change or the manner in which change will be implemented; a second one concerns the relationship between social and economic behavior in changing situations on the one hand and jural rules, ritual and ideology on the other hand. The first raises the question of how behavior patterns associated with a given institution are interrelated, the extent to which institutions are linked and whether a single balanced model can adequately represent the institutions, or if multiple interrelated models, which may contradict each other, are required. The solution to the second problem may reflect the answer to the first. If a monolithic view of institutions adequately explains the nature of processes of culture change, we may expect a one to one correlation between statistical means of actual behavior and jural rules, ritual and ideology. These could be viewed as the institution's charter or blueprint. Any discrepancies between the former and the latter should be short-lived and intrusive rather than intrinsic to an institution. On the other hand, if behavior patterns associated with institutions can be represented only by a multiple model then we may find either one, multiple jural rules, rituals and ideologies associated with alternative modes of behavior, two, a lack of congruence between behavior and the latter or three, a combination of both of these possibilities.

If the second and third possibilities most adequately describe our observations, then jural rules, ritual and ideology can no longer be viewed solely as charters for social interaction. Rather, they must be viewed as symbolic means of communication, i.e. as a code which expresses both similarities and differences between alternative modes of behavior.

In another paper (Buechler, H. 1968) one of us attempted to show that changes in settlement patterns on the Bolivian altiplano could only be understood with a multiple model which was seen as constantly changing over time. In

this paper, we wish to discuss both the means by which
multiple behavior patterns connected with a changing marketing system on the Bolivian highlands are expressed in
symbolic codes and also analyze the content of the messages
communicated.

The formation of market syndicates, or market unions,
in La Paz may be considered a consequence of the Agrarian
Reform of 1953 which transformed the agrarian structure on
the Bolivian high plateau from one dominated by large land-
holdings, or haciendas, where the majority of the peasants
worked for a landlord in return for a subsistence plot, to
one in which most of the land is owned by the peasants
themselves. This reform was part of a vast social revolution
brought about by the Movimiento Nacional Revolucionario, or
M.N.R., a party which came into power in 1952 and which also
promoted universal suffrage, the nationalization of mines,
social laws governing labor, the improvement of rural education, and the opening of frontiers by the construction of
new roads. The agrarian program was accompanied by a growing
interest in the peasantry as a national, political and
economic force. Thus, among other reforms, the government
introduced an albeit unsuccessful program of cooperatives to
promote the improvement of agricultural techniques and
created institutions such as the National Council for
Agrarian Reform and the Ministry of Peasant Affairs, permitting more direct communication between the government and
the peasants. The M.N.R. further contributed to the expanded
political power of the peasantry by replacing the military
by a militia formed by peasants, miners, and workers and
made it possible for educated Aymara and Quechua peasants to
acceed to political positions on the county and provincial
levels, posts which had hitherto been reserved for mestizos.
In La Paz itself, first and second generation migrants from
rural areas began to occupy positions in the lower echelons
of government administration, the militia, and the secret
service.

Concomitant with the change in ownership patterns,
the opening of new roads and the improvement of existing
ones, significant changes were brought about in marketing
patterns which in turn laid the foundation for the market
syndicates. Prior to the reform, the peasant had acted only
as a producer and as a vendor for the landlord in large-
scale transactions in the city as well as for his own
surpluses in local fairs. At the most he was involved in
small-scale transactions with mestizo middlemen who traveled
to the country from La Paz. Direct sales in La Paz were
infrequent. Today he is producer, middleman, vendor, and
consumer both in the country and the city. These changes
have resulted in a market population with very diverse
backgrounds and economic means. The density of today's
La Paz market vendors with 12,000 persons selling on weekdays
and 15,000 on weekends in a city of less than half a million

is in sharp contrast to the pre-reform situation. In
hacienda times, mestizo women monopolized the two major
markets and the tambos or patios where produce was sold
wholesale while the colonos, or serfs were limited to
selling their produce in their patron's patios. Hacienda
produce was sold there as well to metizo vendors and other
landowners. Not only were there changes in number and type
of vendor but also in the quantity and kind of goods sold.
At present larger quantities of manufactured goods and
diversified food crops flow to the rural areas while the
reverse flow of cash crops to the urban areas has increased
as well.

The pre-reform markets and tambos had a rather simple
organization which is still maintained by a number of them.
Each market or tambo had a maestra mayor appointed annually
by her predecessor and one or two aides, the alcaldes mayores
who investigate disputes and settle them either directly in
the market (usually with the advice of other vendors who
flock around the disputants) or at the police stations
located near all larger indoor markets. Sometimes maestras
mayores bring their cases to higher municipal officials in
charge of all La Paz markets. Last but not least they pay
off the market police in order that price and weight controls
be slackened. However, their main functions are of a ceremonial nature. During the year in office they must finance
a fiesta and/or celebrate a mass for the market's patron
saint. Since these functions entail considerable expenditure
only the richer, firmly established market women become
maestras mayores.

The maestrerío provided no link between markets and
although maestras mayores presently do influence marketing
policy e.g. the enlargement of old markets, policy is still
dictated by the municipal government. Post-reform conditions
demanded a more closely linked system. Further the new
multiple role of the peasant and the competitive pressure
called for a more effective regulation of the market than
the municipal police and the traditional maestras mayores,
or market leaders subject to them could provide. The newly
established syndicates address themselves to both the
internal and external affairs of the market. Internally they
act as courts of justice for disputant vendors; they regulate
the distribution and inheritance of stalls in the streets or
markets under their jurisdiction and defend their members
against encroachment by nonmembers. They also arrange market
feasts and occasionally contribute to the welfare of impoverished members. Similarly they purchase land for new
multistoried market buildings which are intended not only to
house the vendors but likewise to provide office space for
the union, a school, kindergarten, nursery, and infirmary
with a full-time nurse in attendance.

Externally the syndicate mediates between the city
government and the market vendors. It seeks to prevent both

police graft and unjust punishment of vendors. Prior to the
formation of the syndicates, persons who could not pay
rentals for their stalls were subject to the confiscation
of produce worth more than the fee. Market women could also
be fined unjustly for alleged failure to comply with the
regulations governing the sanitary condition of their person
and produce. For this reason a set fee has been established
for the different kinds of vendors, i.e. for those with
fixed stalls and for the ambulant ones, and the syndicate
leaders now actively intervene in their behalf. Furthermore
they arrange for the provision of more streets and patios
for marketing. Finally they communicate government requests
for participation in processions on national holidays or
rallies against communism as well as those of labor and
mining unions for support in political manifestations.

The syndicates are grouped into two federations of
La Paz based merchants and these into confederations
including syndicates based in other cities. The main difference between the two federations is the fact that the first
comprises the voters who abstained from voting during the
1966 elections and thus cast a white (i.e. blank) ballot;
the second those who voted for a particular political party
by casting a green ballot. The blancos accuse the verdes of
being bourgeois, capitalists and wholesalers, contending
that they, the small scale retailers alone belong to the true
working class who earns its daily bread by honest toil. This
charge is true to the extent that more vendors of contraband
goods which require a higher capital investment are affiliated to the verde federation. But with this exception, the
federations differ but little as both federations include
syndicates of varying economic status. Rather than reflecting economic differences, the three federations seem to
mirror changing loyalties in the rapidly expanding market.
In fact, rival syndicates competing for a given market area
usually belong to different federations. The confederations
differ by the fact that one includes only market vendors
whereas the latter constitute only a segment of the second
confederation which includes artisans as well.

Each syndicate boasts a roster of twelve officials
devoted to such tasks as conflict resolution, accounting,
charity, public relations, banner bearing, and general
administration. Although few of these leaders spend much
time in their official capacities they are required to be
present at all meetings. Only when general consensus cannot
be reached is a task delegated to the secretary-general
and/or a few particularly active persons. The federations
have a similar roster as the individual unions expanded to
include delegates from each member organization and
confederations.

Syndicate leaders must serve as intermediaries
between the federation leaders and their cadre, federation
leaders between the city government and the department of

labor on the one hand and the individual union leaders on
the other. The highest ranks in the individual unions may
be attained by both men and women, whereas the parallel
positions in the federation are occupied entirely by men,
since the creole tradition which all government officials
follow, does not allow the women the same freedom as does
the cholo, i.e. migrant peasant and mestizo tradition.
Syndicate leaders are retail or wholesale market vendors.
In a sample of eleven syndicate and federation leaders five
were born in La Paz and six elsewhere. The latter, however,
had been in La Paz for an average of twenty-four years. All
except for one set of their parents had not been born in
La Paz. The qualifications deemed necessary for leadership
are vitality, flexibility, energy, oratory skills, and most
important of all, contacts. How these contacts were established must again be understood in the wider perspective of
the social revolution. As we have mentioned earlier, the
M.N.R. recruited a number of persons with peasant backgrounds
to occupy positions in the party machine. These contacts in
turn were essential for the syndicate. Thus, for instance,
two recent secretaries-general of the federation have been acti
in the M.N.R. party. Another lesser leader established herself
by first representing a group of onion vendors from her home,
then becoming standard bearer and finally, at the age of twenty
three , stand-in delegate in one of the federations. She is
now aiming for the highest position in her syndicate.
     Individual market syndicates meet for four hours once
or twice a month, while federation meetings last for the
same length of time weekly. The nature of the business
attended to during the meetings reaffirms our view that
syndicates play a mediatory role in assimilating migrant
vendors into the wider Bolivian society. They provide them
with occasions to express their standpoint vis a vis representatives of other social classes. For instance, the
federation recently invited the newly appointed criollo
market supervisor, a municipal official, to meet the leaders
of the member syndicates and to become acquainted with the
major problems and future plans. The federation leaders had
been in part responsible for the removal of his predecessor
who had been accused of distributing rights to the same
market areas to more than one syndicate. Their attitude
towards this new official reflected both the traditional
self-abasement of "inferiors" in the face of criollo authorities and a newly acquired aggressiveness. Each man and
woman addressing the market supervisor stressed both his
poverty and dependence on the will of the government and his
right to expect certain benefits. The same tone marks the
written petitions to government officials. A considerable
proportion of the time is allotted to the reading of these
petitions in the meetings. The invitations and letters
simultaneously channel the unions' desires to the government,
and transmit the government's wishes, e.g., the participation

of the market women in parades on national holidays and
their support in a demonstration against guerrillas, to the
syndicate leaders.

   The meetings provide an occasion for individuals and
groups within the marketing community to express and define
their mutual relationships too. A sizable part of the
meetings is devoted to what is called "crítica y
autocritica." Actually this phrase does not as one would
expect refer to sessions of criticism and self-criticism,
but a section of the meetings during which persons involved
in quarrels confront each other to obtain appeasement or
clarification of the issues in question. These sessions are
devoted to cases of presumed theft, insults, misuse of union
funds, etc. Although tempers flare on these occasions, they
are intended to prevent and contain the spread of slanderous
gossip. The following is an example selected at random, a
case dealing with insults. The secretary-general of a
street market asked a federation leader present at the
meeting to aid her in settling the dispute. She presented
her case as follows: "I do not want the two women to quarrel,
since we all belong to one syndicate I would like them to
treat each other like sisters. We must collaborate and live
like sisters "compañeras" (comrades), isn't that so
compañero? The confederation leader then took up the exhortations in the oratory style customary in all syndicate
meetings: "Companeras, in truth when dealing with any quarrel
we must consider that we are all human beings. Nevertheless,
because of this very reason [sic] we must respect one
another. This holds true for you, women of humble origin,
as well as for anyone else. I wish that you wouldn't quarrel
for you know as well as I that quarrels carry with them fatal
consequences. If you bring the case to the police they will
fine you of course. What good can come of this, companeras?
Wouldn't this be to your own detriment? Now I would like to
know the reasons for your quarrel." Both parties of the
quarrel presented the issues. The first disputant who had been
raised by the sister of the second disputant resented being
called a "criada" by her 'aunt' with its connotation of
inferiority and servant-like status. Criada means both
adopted child and servant. Adding insult to injury the woman
claimed to have been thrown out of a fiesta held at the home
of her adoptive mother by her 'aunt'. Thereupon the confederation leader recommended a written promise to end the
quarrel (the usual procedure in cases of insult) with a
clause that in case the quarrel continued, the disputants be
expelled from the syndicate. Finally both accepted a verbal
reconciliation even though the elder woman feared that the
rumor would spread that she had acted in a servile fashion
towards her junior. They hugged each other to signify that
they accepted the secretary-general's recommendation: i.e.
that the older woman be as a mother unto the younger and the
latter respect the former's seniority. Then the

confederation leader reiterated that quarrels disrupted the
organization and bothered the vendors. He urged all to live
in harmony and to work for the good of all the members of
the syndicate. Apart from demonstrating the way in which
grievances are aired and conflicts resolved, this case shows
how syndicate members are morally obliged to live, in the
stress on the unity, harmony and cooperation. With respect
to the moral code in which syndicate matters are couched,
the syndicates share characteristics of what Victor Turner
calls "comunitas" (Turner, 1969). Homogeneity and unity are
stressed with respect to the outside (here represented by
the police) and a label (humble women) is attached to the
social position of the members when in fact all markets
include persons from a wide range of social backgrounds and
wealth.

Union meetings are not the only means of communication. The federation now has its own radio announcer,
fluent in both Spanish and Aymara, who broadcasts union
meetings and parade schedules, and transmits calls for aid
on behalf of persons in distress. La Paz radio stations
have become increasingly numerous and have employed more and
more Aymara speakers in order to reach not only the recent
migrant population in La Paz, but the peasants as well.
Radio transmission is an important means of increasing the
power and efficiency of the federations as pressure groups.
In addition groups of leaders present petitions to the mayor
personally. Feasts are another means of communication. For
federation leaders ceremonial functions are among the most
time consuming of all their activities. They are obliged to
attend   most of the vestitures of syndicate leaders of
their member organizations otherwise the new leaders would
feel slighted. Apart from this they must attend the inauguration of new syndicates, cooperatives, etc. Carlos, for
instance, the head of one confederation, is an excellent
master of ceremonies. Apart from making the guests of honor,
e.g. representatives of the municipal government or the
ministry of labor feel at ease, he uses the occasion to
promote the projects of land purchasing and "supermarkets"
construction by informing the guests of recent developments
and making pleas to the invited officials for aid. Since
some of the speeches are broadcast, the general public is
informed as well.

The fiestas all follow the same basic pattern. They
take place in a rented room or in the case of inaugurations,
near the site or building to be inaugurated. Guests arrive
two or three hours after the time indicated on the printed
programs which are handed out a week or so earlier. The
guest list invariably includes government and/or municipal
officials although usually they only attend in person
when it is politically expedient to do so, i.e. before
elections or when the federation has been instrumental in
placing them in office; otherwise they generally send a

representative. The fiesta begins with the playing of the
national anthem and the serving of a few rounds of beer
and alcohol and juice cocktails. A series of speeches by
both syndicate officers and invited officials follows.
Then, sometimes diplomas are presented by leaders and guests
of honor to syndicate members who have been particularly
dynamic with respect to syndicate concerns during the year.
After the foregoing ceremony food is served to all present,
beginning with the guests of honor. At this point most
invited officials leave. Someone appointed as a "godfather"
or "godmother" (sponsor) may provide carnival hats and paper
trumpets. Then the master of ceremonies (often the
secretary-general of the confederation in the case of
"papeleta blanca" fiestas) initiates the dance. Dancing and
drinking then continues for the rest of the day. All the
speeches, diplomas and general conviviality of these feasts
thus serve as a means of informing officials and members of
syndicate activities and to enhance their position as a
corporate group. Informal long and frequent bouts of convi-
vial drinking among syndicate and federation leaders are a
means of channeling information as well. In addition these
informal gatherings constitute a major means of decision
making.

The organization of syndicates reflects the competitive conditions created by the rapidly expanding market
population. Class interests and regional and local loyalties
are the bases for factional conflict within and between
unions. For example within the same market one may find
groups of market women who still owe allegiance to the traditional maestras mayores who were invariably mestizos, as well
as to two or sometimes even three rival syndicates. Such
factions may form when defeated candidates for the position
of secretary-general form their own syndicate with the
dissident membership. For, once a leader has reached a high
position in the syndicate after years of active participation
in syndicate affairs, establishing ties with useful municipal
and national government officials, and other related matters,
he is loath to relinquish his position. Furthermore, his
knowledge often makes him almost indispensable. Rival
leaders constantly vie for allegiance of individuals and
groups who migrated from different localities by accusing
the opposition of collecting unnecessary fees to serve
private interests. These rivalries are an important means
of self-presentation. By stressing the shortcomings of other
syndicates or federations and vaunting their own projects,
leaders are able to build "an image through contrasts" of
their conceptions of syndicalism. A considerable proportion
of syndicate meetings is devoted to harangues against rival
organizations.

Ritualism, i.e. investiture of syndicate leaders,
inaugurations of new syndicates, fiestas marking the purchase

of land, anniversaries, parades held on the occasion of national holidays and the foundation of La Paz, etc., are another means of exposing rivalries.

Investitures for instance are important means of expressing the rivals' strength. If a leader can pay a good brass band for her followers' contributions, serve good food, etc., he or she would certainly be considered a well supported strong leader.

Ritual may also underline disputes directly. At the celebration of the Saints' Day for whom a parcel of land purchased by Carlos' cooperative is named, the vendors belonging to the rival federations danced separately during most of the fiesta and even had separate sponsors for financing part of the costs. In subsequent years as the prospects of an early beginning of the supermarket construction decreased their celebration was held privately and separately by each group. Similarly one leader of the land purchasing cooperative favored by Carlos took advantage of the celebrations marking the expropriation of the land to make disparaging remarks about a rival cooperative. Similarly parades express the cohesion of the federations and at the same time the support for the mayor who organizes them.

A final means of communication and self-expression are politics. The federation leaders often take an active part in politics. The verde federation leaders supported Barriento's candidacy in 1966 while the blanco federation abstained from voting. In 1969 the blanco and verde federations and the blanco confederation all proclaimed their support of the mayor of La Paz as presidential candidate in the 1970 elections for he had initiated the planning and construction of new markets and had helped to expropriate land for the market union's housing cooperative. For once the bitter rivalry between the blanco and verde federation leaders was forgotten at least long enough to hold a joint rally in a large open air theater. In contrast the confederation to which the verde federation is affiliated announced in the newspapers that they would await their national congress to make their proclamation.

As we have attempted to demonstrate in the analyses of meetings, rituals and politics, syndicates employ at least two codes to express marketing relations. One stresses unity and concord, the other diversity. Neither code fully represents reality. Members of the same syndicate vary in interests and social position. Federations to a large extent contain in fact similar membership.

In this paper we have repeatedly stressed the mediatory nature of La Paz syndicates in organization, leadership and rituals. We would conclude that this communicative aspect of the syndicates surpasses their judiciary and economic importance. Furthermore it would appear that the contents communicated are less important than the fact and

quality of communication, i.e. the symbolic self-presentation
of the new markets. The syndicate organization provides more
or less coherent images of the complex composition of the
changing market population. The endless meetings, drinking
sessions held by the leaders, radio announcements, and
celebrations provide the market women with a newly won sense
of identity and direction. Similarly the contact with the
government established by means of letters, calls for invitations to government officials, delegations to talk to the
mayor, and demonstrations per se as well as the quality of
interaction expressed, symbolically relate the markets to
the nation as a whole.

When one questions an individual market woman as to
the nature and importance of syndicates one is given the
definite impression that she understands very little about
their organization and activities. Few maintain that they
themselves have benefited directly. However, the belief
that syndicalism is important is general. This apparent
paradox can be resolved when one examines market syndicalism
not merely from a functional point of view, but from an
interactional one.

From our perspective market syndicalism no longer
appears merely as a means to achieve specific ends. Unions,
which flowered during the social revolution of 1952-53
became a means of self-expression for the burgeoning market
population as well. The La Paz market syndicates thus
provide an example of the processes by which changing interaction patterns are vested with meaning. We would suggest
that in situations of rapid social change behavior and
morphology or social forms (Barth 1967) are not related
causally but are in constant dialogue. Furthermore, new
forms of social behavior are not fixed into pre-established
norms or realms of meaning. Both are being formulated and
reformulated simultaneously.

Postscript

In 1974 a government edict suspended all union
activities. Market leaders were replaced by government
appointed liaison persons. The only corporate activity
allowed is the organization of marketing cooperatives for the
sale and purchase of goods and the construction of market
buildings.

BIBLIOGRAPHY

Barth, F. "Models of Social Organization." Occasional
        Paper No. 23, Roayl Anthropological Institute of
        Great Britain and Ireland, 1967.

Buechler, H. "The Reorganization of Counties in the
        Bolivian Highlands: An Analysis of Rural-Urban
        Networks and Hierarchies," in E. Eddy ed. Urban
        Anthropology, Research Perspectives and Strategies.
        Southern Anthropological Society, Proceedings No. 2.
        Athens: Univ. of Georgia Press, 1968.

--------. "The Ritual Dimension of Rural-Urban Networks:
        The Fiesta System in the Northern Highlands of
        Bolivia," in W. Mangin, ed. Peasants in Cities.
        Boston: Houghton & Mifflin Co., 1970.

--------. The Masked Media: Aymara Fiestas and Social
        Relations in Bolivia. n.d.

Buechler, H. and Buechler, J-M. The Bolivia Aymara.
        New York: Holt, Rinehart, and Winston, 1971.

Buechler, J-M. "Peasant Marketing and Social Revolution in
        the State of La Paz, Bolivia." Ph. dissertation,
        McGill University, 1972.

IDEOLOGY AND SOCIAL CHANGE IN COLOMBIA

E. J. Hobsbawm

1. Ideology. The term "ideology" will be used in this paper in two senses: (a) a formulated and generally recognised system of beliefs about society (often with a recognised brand-name, such as liberalism, nationalism communism, etc.) from which programmes of social and political action can be or are derived; and (b) a similar system of beliefs, which is not formulated as much or consciously held, but which nevertheless forms the basis of social and political action of a given group of men. In other words, "ideology," as used in this paper, includes not only the ideologies commonly recognised and labelled as such, whose significance may be confined to a minority sector of society (the literate or educated) but all systems of ideas about society which determine social and political action. The distinction is of operational importance in a continent such as South America, where ideologies of type (a), at least in their secular post-1789 form, may be politically effective among a restricted stratum (e.g., Comtist Positivism in Brasil and Mexico) but totally unknown or incomprehensible to the bulk of the population. Type (a) will be called socio-political theories, type (b) systems of action. It follows that theories, insofar as they are confined to elite or other politically influential minorities, become effective by imposing a certain pattern of action on the masses, systems of action by mobilising them. It does not follow that either type is confined to any one kind of social group. Thus the social action of Brasilian Positivists was determined not only by their theories, but also by systems of action (e.g., considerations of honour, shame, machismo). Conversely peasant action or inaction was determined not only by systems of action, but also to some extent by theories (e.g., the formulated beliefs of Catholicism). In this paper we are not concerned with other definitions of ideology.

2. Social Change. The term "social change" will be used in this paper in a limited sense. It comprises (a) changes of the type normally referred to as "modernisation" or "industrialisation" and (b) major social revolutions or upheavals. Both are sufficiently recognisable not to need further definition, and the discussions about their nature or the legitimacy of such terminology are irrelevant to the present subject. We are, in brief, concerned with what is by historic or contemporary standards, rapid and drastic social change.

3. <u>Relations between 1 and 2</u>. No <u>a priori</u> model of the relations between ideology and social change will be assumed. Cases where there is such a connection exist, e.g., where a disproportionate number of entrepreneurs is recruited from those who hold a given theory (Protestantism and Capitalism), but the exact nature of the connection cannot be derived from the correlation. It is not improbable that ideologies may have a favourable or unfavourable effect on social change, and indeed this is virtually certain where we are faced with <u>theories</u> which operate through official or state institutions and policies. It would be in the highest degree implausible to suppose that communism had had no significant effect on social change in China since 1949, or the Roman Catholic Church on that of the Papal States in the 16-19th centuries. Nevertheless, we cannot go further than such generalities <u>a priori</u>. In particular, we cannot decide <u>a priori</u> whether and to what extent ideologies reflect or determine the forces of social change in periods before they have become unquestioned forces through their embodiment in government policies, institutions, etc., or the degree of their effectiveness even when so embodied.

4. Ideologies of types (a) and (b) (theories and systems of action) will be discussed separately, for the reasons given in para. 1. Cases where the two merge will be discussed under (b).

5. <u>The case of Colombia</u> (present territory of the Republic). By most indices of economic and social development Colombia ranks between the middle and the bottom tenth of Latin American states.[1] We are therefore not called upon to explain an unusually high degree of economic and social modernisation, nor, on the other hand, an unusual degree of immobility, or an unusually high divergence between indicators, as in Venezuela, or in certain

---

[1]Dividing these indicators into ten levels, where 1 represents the top and 10 the bottom, Colombia occupies the following levels:

Level	Number of indicators
1-4	2
5	5
6	2
7	5
8	3
9	3
10	0

Cf. R. Vekmans and J. L. Segundo, 1963.

respects, Brasil and Mexico. Nevertheless there are a number of peculiarities in Colombian development which are worth listing, since they may have a bearing on the problem of this symposium. They are:

(a) Composition of the population. Though Colombia belongs in the main to the Andean region, i.e., the region of largely Indian settlement, it contains a disproportionately small percentage of people classified as Indians.

(b) Pattern of urbanization. Unlike the majority of Latin American countries, which developed one or at most two relatively giant cities, which far outdistanced other urban centres, Colombia has developed a number of regional cities of broadly comparable size, and not of a different order of magnitude from the national capital: Cali, Medellin,Barranquilla, Bogotá.[1]

(c) Peculiarities of political development. Unlike most other Latin American countries, Colombia has long (since, say 1869) possessed a two-party system with substantial grass roots even in the peasantry. Partly for this reason it has been unusually immune from government by caudillos and military coups, but in return it has suffered from unusually prolonged and savage civil wars.

(d) Peculiarities of social movements. In the absence of serious studies one can only speak of these with the greatest hesitation, but it would seem that movements of social discontent among the peasantry were unusually insignificant until the 1920s, but were followed by unusually active movements of this kind from the 1920s. These culminated in the "violencia" of the years after 1948, which was a phenomenon of revolutionary proportions and may be regarded as a frustrated or aborted social revolution. Possibly because of (c) these movements found only a relatively feeble expression in specific political or revolutionary organizations, such as APRA, Acción Democrática, Communist parties or demagogic populist leaders provided elsewhere.

6. Ideology and social change: "theory". The role of ideology among the political elite of Colombia is unusually clear, but the nature of this role is not clear. Broadly speaking, the two parties of Colombia have had a genuine ideological component of some importance, however much their support was determined by social and geographical

---

[1]The population of these cities in 1962 was estimated at, respectively (in thousands), 700, 700, 500, 1,300.

factors, family connections, etc. The ideological
difference between Conservatism and Liberalism has always
been significant. The major political changes ("revolutions") of Colombian history have always owed a great deal
to groups of the elite mobilised - at least at a crucial
stage of their careers - by specific ideologies. O. Fals
Borda has developed an interpretation of Colombian history
in terms of such periodic "subversions" of the existing
order by ideologically formed "anti-elites," becoming in
due course the elites of the new order. The ideologies of
the 18th century illuminism and of the French Revolution
of 1789 had this function in the era of Independence, or
more exactly, since Fals Borda does not see Independence
as a major social change, the ideologies and example of
the Revolution of 1848 played this role in the revolution
of 1848-54. Communism played an analogous role in the
formation of the anti-elites of the 1920s, which subsequently became the transforming force of the Liberal Party
in the 1930s and 1940s. Fals Borda argues that in the
1960s the time for another "subversion" of this type had
once again come, and discerns the outlines of the new anti-
elite in Camilo Torres and the young Fidelist revolutionaries.[1] Once again, it is irrelevant whether this analysis
is acceptable in detail, so long as the role of ideological
theories as forces mobilising groups of young men of the
actual or potential elite and cementing them together, is
not denied.[2]

The extent to which ideologies not merely mobilised
potential social changers, but determined the shape of the
changes, is a more complex question. It is evident that
revolutionary ideologies, whatever their specific programmatic content, would predispose their adherents to demand
social and political changes more radical than those en-
visaged, or even believed to be possible, by those who
operate within the status quo, whether as conservatives or
piecemeal reformers. It seems probable that their general
characteristics will predispose those who hold them and
exercise political power, to adopt certain types of
policies - e.g., along the lines of secularisation, unre-
stricted rights of property and private enterprise among
19th century liberals, collective action for social welfare

---

[1]Fals Borda 1967

[2]It is equally irrelevant that some members of the
anti-elites belonged to traditional ruling families (cf.
the recurrence of names like Camilo Torres, Restrepo,
Lleras), while others were newly absorbed into them through
their original membership of the anti-elite.

and state economic enterprise among those formed in the
socialist communist mould. But how far does the rise
of ideological anti-elites simply reflect the widespread
consciousness of new problems which require new and radical solutions? How far are the changes due to these
ideological groups the result of their theories and programmes, and how far to mass movements of revolt which
force certain kinds of political action onto the national
agenda? The question is complex. No doubt in 1848-54
and again in 1928-48 the force which transformed Colombian
politics came from popular movements. No doubt the institutional changes which followed found a more suitable
vehicle in the Liberal Party, for partly ideological
reasons - because this party believed in "progress," "economic growth" and "the people" rather than in "order,"
"tradition" and "hierarchy." No doubt the small groups of
radical ideologues who provided the impetus of the change
(in terms of politics and ideas) contributed something
specific to the institutional changes. But what and
how much?

The question becomes even more complex if we bear
in mind two facts generally characteristic of Latin American ideology: (a) its evident debt to foreign models and
(b) the striking divergence between what such foreign
models mean in their countries of origin and in the real
context of Latin American politics. The influence of -
sometimes the tendency to copy - European ideologies such
as utilitarianism, positivism, utopian socialism, marxism,
fascism, etc., is familiar. It is equally well known that
in the Latin American situation the meaning of such ideological labels, and the practical consequences of adherence
to an ideology, may surprise the European or North American,
as witness the political activities of Latin American
groups and men inspired by, or claiming to be influenced
by, the European Fascism of the 1930s. In general all
ideologies have, in the Latin American context, had one or
more of three major objectives:

     (a) to transform backward countries into advanced
          ones
     (b) to transform (formally or informally) dependent
          countries into genuinely independent ones
     (c) to construct a bridge between the small elites
          and the mass of the impoverished and backward
          population.

The essential context of Latin American ideologies
has always been that which characterises the so-called
"emerging" nations today. Their normal form has been one
taken over from among the most suitable, the most fashion-
able, or the most prestigious ideologies of the "advanced"
world, insofar as these are not evidently incompatible with
objectives (a), (b) or (c). The relatively few ideologies

independently evolved in Latin America have had the same
fundamental objectives. They are, characteristically,
combinations of "socialism" and "indigenismo," though in
Colombia such autochthonous ideologies have so far played
only a very minor role.

        In brief, most available ready-made ideologies were
designed for purposes other than those which preoccupied
educated Latin Americans, and therefore tended, when adapted to their purposes, to become unrecognisable or inconsistent. Thus in the generation of 1848 in Colombia
"socialism" could become either (as for the young J. M.
Samper) something which supplemented the insufficient
dynamic of "liberalism," in whose programme he continued
to believe, or a sort of ideology of sour grapes: "since
we cannot catch up with the inhabitants of the Old World
on the road to industry, let us overtake them in the construction of a (just) society." (Colmenares 1966: 2173).
Thus again in the 1930s and 1940s, observing Gaitan, "it
was difficult to establish where the sympathiser of Musso-
lini ended, the Liberal chief began, and the leftist leader
had his roots." (Andrade 1954: 47). It is possible that
ideologies which are both variants of global models and
specifically tailored for the circumstances of Latin
America, may have begun to emerge since the 1950s, but it
is probably too early for a firm judgment.

        So far as Colombia is concerned, it may be suggested
with considerable hesitation, that among the ideologists
of "emergence," the populist objective (c) has been more
prominent than the objectives of economic modernisation
and independence (a and b). It certainly seems to be the
case that neither xenophobic nationalism nor non-populist
"scientific" ideologies like positivism played as important
a role in this republic as in some others (Argentina,
Mexico, Brasil). It might also be suggested that the
ideological champions of progress and - Liberal or national - regeneration, tended to place the primary emphasis
of their thought on democratisation, e.g., Galindo in
1880, Uribe Uribe after 1902 (Fals Borda 1967: 159-60,
166), Lopez and Gaitan between the wars. This may be due
in part to the size and standing of Colombia as a state
and the relative unimportance of foreign capital in it,
until recently, which deprived nationalism of some of its
importance. It may also be due in part to the virtual
extrusion (except at times of major crisis as in the
1930s) of economic growth from the traditional ideological
debate. After all, the most dynamic group of native entrepreneurs, the Antioqueños, have been militantly Conservative in politics since the 1860s and some of the periods
of most rapid development, e.g., 1902-30, the era described
by workers and peasants, according to Fals Borda, as
"cuando llegó el progreso" (Fals 1967: 160) - occurred
under the rule of the party whose official ideology was

committed to tradition and stability and hostility to
change. It has been suggested - again by Fals - that this
may be due to the flight of the new bourgeois groups from
the danger of popular revolution towards the defenders of
"order." Conversely, this may well have led sections of
the Liberal Party, always inclined by its ideology towards
popular government, at least in theory, to compensate for
this loss by seeking the support of "the people." The
junction between populism, anti-imperialism and an ideology of economic modernisation looked like being made in
the 1930s under Lopez, though the consequently emerging
fears of social revolution were eventually to destroy the
New Deal of "la revolución en marcha."

     7. Systems of action: the peasants. Two aspects
of this problem will be discussed: (a) behaviour indicating acceptance or approval of social change among the
masses and (b) acceptance of ideological theories associated with social change among the masses. Both in view of
the poor documentation about mass activities and attitudes
and the general obscurity of the subject, the discussion
must be unusually tentative.

     (a) There are at least four episodes or aspects of
Colombian history which suggest mass modernisation or
mobilisation. They are:

> 1. The large scale transfer from the social cate-
> gory of "Indian" to those of "Mestizo" or "White"
> which account for the unusually low percentage of
> Indians in the present Colombian population.
> (See 5a above). This "de-indianisation" may have
> begun in colonial times, but has certainly speeded
> us since. The chronology remains obscure.
>
> 2. The substantial peasant colonisation of unset-
> tled lands for the purpose of market agriculture,
> and especially of novel export crops, i.e., mainly
> coffee. This developed from the mid-19th century
> and clearly acquired substantial proportions in
> the early 20th.
>
> 3. The mass social movements since 1920 (but
> esp. 1924-1940), which are linked with it.
>
> 4. The mass migration into the cities, which de-
> veloped on the now familiar vast scale since
> the 1930s.

     The decline of Indians in Colombia appears to have
been enforced from above or from outside. It seems to

have been due partly to the gradual erosion of <u>resguardos</u>
(protection) by pressure from non-Indian settlers and
landowners, with the consequent break-up of the Indian communities or their scattering and individual assimilation
of their former members, partly to the official dissolu-
tion of communal properties by 19th century legislation
and the consequent disruption of the social organisation
of the population established on these lands. The first
process (which still continues on the frontiers of Indian
territory in the Southeast and Northeast) has been studied
by various historians and anthropologists. (G. Reichel-
Dolmatoff 1953, Friede 1943, Friede 1944, Friede 1963),
the second has been little studied (Fals Borda 1962, Sylvia
M. Broadbent 1964). It would appear that in the Chibcha
heartland both the resguardo system and an Indian population recognised as such survived until the 1830s-40s. The
Indians were victims of history and not its makers, and
consequently it hardly matters what they thought about it.
At most it may be suggested that the colonial system and
ideology, which Fals Borda claims to have been unusually
successful in creating a genuine "pax hispanica" in Colombia (Fals Borda 1967), may have diminished the capacity of
collective resistance of the central bloc of Indians.
Though a powerful nativistic movement developed in 1781
(that of the Comuneros), he argues that it was less ambitious, less intransigent and less determined than the
contemporary Tupac Amaru movement. Insofar as the colonial
ideology was (for reasons not yet clarified) internalised
in this manner by the Colombian Indians, ideology played a
part in their unusually successful assimilation to
mestizo status.

No ideological element is necessary to explain the
present colonisation. There is no evidence that a modern-
ising ideology is needed to convince some peasants of the
advantages of making money by selling their produce when
the opportunity of doing so arises; or of the desirability
of adopting new crops which can be seen to be very advan-
tageous. The existence of an element of economic calcula-
tion in a peasant economy must not be confused with the
substitution of a system of market rationality for one
of peasant economy. Nor must the adoption of new crops on
the basis of a traditional technology be confused with the
systematic adoption of novel and constantly improving technologies. Granted the absence or disappearance of a traditional communal organisation of the Indian type, Colombian
peasant colonisation requires no explanation except in
terms of relative overpopulation, availability of land, and
the development of a market for agrarian produce. To what
extent the civil wars speeded up this dispersal of the
peasantry is a question which remains to be fully studied.

No ideological explanation is required for the
process of mass migration to the cities.

The social movements of the period since the 1920s
have been, however, associated with ideological movements
and groups which have sometimes provided the masses with a
framework of organisation, leadership, programmes and
formulated aspirations. However, it is probable that these
movements, which were rather widespread and took the form
of "a decentralised kind of initiative ... a decentralised
violence" (Hirschmann 1963) occurred in areas unaffected
by leftwing agitation and organisation as well as in areas
where this was influential. Nevertheless, insofar as
leadership or inspiration from outside the traditional
environment of peasant action provided local movements
with a more effective and lasting policy and framework
than might otherwise have been expected, the role of ideology is significant. They were clearly significant in this
sense in certain areas, notably of Cundinamarca, Tolima,
among the Indians in Cauca, and in the banana zone of
Magdalena. We shall consider under 7(b) below to what extent the actual behaviour of these peasant movements correspond to the ideologies that were supposed to inspire
them.

The precise manner in which outside ideological
movements penetrated the peasantry, and the extent to
which they were effective mobilisers of action, is not
clear. The following brief sketch may suggest some of the
obscurities and complexities of the problem. There is
little doubt that the unrest of the 1920s and 1930s arose
out of the accumulated agrarian tensions (especially the
conflicts between estate-owners and peasant settlers, both
expanding into hitherto empty territory) of the imperialist
era 1900-1929. Evidence of tension before the slump is
strong, though the collapse of the international primary
products market sharpened an already acute social crisis.
Foreign-owned enterprise such as United Fruit provided a
natural spark-plug for explosion, though its significance
in the Colombian economy at the time was limited (Dix
1967). It does not seem that outside ideological bodies
played any significant part in the movement until after
the 1928 banana strike of Santa Marta, where radical elements played some part - though the communists among them
appear to have held back initially (Kepner and Soothill
1935: 323 ff, Rippy 1931) - and both communists and left-
wing liberals made this dispute into the starting-point
of a much wider subsequent agitation. On the other hand
a much more traditional factor appears to have helped in
crystallising peasant unrest from the early 1920s, namely
the machinery for bringing disputes about land-ownership
before the courts. It has been persuasively argued (Lynn
Smith 1968: 81 ff, 247) that the precipitating factor was
a Supreme Court decision of 1926 that land-titles should
be voided if the owners, i.e., estates, could not produce

the original title-deeds, i.e., that in such cases the
rights of cultivating squatters should be recognised de
facto. The famous Law 200 of 1936 gave legal sanction to
such occupations after years of intensive social agitation.
   The movements of the late 1920s and 1930s were un-
doubtedly - or increasingly came - under the leadership of
the ideological left, partly communist, partly populist-
liberal, partly (as perhaps in Sumapaz) grassroots peasant
organisers influenced by socialist or communist ideologies.
It is a curious fact that the Colombian Communist Party,
officially formed in 1930, complained to the International
in 1935 that its membership was insufficiently proletarian,
being composed primarily of peasants and Indians, rather
than workers (International Press Correspondence 1935:
1348). There can be no doubt that the institution of
local land-reforms - i.e., the forced sale of estates to
the peasants cultivating them - in the early 1930s, as in
parts of Cundinamarca and Valle (Informes 1934) was largely
due to such organised movements, which obviously also affected the subsequent national legislation of the Lopez
government. A glance at the map also demonstrates that
the areas in which communist or other leftwing "armed
self-defence" was successfully organised in the 1950s are
largely those in which the movement of the early 1930s had
been strongest and best organised (e.g., Viota, Sumapaz,
Mariquita-Marquetalia), so that we have here a history of
upwards of thirty years of peasant organisation.

   (b) How far does this indicate the acceptance by
peasants of ideologies of the modern type? The subject may
be discussed under two headings; (1) liberalism, (2) communism. The problem of christian democracy may be left
aside, since until very recently the dominant religious
ideology of Colombia was strongly traditionalist.
   (1) There is no doubt that from the middle of the
19th century liberalism had mass roots, so that to speak
of a peasant as Liberal means that he recognised a personal
political loyalty as well as clientship of a patron who
happened to support the Liberal Party. At the same time
there is no evidence that this loyalty had any direct ideological implication. It appears to be rather "a collective
defense mechanism" "dictated by a desire for mutual defense
during times of attack by outsiders" (Fals Borda 1962: 42),
so that it is irrelevant - except for the historian -
whether a vereda happened to be Liberal or conservative,
so long as it was one or the other collectively. And
indeed politically equally divided neighborhoods are rare.
The major political aspirations of 19th century Liberalism
appear to have been irrelevant.
   In the second quarter of the 20th century a new
element entered, as a genuine political consciousness began

to emerge among peasants. At this point a tendency to chose Liberalism as the party "of the people" makes itself felt, encouraged by the development of socially conscious or "New Deal" forces within the Liberal Party. Though Gaitanismo appealed more powerfully to the urban poor than in the countryside, there is some evidence that the great populist demagogue made a significant impact among the peasantry. Given the numerical prevalence of Liberalism which emerged in the 1930s,[1] a growing politisation of the masses under its aegis might have been expected, but events after 1948 distorted this development. Since the Liberal Party represents not only a rank-and-file ideology but also a part of the official power-structure, the specific character of grass-roots Liberalism in the countryside today is difficult to determine without ad hoc research. However, there is evidence that some otherwise "non-political" Liberal peasant band-leaders in the later stages of the Violencia acquired at least the vocabulary of a social programme (Guzman, Fals Borda, Umana Luna 1964), e.g., the redoubtable "Chispas," who is said to have supported the M. R. L. (ibid.: 336, personal information C. Torres).

(2) We are in a better position to say what communism meant to the peasants supporting it. It did (does?) not stand primarily for economic collectivism. In Viota, long controlled by the C. P., not even cooperatives appear to have been instituted; in Sumapaz the only economic activity organised in common was the distribution of water, traditionally a collectively planned matter. The simplest definition of its actual significance is that it stands:

    a. for a movement of men who demand their rights – not so much "natural" or new rights as legal old rights.

    b. for the legitimisation of an economy of independent peasants operating in the manner to which the local peasantry is accustomed, but where necessary with formal sanctions, for example non-compliance with customary mores (mutual aid, etc.), as in Viota. In Sumapaz informal social pressure and solidarity appear to have made such formal sanctions rare.

    c. the establishment of a peasant autonomy at the subordinate level which peasants regard as proper to them. Thus in both Viota and Sumapaz small crimes and disputes were settled in the community, serious ones were left – or handed over to official justice, except during periods of enforced independence (as when engaged in war against government forces). Then Sumapaz supplied all its own justice, but without jails, the penalties being either fines or death. Similarly, commercial and credit transactions

were under the state system, and indeed the
commercial centres to which peasants brought
their produce were not in the grass-roots
communist system.

d. a formal structure of social organisation through
membership of the Party to which the majority
of adult men in Sumapaz belonged in the 1950s.
It would seem that the Party undertakes the
maintenance of good custom and morals, either
directly or through local councils (cabildos).
Thus Guzman reports that the communist guerrilla
unit in the Alto Meta obliged guerrillas to take
formal responsibility for their women, drawing
up a document of which the original remained
with the unit commander, the couple and the
parents of the woman receiving copies. Sumapaz
discouraged fiestas, even for fund-raising purposes, as likely to lead to drinking and fighting, though Viota was less puritanical.

e. an educational system - always a matter of major
importance to politically conscious peasants.
Political education for adults was practised in
both Viota and Sumapaz, independent schools were
founded and the right to appoint suitable teachers in state schools was tenaciously demanded,
and indeed informally accepted in long-autono-
mous peasant neighborhoods.

(The above paragraphs are based primarily on personal information.)

We may conclude that, insofar as it is a grass-roots
movement of peasants, Colombian communism seeks to establish
or re-establish the traditional norms and values of peasant
society. It is a movement of modernisation chiefly insofar
as it established the possibility of effective and organised peasant action, links this with an ideology of modernisation, provides a powerful impetus to and mechanism of
education, and probably also a method by which potential
leaders and cadres can be recruited, developed and trained
from among the peasantry. We may conclude further, that,
where left to themselves, the peasants select from the communism which reaches them from the outside those elements -
and probably only those elements - which make sense to them
in terms of their previously held aspirations. It does so
almost irrespective of the Communist Party official views.
Thus it seems that the general analysis of the situation of
the Arauco Indians in the communist or communist-influenced
literature circulated in the Sierra Nevada is extremely
remote from their reality (Friede 1963). The local labour
organisations and the Liga de Indígenas have nevertheless

maintained a permanent presence and occasional influence insofar as they have been the only organisations through which the Indians have been able to make their protest heard. Where, as in Viota, that protest has at some point achieved its object under communist leadership, a more permanent relationship between the peasantry and the movement develops. The peasants "became communist" and remain so. However, though sociologically and politically interesting, the communist peasant communities in Colombia are quantitatively of very limited importance.

8. <u>Final remarks</u>. A number of observations have been made in the course of the discussion above, but the gaps in our knowledge - or at least in the published literature - about Colombia are such, that it would be unwise to summarise them under so formal a heading as "conclusions." If there is one conclusion, it is that systematic research is needed in many fields, and both facts and explanations must be tested, rather than just asserted. (The recent critique of Everett Hagen's thesis about the Antioqueños is a good example.) Where information is so relatively thin, the danger is that the only available source of it comes to bear a heavier weight than it may often be able to.

The only concluding remarks worth making at the end of so tentative a discussion are, (a) that much of what has been said plainly applies not only to other Latin American countries but also to emergent countries elsewhere, but (b) the Colombian situation is peculiar in important respects (e.g., the relative weakness of social-revolutionary and populist movements outside the two-party system or of autochthonous ideologies). Insofar as these peculiarities are explicable without resort to ideological factors (e.g., the disappearance of a large Indian sector which might have provided the basis for "indigenist" ideologies), they derive from the historic peculiarities of this region, which still remain in some obscurity. Insofar as ideological factors must be regarded as primary, they derive from, or are dominated by, the liberal-conservative dichotomy, the nature and permanence of which also raises numerous unsolved problems. Until we (or at least the writer of these notes) understand these things better, firm opinions are best postponed.

REFERENCES

Andrade, Raul
 1954 -- La Internacional Negra en Colombia y Otros
        Ensayos. Quito.

Broadbent, Sylvia M.
 1964 -- Los Chibchas, Organización Socio-Política.
        Bogotá.

Colmenares, German
 1966 -- "Formas de la Conciencia de Clase en la Nueva
        Granada de 1848-54." In Boletín Cultural y
        Bibliográfico, Banco de la República, IX.

Dix, Robert H.
 1967 -- Colombia: The Political Dimensions of Change.
        New Haven and London.

Fals Borda, Orlando
 1967 -- La Subversión en Colombia. Bogotá.

Friede, Juan
 1943 -- Los Indio del Alto Magdalena. Bogotá.
 1944 -- El Indio en la Lucha por la Tierra. Bogotá.
 1963 -- Problemas Sociales de los Araucos. Bogotá.

Guzman, German, Orlando Fals Borda and Eduardo Umana Luna
 1962 -- La Violencia en Colombia. Vol. I. Bogotá.
 1964 -- La Violencia en Colombia. Vol. II. Bogotá.

Hagen, Everett E.
 1962 -- On the Theory of Social Change. Homewood III.

Hirschmann, Albert O.
 1963 -- "Land Reform in Colombia: Some Ideas." In Land
        Reform and Social Change in Colombia. Land Tenure
        Center, University of Wisc. Discussion Paper 4. Nov.

Informes de los Señores Gobernadores
 1934 -- Intendantes y Comisarios Especiales. 1930 a 1934.
        Bogota.

International Press Correspondence
 1935 -- Vol. 15. London.

Kepner, C. D., and Soothill, J. H.
 1935 -- The Banana Empire: A Case Study of Economic
        Imperialism. New York.

Reichel Dolmatoff, G.
    1953 -- "Contactos y Cambios Culturales en la Sierra
           Nevada de Sta. Marta: los Kogi." <u>In</u> Rev.
           Colombiana de Antropología I.

Rippy, J. Fred
    1931 -- The Capitalists and Colombia. New York

Smith, T. Lynn
    1968 -- Colombia. Gainesville.

Vekemans, Roger and Secundo, J. L.
    1963 -- "Essay of a Socio-Economic Typology of the Latin
           American Countries." <u>In</u> Social Aspects of Eco-
           nomic Development in Latin America.   E. DeVries
           and J. Medina Echevarría, ed. UNESCO.

POPULISM AND POLITICAL CONTROL

OF THE WORKING CLASS IN BRAZIL[1]

Kenneth Paul Erickson

Introduction

Political activists and scholars alike, writing in
the early 1960s, claimed that Brazil was on the verge of a
social revolution.[1a] That their predictions proved wrong is
an understatement, for when a conservative civil-military
coalition seized power in 1964, the working class and
peasantry--the social sectors most closely associated with
the image of revolutionary Brazil--offered almost no resistance. Why did activists and scholars incorrectly assess
the prospects for revolution in Brazil? In particular, what
accounted for the political weakness of the supposedly
revolutionary sectors? To address this question, we will
examine the relationship between Brazil's leading politicians
and the labor movement in the decades before the coup. We
will see that populist politics played a major role in crip-
pling the workers' organizations.

One of the least studied and most misunderstood
phenomena in Brazil, and indeed in all Latin America, is
populism. This term, as it is used in Latin America, refers
to a type of nationalist political movement which appears
when incipient industrialization brings on rapid social
change. Populist movements enjoy mass support among the
lower classes, espouse apparently anti-establishment policies, but are organized and led by politicians from the
ruling class.* In serving the class aims of their leaders,
these movements channel the political participation of the

---

*At the broadest conceptual level, "ruling class"
denotes the owners of the means of production as well as
their allies and subordinates holding top positions in such
key social and political institutions as government, military, and Church. At a narrower level of analysis, "elite"
refers to the top decision makers in a specific sector:
e.g., agricultural elites, military elites. Readers who
expect to find a three class social structure in Latin
America should consult Richard Adams, "Political Power and
Social Structures," The Politics of Conformity in Latin
America, ed. Claudio Veliz (New York: Oxford University
Press, 1967), 15-42. Adams argues that, in terms of
political behavior, only two classes exist in Latin America.

urban masses and the peasantry into activities which do not
challenge the existing social structure.   Latin America's
most notable populist leaders include Argentina's Juan
Domingo Perón, Mexico's Lázaro Cárdenas, and Brazil's Getúlio
Vargas and João Goulart.   All four enjoyed massive working
class support.

We will trace briefly the development of populism in
Brazil.   In the 1920s, ruling class spokesmen including
President Washington Luiz considered labor union demands and
activities to be simply a matter for the police.[2]   Vargas,
who overthrew Washington Luiz in Brazil's "Revolution of
1930" and ruled for the next 15 years, recognized the legitimacy of union demands as well as the valuable political
support workers could supply.   He decreed co-optive, corporative labor legislation which provided workers with social
welfare and workplace benefits but deprived them of organizational autonomy.   Such benefits won him broad labor support
as well as the enduring nickname, "Father of the [Common]
People."   (Pai do povo)   After Vargas' overthrow in 1945, the
members of the constituent assembly expanded suffrage,
established direct elections, and founded liberal democratic
executive and legislative institutions, but they left
untouched Vargas' labor law and the corporative institutions
it created.   This labor law enabled the ruling class to
supervise and manipulate the political participation of the
working class through governmental regulation of strikes and
trade union (sindicato) funds, activities, and elections.

With the advent of direct elections after 1946,
populist appeals and corporative institutions together
provided the carrot and stick for political control over the
working class in Brazil.   Populist politicians offered
perquisites and sinecures to labor leaders in exchange for
their support, and they applied the corporative labor law
strictly to harass, punish, or remove uncooperative union
heads.   The nature and impact of the Brazilian corporative
institutions are described in detail elsewhere, so we will
confine our discussion to Brazilian populism.[3]

During the period of electoral democracy between 1946
and 1964, and particularly toward the end of it, populist
politicians built increasingly vocal and active mass movements.   Not only did these politicians promise their
constituents such legislated benefits as minimum wage hikes
and social welfare measures, but they created the impression
among observers on right and left alike that the working
class, through the populist coalition, actually wielded
power.   Strikes increased in frequency and intensity as
spiraling inflation forced workers to defend their real wage
levels with growing militancy.   Populist politicians often
lent their prestige and support to the strikers by marching
in picket lines,[4] and labor leaders ultimately won easy
access to President Goulart and other important government
officers.[5]   The Friday the Thirteenth rally in March 1964

illustrates the apparent power of labor leaders. President
Goulart shared a small compartment on the dais with his wife
and Osvaldo Pacheco, the Communist leader of the militant
port workers. Before them were assembled 200,000 persons,
most of them workers turned out by their union heads.
Discarding his prepared text, the president delivered a much
more radical impromptu speech, incorporating Pacheco's
whispered suggestions which were audible over the public
address system.[6]

The rally served as catalyst to the military coup
that overthrew Goulart at the end of the month, bringing to
an end Brazil's populist era. Despite the widespread belief
that workers and their organizations wielded substantial
power, the military executed their takeover with great ease.
Civilian institutions, and notable among them the labor
movement, lacked the strength to block the coup. Few studies
have analyzed the causes of this institutional weakness and,
in particular, the important role populism played in causing
it.[7] We will address this question by examining the causes,
characteristics, and consequences of Brazilian populism and
particularly its role in debilitating working class
institutions.

Commentators and critics applied the populist label
to many Brazilian politicians and movements in the twenty
years before the coup, but only a handful of scholars really
sought to develop populism as a useful concept for political
analysis.[8] Between 1946 and 1964, when populism flourished
in Brazil, such neglect owed to wishful thinking of analysts
who considered populism a transitory and declining political
style and thus focused their studies upon interest-group or
ideological-class patterns of politics--models they desired
to hasten into being.[9] And now that the military have
definitively laid Brazilian populism to rest, most scholars
are pursuing topics which show more apparent contemporary
vitality, again neglecting this critical concept. This
article, then, proposes to exhume the corpse of populism in
order to appraise its impact upon working-class politics in
Brazil. The evidence below casts populism in a negative
light. Hopefully, it will lead workers and scholars to
consider extremely cautiously the appeals of politicians who
promise material benefits but prevent workers from building
autonomous organizations.

Many movements in many countries over the last 150
years have been called populist. This article first presents
characteristics common to these movements in order to place
the Latin American variant within the broader family of
populisms. It then relates the emergence of populism to
Brazil's changing class structure, and finally it examines
populism's consequences for the working class in particular.

Analysis of government financial records and of the
political behavior of the Ministry of Labor will show that
populism provided few material benefits for workers. More

important, in combination with Brazilian corporatism, it
hindered the development of strong and autonomous working
class organizations. Without such organizational weapons,
Brazil's workers possessed no means to block or mitigate the
military intervention in 1964, and since then, to prevent
the erosion of their real wages which redistributed their
income toward wealthier social strata.

General Characteristics of Populist Movements

In most cases, the term "populism" has referred to
movements based on rural masses.[10] In Latin America,
however, populist movements are principally urban phenomena
based upon the lower socio-economic groups but led by members
of the upper and middle strata. Leaving aside the rural
component, though, most of the other attributes of populist
movements are observed in the Latin American variant. The
remainder of this section will present these attributes and
illustrate them with Latin American data.

Nationalism, stemming from political and economic
dependency, marks all populist movements. These movements
have always arisen in underdeveloped countries (or regions,
as in the United States), where they constitute a reaction
to increasingly apparent domination by developed capitalist
countries (or regions). In a dependent setting, the expansion of industrial capitalism fuels this nationalistic sense
of discontent. Local handicrafts in agrarian societies
succumb to mass production industries located in far-off
places and basic decisions on pricing, credit, and land use--
decisions affecting most people in the society--move farther
and farther from the point where their effects are felt,
sharpening resentment toward outsiders. Incipient industrialization in Third World areas such as Latin America works
even more profound changes in social structure, destroying
the means of livelihood of many craftsmen and shopkeepers
while enabling some workers with industrial or technical
skills to ascend the social ladder. Most rank-and-file
participants in populist movements come from these socially
mobile strata, and they blame real or threatened downward
social mobility or blocks to further upward mobility on the
tightening integration of the national economy into the
world economy.

In the Latin American case, public awareness of
increasing foreign economic penetration inevitably grew more
acute during the post-war industrial surge when articles
consumed daily began to carry such names as Colgate,
Palmolive, Tide, and Coca-Cola, and at the same time, the
press and politicians began linking domestic economic difficulties to profit repatriation by foreign firms and to
foreign banks' and governments' credit policies. Details

differ from one country and/or decade to another, but
everywhere this process intensified nationalistic feelings.

A debate exists over whether populism refers to an
ideology or simply to movements. In the Latin American
context, however, populism can only refer to movements.
These movements have never generated ideologies, in the
sense of codified, rationally elaborated systems of thought
which illuminate the causes of man's problems and describe
paths of action for remedying them. At best, Latin American
populist movements reflect what Theodor Geiger defined (in
contradistinction to ideologies) as mentalities, i.e., non-
codified ways of thinking and feeling which are more
emotional than rational. To Geiger, such mentalities derive
generally from the past or present and lack the future
orientation of ideologies.[11] For a striking example of the
philosophical weakness of populist "ideology," one need only
consult the post-hoc ideology which the Peronist movement
created.[12]

Their philosophical value aside, most populist
platforms are programmatically and rhetorically similar,
again because they arise in economically and/or politically
dependent nations. They seek to limit dependence upon
foreign capitalism through domestic industrialization and
the nationalization of key economic sectors. Only if all
social classes collaborate in this effort, populist politicians argue, will national autonomy be assured. Political
rhetoric suggests that the evils of capitalism, a foreign
economic system, will vanish under economic development
guided by the state and managed by the national bourgeoisie
--an apparent contradiction in terms, but one which raises
few objections during populist heydays. In the inter-class
alliance to secure domestic development, the industrial
bourgeoisie seeks and usually gets credits, protective
tariffs, and tax benefits. Political leaders win workers to
the coalition by tolerating and often encouraging strikes,
particularly where employers are foreign, and they promise
the peasants agrarian reform, though in most cases with
abysmally little follow-through.

Even where radical populists attain power and actually
make visible improvements in the lives of the lower classes,
however, such gains prove short-lived. Benefits are transitory because the workers have not won them through pressure
from their own autonomous, militant organizations; rather
they received them as favors granted by populist politicians.
Because they have not forged their organizations in struggle,
they lack the collective strength to defend their gains once
their patrons leave office. Real wage data support this
conclusion. See Table One, which summarizes these data for
the Brazilian case and for the two Latin American populist
presidents best known as patrons of the working class.

Mexico's Lázaro Cárdenas, for example, probably
achieved more for the lower classes than any other twentieth

TABLE ONE

REAL WAGE INDEX FOR POPULIST PRESIDENCIES AND FOR
FOLLOWING DECADE IN ARGENTINA, BRAZIL, AND MEXICO

	ARGENTINA		BRAZIL		MEXICO
Year	Real Wage Index (1943=100)	Year	Real Wage Index (1960=100)	Biennium	Real Wage Index (1940-41=100)
1939	100	1952	95	1934-35	109
1940	97	1953	83	1936-37	99
1941	97	1954	115	1938-39	103
1942	97	1955	113	1940-41	100
1943	100	1956	105	1942-43	75
1944	111	1957	134	1944-45	67
1945	106	1958	101	1946-47	73
1946	112	1959	115	1948-49	79
1947	140	1960	100	1950-51	66
1948	173	1961	115		
1949	181	1962	100		
1950	173	1963	92		
1951	145	1964	90		
1952	135	1965	82		
1953	135	1966	76		
1954	153	1967	75		
1955	140	1968	73		
1956	164	1969	71		
1957	134	1970	69		
1958	148	1971	n.a.		
1959	119	1972	n.a.		
1960	120				
1961	130				
1962	127				
1963	125				
1964	131				
1965	n.a.				

NOTE: Years of pro-labor radical populist leadership
(Perón in Argentina, Cárdenas in Mexico, and Vargas and
Goulart in Brazil) are in boxes.

SOURCE: For Argentina, Gilbert W. Merckx, "Sectoral
Clashes and Political Change: The Argentine Experience,"
Latin American Research Review, IV, 3 (Fall 1969), 97.
Merckx uses tables which subsequently appeared in Carlos F.

Díaz-Alejandro, Essays on the Argentine Economy (New Haven:
Yale University Press, 1970), 538, for 1939-1950 and Clarence
Zuvekas, Jr., "Economic Growth and Income Distribution in
Postwar Argentina," Inter-American Economic Affairs, XX, 3
(Winter 1966), 28, for the years 1950-1964. The Brazilian
index results from dividing the legal minimum wage by the
monthly cost-of-living figures for Guanabara published
regularly in Conjuntura Economica and then averaging the
twelve months each year. For Mexico, the index is presented
in James W. Wilkie, The Mexican Revolution: Federal Expenditure and Social Change Since 1910 (Berkeley: University of
California Press, 1970), 187. Wilkie uses data from
Cincuenta Años de Revolución en Cifras (Mexico: Editorial
Cultura, 1963) to compile his index.

century populist president in Latin America. He fostered
urban and rural unionism, substantially raised workers' real
wages, and distributed 10.2 percent of Mexico's land surface
to 41.5 percent of those who worked it.[13] Table One shows,
however, that soon after he left office, inflation eroded
the gains in real wages; land redistribution also slowed to
·a crawl. Mexico's labor organizations, dominated by the
nation's official political party, were powerless to prevent
these severe losses. The Argentine pattern is similar. The
table shows that the Argentine real wage curve rose sharply
during Perón's first years and, while declining some during
the latter half of his presidency, remained above their
pre-Perón levels. As in Mexico and Brazil, real wages
declined after Argentina's populist leader left the presidency, and Argentine labor organizations failed to reverse
this decline. Even Perón's widely heralded achievement of
creating a massive labor movement should be put in proper
perspective. While he expanded unionism greatly, he built
his movement upon a core of existing, militant unions which
had successfully maintained their institutional integrity
during the repressive period from 1930 through 1943.[14]

Populist movements, because they seek a social base
in the lower class and their rhetoric emphasizes economic
nationalism, state enterprise, and equitable distribution of
goods and services, are sometimes confused with socialist
ones. This is a fundamental misunderstanding for several
reasons. Unlike socialism, populism fails to address itself
to two important aspects of production. In the first place,
populist movements fail to confront squarely the issue of
the social relations of production--particularly the role of
the worker as producer. Because they lack a comprehensive
ideology, they see workers merely as consumers and thus focus
mainly on distributing goods and services to them. Brazilian
survey results will illustrate this point in the following
section. Secondly, their exclusive focus on distribution
leads them to neglect the saving and investment necessary to
create the goods and services. Such fundamental economic
shortsightedness ultimately causes the economic and political
collapse of populist movements which do attain power.[15]
After their collapse, right-wing, anti-labor governments have
usually replaced them.

Why have populist movements failed to develop
comprehensive ideologies? To answer this question, let us
juxtapose the class origins and aims of populist leaders with
those of their followers. Leaders come from the ruling class
and seek mass support for their political careers. They
distribute material benefits to their followers in exchange
for their support, but they do not permit their followers to
create autonomous political organizations. Indeed, they
suppress potential working class leaders who strive for
autonomy.

Populist politicians, therefore, seek to prevent adoption of a radical ideology which would lead workers to create organizations independent of the present ruling class. Populism thus contrasts dramatically with Marxism-Leninism, for the latter directs a revolutionary elite to build a movement which will eventually take control of the state and establish a dictatorship of the proletariat. Populist movements have failed everywhere to emphasize the necessity of creating enduring political institutions to safeguard the just society they seek to establish. While they appeal to the state to rectify social and political ills, they possess no analytic program which would compel the state machinery, over both short and long run, to implement policies favorable to workers and peasants. Hope for social justice rests instead with a hero-figure who will create with one blow the just society. Even if a saviour could work such wonders, however, no political institutions would exist to preserve them after his and/or her demise. The lack of an analytical, programmatic ideology such as socialism therefore dooms populist movements to be of little long-term benefit to workers.16

Mexico's Lázaro Cárdenas in some ways fits the populist hero image, and indeed the benefits which he granted the lower classes began to erode even before the end of his presidency (1934-40) and were completely wiped out afterward.17 The same holds true for Perón and the material rewards of his presidency. The fortunes of the working class always decline precipitously after the patron-leader passes from power because the movements placed no emphasis on the value and, indeed, necessity of autonomous organization. No concise, programmatic work of applied ideology like Lenin's What Is To Be Done? has ever guided a Latin American populist movement. The industrial bourgeoisie hoists the banner of nationalism in these dependent capitalist countries and, in the absence of a well articulated counter-ideology, capitalism wins by default. Even Cárdenas, who often spoke in socialist terms, laid the bases for a strengthened capitalism in Mexico.18

The defects of populist movements necessarily prevent them from working long term radical changes on their nations. In dependent capitalist societies, having no ideology is equivalent to accepting capitalist ideology. If weak working class organizations with no analytic program ally with populist politicians, they will remain just as they were--weak and, therefore, subordinate. Political control will remain in the hands of the industrial bourgeoisie and state elite. The populist mentality sees the masses as virtuous and the elites as decadent, but populist leaders, with the possible exception of Cárdenas, have come from the ruling class and have enjoyed or aspired to elite status. Even in terms of their own world view, then, these movements have bargained with the enemy and must fail to achieve their aims. Populism in power, therefore, must necessarily be a transitional, short-lived phenomenon.

The political dynamics of late industrialization in Latin American countries will probably limit populism's legacy to one of two outcomes. First, if labor leaders take advantage of the political freedoms of the populist era to establish their own organizational integrity and if they channel the spontaneous awakening of the working class into meaningful union activities, they will surely establish greater organizational strength for the working class. The organizational strength of Argentina's working class, for example, enabled workers there to retain some of their gains after Perón's radical populist rule while their Mexican and Brazilian counterparts lost all of theirs afterwards.

On the other hand, if workers fail to develop such organizational independence, they will not only lose the short-term material benefits provided by populist leaders, but they will also lose what few trade-union freedoms they had won. In Brazil, for example, labor leaders devoted more attention to gaining short-run material benefits from politicians than to securing and developing organizational autonomy and integrity. Populism culminated in right-wing repression in 1964.

Two processes--the growth in political agitation by labor and other nationalist groups and the maturation of dependent capitalist development--combined to produce this outcome. In the first place, workers followed populist politicians because those politicians promised such material benefits as minimum wage increases, social welfare outlays, expanded public employment, and the like. When Brazilian politicians failed to make good on those promises after the late 1950s, workers responded by striking more frequently and by demanding fundamental reforms. Faced with an economic slowdown in the early 1960s, a nationalist coalition with participation by politicians, workers, peasants, and students laid the blame to foreign capital. These groups led strikes, protests, and demonstrations which provoked the anti-populist sectors of the ruling class to denounce striking and protesting workers and to castigate the populists for conceding too much to the workers. Conservative figures, alarmed because the calls for reform implied at the very least a substantial revision of the capitalist system, overthrew President Goulart and instituted an authoritarian regime based on the military.

A second process, that of the maturation of dependent capitalist development, turned the industrial bourgeoisie and technical middle strata against the workers and thus hastened the coup. In the early phase of industrialization, pro-industrial members of the ruling class initiated the cross-class populist alliance to strengthen their hand in shaping national economic policies. They needed worker support to obtain favorable government credit, tariff, and

investment policies. Recent research has shown, however,
that Brazilian industrialists ceased to view the workers as
useful allies once their enterprises established secure
foreign sources of capital, credit, and technology.[19]
        Another dimension of dependent capitalist
industrialization drove a wedge between the populist movement
and the technically skilled middle and upper strata.
Technocratic roles, i.e. roles which originated in the
already industrialized countries and which involve application of modern technology, had spread through the economy,
public bureaucracies, military, and media. As these roles
proliferated, their incumbents came into increasing contact
with each other, developed a sense of solidarity, and came to
believe in their capacity to govern. Since the social
context of the countries where these technocratic roles
originated is quite different from that in Third World
countries, the holders of these roles experience "severe
frustration stemming from a 'failure' of the context to meet
their expectations."[20] They came to believe they could
govern far better if they could eliminate the disruptive
encumbrance of democratic procedures. These technical
strata, moreover, believed their own material well-being
had declined during the economic slowdown of the early
sixties because of distributive populist programs and labor
unrest. They therefore supported the military coup which
put an end to populist politics and gave them, the
technocrats, the freedom to reshape the social context to
conform to their own expectations. Thus, two important
socio-economic groups--industrialists and holders of technocratic roles--withdrew from the population coalition, thereby
isolating the populist politicians, workers, and peasants.
        This discussion has highlighted populism's principal
characteristics. The following sections will examine its
rise and decline in Brazil.

Social Class and Brazilian Populism

        The very term "populism" carries misleading
implications. Its reference to the lower class (massas or
classes populares in Portuguese) suggests that these lower
social sectors have an important policy input and thus masks
the fact that political elites from the ruling class lead and
control populist movements. Nonetheless, the lower classes must
play some   political role, usually in electoral politics,
before populism can flourish. The electoral data in Table
Two graphically differentiate the populist period (1946-1964)
from its predecessors. Under the Old Republic (1891-1930),
narrow state oligarchies controlled the political system,
voters in presidential elections averaged only 2.7 percent of
Brazil's population, and the winning candidate topped
90 percent of the vote in six of eleven races and pulled more

TABLE TWO

RESULTS OF DIRECT PRESIDENTIAL ELECTIONS IN BRAZIL, 1894-1960

Date	Total Population	Total Votes Recorded	Voters As Percent of Total Population	Winner	Votes For Winner	Winner's Votes As Percent of Total Vote
1894	15,583,000	345,097	2.21	Prudente de Morais	290,883	84.29
1898	17,145,000	482,188	2.70	Campos Sales	420,286	90.93
1902	18,782,000	645,531	3.44	Rodrigues Alves	592,039	91.71
1906	20,427,000	294,401	1.44	Afonso Pena	288,285	97.92
1910	22,216,000	707,651	3.19	Hermes da Fonseca	403,867	57.07
1914	24,161,000	580,917	2.40	Venceslau Bras	532,107	91.59
1918	26,277,000	390,131	1.48	Rodrigues Alves	386,467	99.06
1919	26,835,000	403,315	1.50	Epitácio Pessoa	286,373	71.00
1923	28,542,000	833,270	2.92	Artur Bernardes	466,877	56.03
1926	30,953,000	702,612	2.27	Washington Luís	683,528	97.99
1930	33,568,000	1,890,524	5.65	Júlio Prestes	1,091,709	57.74
1945	46,215,000	6,200,805	13.42	Eurico Gaspar Dutra	3,251,507	52.44
1950	51,978,000	8,254,989	15.88	Getúlio Dorneles Vargas	3,849,040	48.63
1955	58,458,000	9,097,014	15.56	Juscelino Kubitschek	3,077,411	33.83
1960	65,743,000	12,586,354	19.14	Jânio Quadros	5,636,623	44.78

NOTE: These are the only direct presidential elections ever held in Brazil.

SOURCE: Alberto Guerreiro Ramos, A Crise do Poder no Brasil (Problemas da Revolução Nacional Brasileira) (Rio de Janeiro: Zahar, 1961), p. 32.

than 70 percent in two others. The Revolution of 1930 terminated the Old Republic and for 15 years no direct presidential elections took place, although suffrage expanded in elections for lesser offices.

The electorate soared in the limited liberal democratic regime between 1946 and 1964, averaging 16 percent of the population--a figure five times that of the Old Republic. Though the literacy requirement of the 1946 Constitution still deprived most of the rural population of the vote, the broadened urban electorate provided one of the necessary conditions for the emergence of populism. We will better understand dynamics of populism in this setting, if we relate its emergence to changes in the Brazilian class structure.

The upper class was not a monolithic body. A new industrial bourgeoisie appeared alongside the coffee, cattle, and sugar barons who had controlled the polity prior to the Great Depression. This split in the ruling class illustrates the second necessary condition for populism. Not only must there be an electorate to be manipulated, but some members of the ruling class must have an interest in enlisting the support of this mass of voters. Populist movements have appeared in Latin America only when a split within the ruling class has caused at least one faction to try bolstering its position by promising the lower class benefits in exchange for support.

The economic turmoil of the Great Depression and the Second World War hastened the split within the Brazilian upper class. The Depression all but eliminated Brazil's foreign markets for coffee and other primary products, and although sales increased during the war, Brazil could not spend its receipts while the world's major industrial economies produced principally for their own war efforts. This situation protected domestic industry from foreign competition and enabled the industrialists to strengthen their position before the war ended.[21] Afterwards, however, such natural protective mechanisms disappeared as foreign trade expanded and industrial imports again became available. Politicians representing urban and industrial interests, facing an agrarian export sector which wished to establish free trade policies, therefore enlisted the electoral support of the urban masses. In the end, Brazil adopted policies to protect domestic industry.

Why did workers succumb to the blandishments of populist politicians if the latter did not move the locus of political power down the social pyramid? Immediate material benefits, of course, provide one answer, although data in the following section will show that even on this score, what Brazilian politicians gave with one hand, they took back with the other. More important is the fact that Brazil's workers had not yet developed a sense of class consciousness. That the workers felt a vague sense of social solidarity is not under dispute here. It might be more appropriate to label

this a sense of similarity rather than of solidarity,
however, for it merely reflected their common status as poor
people. Because workers had not generated a political
self-image as a class, they lacked the stimulus to form
active pressure groups, as liberal theory would have it, or,
in keeping with Marxist theory, to organize and assert
themselves as the dominant class in industrial society.

In documenting this point, a brilliant attitudinal
study of Brazilian auto workers clearly reveals the distance
between socialist ideology and the populist mentality.
Participants in populist movements see themselves as
consumers of benefits issuing from the state rather than as
builders of enduring political institutions which will
secure their interests. Similarly in economic matters, their
mentality leads them to focus on consumption and to overlook
the fact that they themselves are producers. This prevents
the self-confidence upon which labor leaders could build the
revolutionary class consciousness necessary for a truly
ideological movement.[22]

The auto-worker study examined three major attitudinal
components in the process of class formation. Very briefly,
for a revolutionary class consciousness to emerge: (1) the
workers must conceive of themselves as a class which offers
an essential input to production, and they must have pride in
themselves for that; (2) they must conceive of the employer
as an adversary who exploits them and unjustly takes the
fruits of their labor without contributing any real inputs to
production; and (3), they must conceive of the social and
political organization of their nation as growing out of
industrial economic activity and as shaped and controlled by
the class which controls the utilization of labor and the
distribution of its product, i.e. the bourgeoisie.

The respondents of this survey manifested a most
negative and pathetic self-image. To them, the worker is
humble, crude, and poor, and is bossed around and has to
obey. Labor itself is seen as manual, dirty, and degrading--
not as productive labor. The workers perceived the enterprise, which paid relatively well, supplied good food in the
company restaurant, and offered transport to the factory, as
the key to their social ascent rather than as the cause of
their poverty and degradation. Finally, they saw society
divided into rich and poor rather than into social classes
whose social positions are determined by control over the
means of production. "Poverty, and even more, submission,
appear thus as a natural condition, which leads to fatalism
and resignation."[23] It is not surprising, in view of the
low esteem in which they hold themselves and their class,
that such workers looked to populist politicians from the
upper class rather than to themselves for the alleviation of
their burdens.

Why have these attitudes persisted? The manner in
which Brazil's working class developed holds some potential

explanations. First, these workers were largely of rural origin; unlike many European workers during industrialization in their countries, hardly any Brazilian workers had been independent artisans who owned their own tools. They therefore did not consider it unjust that the industrial firm owned the means of production. Furthermore, they lacked the sense of pride in their product and hence in themselves which arises from the knowledge that they had once controlled the technology of their trade before it fell into the hands of factory owners.

Second, Brazil's political elites successfully smothered workers' attempts to build strong autonomous class institutions. Repression was the major governmental tool prior to the Revolution of 1930. Afterward, government officials relied more heavily on co-optation of labor leaders and strict legal controls over their activities. Getúlio Vargas, who governed from 1930 through 1945, established corporative political institutions fashioned after those of contemporary Portugal and Italy. The corporative framework gave Brazilian labor organizations the legal right to exist for the first time, but it imposed so many constraints upon their leadership, finances, and bargaining activities that one may justly call them captive labor unions.[24] The labor code, promulgated during Vargas' corporative dictatorship (1937-45), for example, still specifies that the first duty of trade unions is "to collaborate with the public authorities in the development of social solidarity."[25] Since the 1930s, the government has effectively combined co-optation and repression to crush or muzzle revolutionary workers' movements which sought to develop class consciousness. When co-optation failed to contain two brief but important post-war surges of labor union activity, repression in 1947 and again in 1964 crushed them.

Finally, Brazil's employment structure may have weakened the development of working class consciousness. Historically, industrial employment has contributed most heavily to generating such a consciousness, yet a large proportion of Brazil's urban labor force has never worked in industry. Table Three demonstrates that urbanization outran industrialization by a wide margin in the period under study, so many of the urban poor therefore either lacked steady jobs or worked in the rapidly expanding tertiary (service) sector rather than in the secondary (manufacturing, processing, construction) sector.

Populist politicians, then, tended to benefit from and to perpetuate this situation in which class relations were only dimly perceived by the mass of voters. The politicians held initiative within their own hands and owed little to the masses, as an insightful essay on Brazilian populism makes clear:

TABLE THREE

URBANIZATION AND EMPLOYMENT BY SECTORS
IN BRAZIL, 1940, 1950, AND 1960

Population Distribution

Year	Total Population	Urban Population	Urban as % of Total
1940	41,236,315	8,718,212	21.1%
1950	51,944,397	13,925,769	26.8
1960	70,967,185	25,550,857	36.0

Employment Distribution (%)

Year	Primary	Secondary	Tertiary
1940	64%	12%	24%
1950	58	16	26
1960	52	15	33

SOURCE: Employment distribution figures from Brazilian census data, as reported in Gláucio Ari Dillon Soares, "The New Industrialization and the Brazilian Political System," Latin America: Reform or Revolution?, ed. by James Petras and Maurice Zeitlin (Greenwich, Conn.: Fawcett, 1938),pp. 192-194; population distribution figures from Brazil, Serviço Nacional de Recenseamento, Censo Demográfico 1950 Serie Nacional, Vol. I, (Rio de Janeiro: 1956), pp.270-277; and Sinopse Preliminar do Censo Demográfico 1960, (Rio de Janeiro, 1962),pp. 10-19.

The urban population figures used here refer to population in centers with 5001 or more inhabitants. Official Brazilian figures for urbanization include all cidades and vilas (município and distrito seats), some of which have fewer than 501 and 101 inhabitants, respectively. According to official calculations for the three census years, respectively, Brazil was 31.2, 36.2, and 45.1 percent urbanized.

> In all crises since 1945, the
> intervention of the [common] people
> (povo) has appeared as a possibility,
> but so far the game has consisted of
> evaluating the weight of this
> intervention and bluffing on the
> estimate. In the debates we witnessed
> on the Basic Reforms, in the early
> 1960s, for example everyone--even the
> most radical politicians--hoped to find
> a "formula" which would render such
> participation unnecessary.[26]

Once the upper class has split and the urban masses
have the vote, the final necessary condition for a populist
movement to emerge is the appearance of a politician who can
win the confidence of the masses. Observers often label
populist leaders charismatic, but they seldom meet Weber's
rigorous, almost religious, definition of the term.[27] While
personal appeal or credibility similar to that of charismatic
leaders helped their campaigns, these populist politicians
also won supporters through material performance in a manner
reminiscent of American urban machine politics. They
promised supporters the jobs, favors, and services which
public office enabled them to dispense. Generally, a
patronage chain extended downward from these leaders through
ward healers (cabos eleitorais) to their constituents.[28] The
patronage mechanism which anchored the populist politicians'
machines rewarded individuals, not social classes, and
further prevented the development of working class
consciousness.

One student of populism has hypothesized, with Weber,
that charismatic leadership is the least rational form of
legitimizing political power relationships and that it may be
shattered if the miracles which followers expect of the
leader do not materialize. The Brazilian politician who most
closely approached Weber's charismatic model, Janio Quadros,
held the presidency only nine months before resigning in 1961
and, for many, hopes for miracles came to an end with his
exit.[29] After this point, many labor leaders apparently
tried to go beyond the populist stage of development, i.e. to
rely more heavily on the strength of the workers they
represented. The surge in working class activity between
Quadros' resignation and the military coup of 1964--most
notably the two general strikes of 1962 and the emergence or
self-assertion of many politically active labor organizations
such as the General Labor Command(CGT) and its regional and
local affiliates--supports this hypothesis.[30]

Why did the military so easily crush these activities
and organizations in 1964? Obviously the leaders had little
time to consolidate their movement. More important, however,
they did not build their movement upon a militant, tightly

organized mass of workers. Throughout this period, few
labor leaders attempted to bolster the tenuous links between
themselves and the rank-and-file workers. Even the major
"political" strikes between 1960 and 1964 had only the most
tenuous organizational backstopping. Labor leaders instead
sought to derive power from positions which populist politicians offered them in the Brazilian corporative state rather
than by accumulating organizational strength through a disci-
plined workers' movement. Had their thought and actions been
informed by an analytic ideology stressing the value of
organizational autonomy, they would have sought to derive
power not only from such sources outside the working class
but also (and more importantly) from campaigns to raise union
membership, develop class consciousness, and make the unions
more relevant to workers in the intervals between contract
disputes. As it was, most of the radical labor movement collapsed
with Goulart's populist government when the military took
power in 1964, because the labor leaders' strength did not
originate within the working class.

The Labor Ministers and Control of the Working Class

This section and the following one compare the
promises of populist politicians to the substance of the
policies they implemented through the Ministry of Labor, the
government agency specifically charged with labor affairs and
the one in which the substance of policies toward the working
class may be most clearly discerned. Data on labor
ministers' actions and on resources spent for workers underscore the point that, with one exception, even the most
radical populist politicians sought the political support of
the workers while actively impeding their development of
organizational autonomy.
Scrutiny of the background and actions of the labor
ministers reveals two major patterns in the official relationship between the political elites and the working class.
These patterns (summarized in Table Four) are: (1) classical
populist, or paternalistic-administrative, and (2) radical
populist. Both are variants of populism, since in both the
dominant politicians build their movements upon a mass base
which exercises little independence.
Throughout most of the period since 1930, relative
ruling class solidarity, which the factional disputes
disturbed but did not destroy, and the absence of revolutionary ideology and organizational autonomy among workers
allowed the classical populist or paternalistic-
administrative pattern to predominate. After the Revolution
of 1930, politicians for the first time made major rhetorical
overtures to workers, created state agencies to serve them,
accorded legal recognition to their unions, and promised them
substantial improvements in status and material well-being.

TABLE FOUR

PREDOMINANT PATTERNS IN THE RELATIONSHIP BETWEEN POLITICAL
ELITES AND THE WORKING CLASS, 1930-1975, AS DERIVED
FROM LABOR MINISTERS' CAREER PATTERNS AND POLICIES

Years	Pattern
1930-1953	Paternalistic-Administrative
1953-1954	Radical Populist
1954-1955	Paternalistic-Administrative
1956-1962	Mixed, with paternalistic-administrative dominant
1963-1964	Radical Populist
1964-1975	Paternalistic-Administrative

SOURCE: Op. Cit., Table 4.1.

This traditional form of elite control has prevailed through thirty-four of the forty-five years since the Ministry of Labor was founded. It is deeply rooted in the paternalism of Brazil's traditional rural culture and in the long-standing Brazilian practice of giving state elites predominance in almost all spheres of social activity.[31] João Cafe Filho, Vargas's vice-president who succeeded to the presidency on the latter's death in 1954 illustrates this paternalism in his description of audiences with ordinary citizens:

> In a sense, the President and even the
> Vice-President of the Republic perform
> a paternal function in the feelings of
> the people; the President is the head
> of a great family to whose protection
> one may run. Whatever the President
> and Vice-President might do and say
> will be accompanied with gratitude and
> confidence.[32]

"Radical-populist" describes periods in which government officials raised hopes or fears that they were actually transferring power to the working class. These officials, usually the president and labor minister, suggested that they would redistribute social, political, or economic resources to the nation's workers. References to class or economic conflict rose in official rhetoric, and governmental toleration of strikes increased markedly. Although "populist" describes the behavior of most politicians between 1930 and 1964, only two brief periods (1953-1954 and 1963-1964) qualify as radical populism in power. These short periods are crucial to our analysis, because the action of politicians in office offers far more substantial evidence about the nature of their movements than their rhetoric when out of power.

The two types of populism, classical and radical, become clearly defined when we analyze the actions, backgrounds, and career patterns of the men who implement official policy as well as actual government spending for workers. By studying the reality of labor policy rather than the official intentions stated in politicians' rhetoric, we see that turnover in the nation's top office rarely changed the patterns of official labor policies. Both presidents who appointed radical populist labor ministers, for example, did so in the middle of their term. Only with the election of Juscelino Kubitschek in 1956 and the military coups of 1954 and 1964 did discernible policy shifts accompany presidential changes. Even such a fundamental constitutional change as the shift from Vargas' authoritarian Estado Novo (1937-1945) to electoral democracy in 1946 made almost no impact on labor policy. And analysis of the labor ministers' career patterns wipes out any distinction between the Estado Novo and most

years between 1946 and 1964. Background data for the
twenty-seven labor ministers between 1930 and 1964 reveal a
very high level of education, which suggests they came from
middle or upper class families. Twenty-two of them had a
university education and two more were trained in the
military academy. Only two, one of whom became a highly
successful businessman and the other a journalist, did not
go beyond secondary school. (Educational data are unavail-
able for one.) Very few Brazilians--well under 2 percent of
the 18-21 year-old age group--reached the university during
this period, and nearly all of those who did came from middle
or upper socio-economic strata.[33]

A significant contrast in age occurs between the
populist ministers, who averaged 36 years on assuming the
post, and those of other periods, who averaged 48 years.[34]
This distinction suggests that the younger ministers, less
socialized by time and experience into accepting the status
quo and less firmly integrated into the power bases of the
establishment than older men, were thus more disposed to
offer concessions to the lower class.

The Ministry's essential function during the
paternalistic administrative periods, of course, was to
control the working class. The career patterns of the twelve
ministers prior to the first break with the paternalistic-
administrative pattern graphically illustrate this point, for
s ven of them had previously served in one or more of the
following capacities: police chief, police commissioner,
public prosecutor, or interventor (chief executive of states
appointed by President Vargas during the authoritarian
period, 1930-1945). These seven men occupied the Ministry
for 187 of the 262 months between 1930 and 1953.[35]

Vargas' elective presidency (1951-1954) illustrates
the contrast between classical and radical populism. He
clearly dictated a paternalistic-administrative approach
during his first two and one-half years. Indeed, in his
Christmas eve address of 1951, he counseled the workers: "You
don't need strikes or appeals to extreme methods; don't let
yourselves be moved by agitators and those who disrupt order
and entice you with ideologies that conceal ambitions of a
very different kind."[36] He selected his two labor ministers
from 1951 to 1953 for their ability to control the working
class. One had served the Estado Novo in several capacities,
including chief of police for the industrial state of
São Paulo. His replacement had once been a public prosecutor, but he spent most of his career in the Ministry of
Labor bureaucracy. He had co-authored the labor code which
so carefully circumscribed organized labor's activities.

In 1953, for reasons which the next section will make
clear, President Vargas broke with the classical populist
tradition when he appointed thirty-five year old João Goulart
to the Ministry. Goulart, then a popular young politician
from Vargas' home state, personified the government's new

radical populist style. Immediately before his appointment, he had supported a maritime strike opposed by the labor minister.[37] As this incident occurred when Goulart was Vargas' house guest in the presidential palace, it signaled a dramatic change in the president's policy toward strikes and labor. The incumbent minister therefore resigned, and Vargas appointed Goulart.[38]

The young appointee, unlike his predecessors, applied his control of the Ministry to the task of building a militant political base in the working class. He intervened in the Federation of Maritime Workers to replace the unpopular president who had opposed the strike.[39] This raised the hopes of many workers that the government would allow a new, responsive labor leadership to take the place of the corrupt, state-dominated pelegos.* He courted sympathy by decrying financial mismanagement in the Ministry and by urging all unionized workers to report violations of the labor law so administrative or judicial action could be taken.[40] The ministerial power of appointment served to multiply his supporters. And he also changed the composition of the local minimum wage commissions, for example, so they would approve a 100 percent minimum wage increase in their districts.[41]

The proposal to raise the minimum wage gained many supporters among the masses, but the opposition which it aroused brought his ouster in a civil-military crisis in February 1954. The financial situation of the early fifties had put a squeeze on the military budget, and a colonels' memorandum to the minister of war protested the deteriorating physical conditions of the military installations and declining remuneration of the officer corps relative to comparable civilian posts. The colonels opposed Goulart's intention to double the minimum wage, claiming that in the big cities it would approach that of warrant and senior non-commissioned officers.[42] Though Vargas gave in to the pressure and ousted Goulart, he did follow through with the 100 percent minimum wage hike on Labor Day in May. This wage decision fueled already rising political tensions. In August, these culminated in a military ultimatum that Vargas resign and, in response, his suicide.

The military-dominated regimes which followed Vargas' death reinstated the paternalistic-administrative pattern. In the 1956 elections, however, Juscelino Kubitschek won the presidency and João Goulart the vice-presidency. Tension between the two types of populism characterized the Kubitschek presidency, therefore, because Goulart sought to

---

*The relatively docile heads of labor organizations who were satisfied to enjoy the perquisites of their position without fighting aggressively for their class were dubbed pelegos, after the sheepskin horseblanket which makes it easier for the horse to bear the burden of the rider.

expand labor activity while the president sought to restrain
it. This mixed pattern continued when Goulart, now
president, opted for radical populism.

The ministers appointed during this second brief
radical populist period were also in their thirties and they
sought labor support as actively and with the same tactics
as Goulart had a decade earlier. One of them, Almino Afonso,
transgressed the unwritten rules of populist politics by
supplying labor leaders with sources of real political
leverage, but this approach cost him his job. This article
will examine his six months as labor minister after first
analyzing ministerial expenditures.

Expenditures for the Working Class: The Ministry of Labor Budget

Radical populist presidents claimed to do more for
the workers than their predecessors. Promises of public
officials, however, are seldom reliable indicators of the
policies they pursue. Do radical populists in power actually
increase spending on workers? Can they force other social
sectors to transfer resources to workers? This section
evaluates Labor Ministry budgets and accounts, i.e. concrete
yardsticks of actual governmental performance toward the
working class.

Indeed, economic data illuminate both cause and
content of the radical populist periods. Economic output
figures show that both populist periods coincided with brief
economic crises which put a sharp pinch on governmental
resources. Real economic output grew only 3.2 and 1.6
percent in 1953 and 1963, respectively, compared with annual
averages of 6.2 and 6.7 percent over the preceding five-year
periods.[43] The economic crises deepened divisions within
the ruling class and caused the presidents to look to the
working class for additional political support.[44] In both
instances, the government courted labor by permitting greatly
increased strike activity and by heightening rhetoric that
exalted the working class. In sharp contrast with the
high-sounding rhetoric, however, the Ministry of Labor
substantially reduced allocations for social welfare,
hospitalization, and pensions for workers. The economic
crises had made it difficult for the state to finance the
paternalistic welfare apparatus, forcing Presidents Vargas
and Goulart to establish a new pattern of relations with
the workers at a time when their governments needed mass
support more than ever.

The impact of reduced funding for the workers' pension
and welfare programs would be felt only after some time had
passed, but promises, passionate rhetoric, and a new toleration of strikes provided workers with immediately perceptible
indicators of an apparently favorable policy change. One may

conclude, then, that the government increased its radical
rhetoric in order to obscure from the workers the reductions
in financial support for worker oriented programs. Let us
examine the radical populist periods more closely, first
contrasting the two classical populist years after President
Vargas' election in 1950 with his radical populist years,
1953-54.

The annual budget, which the president submits and
Congress passes prior to each fiscal year, reflects the
government's promises and rhetorical commitments. Throughout
Vargas' elective presidency (1951-54), the budget programmed
no significant drop in spending on labor. Analysis of the
Labor Ministry's books, however, establishes that Ministerial
expenditures during the first radical populist period averaged 1.4 percent of total annual federal outlays, while
during the preceding two years, they had averaged 2.4 percent.[45] Vargas obviously did not wish to publicize these
spending cuts in advance, so only when the Ministry of
Finance had processed the accounts of actual expenditures
several years afterward did the contrast of performance with
rhetoric become clear.

The biggest bite came out of social security funds.
Statutory contributions from employees, employers, and the
government make up the budget of the Brazilian social
security system. The national budget allocates the government's annual contribution to the Ministry of Labor, which is
supposed to transfer it to the appropriate social security
and welfare organizations. In no year has the government
transferred all of those funds to the appropriate agencies,
though the proportion released differs greatly from one year
to the next. In Brazil's chronically inflationary economy,
the government reduced inflationary pressures in some
measure by holding these funds rather than transferring them
to agencies which would spend them. Services for workers,
who had already contributed their share through automatic
payroll deductions, suffered accordingly.

In 1951 and 1952, the Ministry released the very high
average (for Brazil) of 79 percent of the transfer allocations for social welfare, demonstrating Vargas's reliance on
the paternalistic element in the administrative tradition.
These transfers, however, dropped to less than half that
figure (37 percent) in the last two years of his presidency.
The currency exchanged for labor support, therefore, did not
come from the national treasury. However, government actions
doubling the minimum wage and allowing strikes forced the
private sector to provide immediate material benefits for
workers. Despite the damage to long-range welfare programs,
therefore, the first radical populist period provided some
material benefits. No evidence, however, supports the
contention that the government sought to transfer power to
the workers.

In significant ways, the circumstances surrounding the establishment of radical populism in 1963 echo those of a decade earlier. Economic crisis and sharp divisions within the ruling class marked this period as well. Again, the government appeared unable or unwilling to finance its paternalistic welfare apparatus. In 1962, the Labor Ministry released only 32 percent of its welfare allocation. Though it did much better in 1963, releasing 62 percent, it fell back to 43 percent in 1964. Once again, political leaders honored the working class with symbolic, rhetorical outputs while state services deteriorated. And due to the more serious nature of the economic slowdown in the 1960s, the government could not force the private sector to play a compensatory role: minimum wage hikes failed to keep pace with the soaring cost of living.

By comparing personnel costs with social security outlays, we shed still more light on the radical populist phenomenon. In these years, the government transferred even less of its statutory obligations to the social welfare apparatus than in other years, yet personnel costs increased dramatically. Although Brazil's chronic inflation required regular salary hikes, the jumps in personnel expenditures during radical populist periods went well beyond the norm for other years. For the four radical populist years, personnel increases averaged 73.3 percent annually--more than twice the annual average of 34.4 percent for the other 15 years between 1946 and 1964. When we contrast the decline in overall Ministry expenditures with the rise in personnel outlays, therefore, we conclude that the initiators of radical populism consciously opted to protect their own political careers at the workers' expense. They reduced service to the working class as a whole and then directed some of the money saved, in the form of patronage, to labor leaders, politicians, and bureaucrats--key individuals in the corporative structures whom they expected to <u>control</u> the working class.

With the significant exception of Almino Afonso, whose case will be discussed below, radical populist ministers did not emphasize efficient performance by the administrative agencies. Rather, they combined heavy emphasis on traditional clientelistic politics with radical but unfulfilled rhetoric.

Radical Populism and Political Change: A Case Study

Brazilian economist Celso Furtado observed that rewards conferred upon the lower classes by populist politicians at first tend to numb class consciousness, because the recipients have not won them through pressure from their own autonomous organizations. He added however, that if labor or peasant leaders take proper advantage of benefits accorded them in this struggle among political elites--particularly benefits which enable them to develop their own organizational strength--they may be able to accumulate power which can then be used to pressure politicians for ever-increasing concessions. By making demands which further advance the institutionalization of autonomous organizational structures, the working class and peasantry can establish an independent power base which will ultimately allow them to share or attain political power.[46] In essence, populism would create conditions for its own replacement by a socialist or a trade unionist movement.

This description of populism and its capacity to evolve away from elite domination provides a framework for analyzing Labor Ministry relations with workers' organizations during the fifties and sixties. From this perspective, Goulart's six months as labor minister in 1953-54 fit within the early stage of radical populism when apparent concessions or benefits to the workers served primarily to advance the careers of individuals in the established political elite while numbing the recipients' class consciousness. This holds true through the transitional period of the fifties.

Populism began to yield some political leverage once a more able leadership replaced the old pelegos at the command of the most important labor organizations in the early 1960s. During the fifties, the pelegos had been content to treat whatever benefits came their way as purely personal profit. They did not seek to convert them into autonomous power or real material benefits for their constituents. The new leaders, on the other hand, consciously set out to take advantage of major organizational gains described below to increase their power within the political system. Their success marks the later stage of populism, which provided increasingly meaningful participation to the working class, and in an incipient form, to the peasantry. As Furtado cautions, however, the positive benefits of populism can be wiped out if worker- or peasant-based political groups make a false move before they have achieved firm organizational autonomy.[47] This caveat, written before the coup of 1964, proved prophetic of Goulart's overthrow and the return to the administrative tradition.

Let us examine the process by which labor leaders began to build their political power. The social security law of 1960 provided them with their major lever.[48] It assured them one-third of the seats on the governing councils of all social security agencies. Chairmanship of the councils now rotated among the three participant groups: labor, government, and employers. Prior to 1960, labor had no delegate on the executive bodies, and the chairman had always been a Ministry official or an appointed expert in social legislation.

This new law, therefore, considerably augmented the political influence of labor leaders by giving them a firm foothold in patronage, a major currency in Brazilian politics. The social security agencies employed nearly 100,000 of Brazil's 700,000 federal civil servants and disposed of a budget larger than that of any state except São Paulo.[49] The legal autonomy of these councils offered protection against control from above, and their political use of the power of appointment, even in defiance of the president and the labor minister, has been documented in a case study of patronage.[50]

From Goulart's occupancy of the Ministry in the fifties through the transitional phase, little danger existed that ultimate control of the labor movement would slip from the hands of the political establishment. The passage of the social security law, however, increased its likelihood. Although the government still possessed certain controls, labor leaders used their social security offices and their leadership of strikes to extend their autonomy vis-à-vis establishment politicians like President Goulart. For example, top labor leaders planned a series of strikes and demonstrations between 1962 and 1964 with an eye toward increasing their leverage within the political system. In July 1962, they ignored Goulart's personal plea to cancel a major general strike, and they forced policy concessions from him in another general strike two months later.[51]

Labor Minister Almino Afonso, appointed in early 1963, sought further to increase that autonomy against the wishes of the chief executive. His six-month tenure in the ministry illustrates the later stage of radical populism, when major political actors seek to convert populism into another type of movement, in this case a socialist one. Almino, the youngest labor minister ever at age 33, was committed to achieving social justice through socialism. Two major thrusts of his program aimed at (1) increasing the efficiency and output of the Ministry and social security agencies, and (2) creating a power base for socialists and left-wing nationalists in the government bureaucracy. Success in the latter served to undermine the old-time wheelhorses of his own party, the Brazilian Labor Party (PTB), whose major source of patronage and political influence derived from control over the social security institutes.

Each of these goals reinforced the other. He first highlighted the corruption of the social security institutes in order to discredit their directors. For example, he berated the bureaucrats for self-indulgence, citing the flagrant example of the doubling of the institute treasurers' salaries two years earlier. He then decreed these increases null and void and ordered the excess returned to the public coffers.[52] This type of maneuver garnered popular support while giving him a justification for subsequent personnel transfers. In the process, he replaced officials loyal to traditional PTB leaders with individuals who shared his desire for substantial reform of the system.

The government representatives on the tripartite councils became his major targets, because appointment of their successors fell within his prerogatives. Allied with the left-wing labor representatives on the boards, his new appointees commanded a voting majority for improvements in service. Of more long-term importance, however, these appointees deprived the traditional political machines of the patronage so necessary for their sustenance and—equally important—channeled that same patronage into efforts to build a socialist movement.

The shake-up of the giant Industrial Workers' Social Security Institute (IAPI), with 28,000 employees and 3.2 million persons insured, provides a concrete example.[53] After implicating the president of the IAPI Administrative Council in corrupt dealings, Almino convinced President Goulart to replace the council head with one of his (Almino's) own proteges. The ousted man served as a key patronage conduit for the São Paulo PTB machine, and his departure deprived it of one of its principal sources of patronage and political leverage.[54] Within four months, Almino had moved against three other major social security bodies and had announced plans to dynamize other ministerial dependencies by substituting the government representatives there also.[55]

The only labor minister in the populist periods who actually tried to alter the political system in a fundamental way, Almino posed a threat to the social status quo and the president. Goulart predictably ejected him from the cabinet in June. The extent of the threat may be estimated from the fact that after only a few months in office, Almino had assembled and strengthened such a constituency on the left that he successfully frustrated for two months the president's desire to sack him. Through pro-labor policies and astute use of his power of appointment, Almino had successfully courted the General Labor Command (CGT), an extra-legal confederation uniting labor leaders of the radical, nationalist left. Considerable political influence had accrued to these leaders from their apparent control over strikes, and they outspokenly sided with the minister in his clash with the president. If Goulart had removed Almino from the cabinet, he would have faced the threat of an economically damaging and socially divisive general strike.

Confronted with opposition based in the labor movement and vocally led by a member of his own cabinet, the president withdrew his support of the CGT (which he had hitherto backed) and then lent the prestige of the presidency to a parallel but much weaker central labor organization. The threat to withdraw the prestige, patronage, and financial resources which accompanied good relations with the government forced the CGT leaders into retreat, facilitating the ouster of the labor minister.[56] The episode is significant because it disproves the argument that Goulart had shifted

to the left during this period.[57] To the contrary, he had
moved right by weakening labor's left wing and preventing
working class leaders from amassing real power in their own
hands. This is precisely what one should expect of populist
politicians, for they see the working class as an electoral
mass to manipulate and, whatever their humanitarian considerations, only the rarest exceptions among them willingly
allow workers to gain access to the levers of power.

Conclusion

Populist movements occur in industrializing countries
as nationalistic responses to increasingly apparent foreign
domination. Brazilian data support the observation that
these movements arise only where the lower strata play a
political role and where a split within the ruling class
leads one of its factions to seek lower class support.
Economic development, and particularly industrialization,
provoked the initial split within the Brazilian ruling class.
The faction favoring industrialization promised the urban
masses welfare programs and higher wages in return for their
backing. Implicit in the appeals of such populist politicians was the notion that the nation's workers would
ultimately share in political power.
President Getulio Vargas established a populist
relationship with the urban masses after the Revolution of
1930. He created the Ministry of Labor within a month of
taking office, and his first labor minister's inaugural
address referred to it as the "Ministry of the Revolution."[58]
For more than 20 years, however, Brazil's dominant politicians treated the workers in a paternalistic manner, carefully supervising their organizational activities while
disbursing welfare benefits through the state administration.
This is the essence of classical populism.
On two occasions--in 1953 and 1963--Brazilian
presidents initiated radical populist policies and raised
hopes or fears that they were transferring a share of political power to the working class. They did not make this
policy shift in response to overwhelming pressure from
workers' organizations, however,for the Brazilian working
class movement did not possess sufficient force to impose
such policy departures upon the chief executive. Rather,
these presidents changed policies because deteriorating
economic conditions had exacerbated internal divisions within
the ruling class and thus weakened their governing
coalitions.
Reaching out for additional support from the workers,
they appointed labor ministers who relaxed governmental
resistance to strikes and lavished the workers with rhetoric
promising social justice. Despite the tone of this rhetoric,
though, these two radical populist governments actually

reduced programs for the working class. Ministerial spending
patterns rebut conclusively the claim that they channeled
additional resources to the working class.

Radical populist politicians, moreover, did not seek
to transfer power to the workers. Those in office did not
attempt to alter the class base of participation in political
decision making but only sought to strengthen the mass base
of their own support. Only once did a labor minister--Almino
Afonso--actively promote an increase in the power of organized labor, and this audacious step led President Goulart, a
more typical populist, to eject him from the cabinet.

Without political power based on an autonomous
bargaining capability, therefore, workers reap only those
rewards which their populist patrons see fit to bestow upon
them. Economic data demonstrate that the material benefits
Brazilian workers received were at best meager and short-
lived even under the radical populist presidents. Having
failed to develop an ideology or scheme of analysis to guide
their construction of strong, autonomous class institutions,
the workers found themselves unable to control or influence
the terms of their alliance with the populist politicians.
This left them unprepared for the military takeover which
brought Brazil's populist era to an end. Only when Latin
American workers look to themselves rather than to the ruling
class for the improvement of their lot is their powerless-
ness, and with it their privation, likely to end.

NOTES

1. This article is reprinted from the Proceedings of the Pacific Coast Council on Latin American Studies, Vol. 4 (1975), pp. 117-144. I wish to acknowledge the valuable suggestions and criticism offered by Patrick V. Peppe and Hobart A. Spalding, Jr. during several stages of the development of the thoughts and material presented here. I am also indebted to Gil Carl AlRoy, Michael M. Hall, Timothy F. Harding, and Amaury de Souza for their critical readings and valuable comments on earlier drafts.

1a. Many book and article titles reflected the imminence of revolution, e.g., Irving Louis Horowitz, Revolution in Brazil (New York: Dutton, 1964); see also the Brazilian press from 1961 through 1964 for expressions on revolution.

2. José Albertino Rodrigues, Sindicato e desenvolvimento no Brasil (São Paulo: Difusão Europeia do Livro, 1968), pp. 68-69.

3. Kenneth Paul Erickson, The Brazilian Corporative State and Working Class Politics (Berkeley: University of California Press, forthcoming).

4. Leôncio Martins Rodrigues, Conflito industrial e sindicalismo no Brasil (São Paulo: Difusão Européia do Livro, 1966), p. 73.

5. Erickson, op. cit., Chapter 6.

6. Edmar Morel, O golpe começou em Washington (Rio de Janeiro: Civilização Brasileira, 1965), pp. 71-72.

7. Ronald M. Schneider, The Political System of Brazil: Emergence of a "Modernizing" Authoritarian Regime, 1964-1970 (New York: Columbia University Press, 1971), p. 30, laments the fact that "The crucial concept of populism in Brazilian politics is still very much understudied."

8. The first insightful analysis of Brazilian populism is: (anonymous), "Que é o adhemarismo?", Cadernos do Nosso Tempo, No. 2 (January-June 1954), pp. 139-149; see

also a series of important articles on Brazilian
populism by Francisco C. Weffort: "Clases Populares y
Desarrollo Social (Contribución al estudio del 'Popu-
lismo')," Revista Paraguaya de Sociología, V
(December 1968), pp. 62-154; "Estado y masas en el
Brasil," Revista Latinoamericana de Sociología, I
(March 1965), pp. 53-71; "Política de massas," in
Política e Revolução Social no Brasil, by Octávio
Ianni et al. (Rio de Janeiro: Civilização Brasileira,
1965), pp. 195-198; "Raizes sociais do populismo em
São Paulo," Revista Civilização Brasileira, I (May
1965), pp. 39-60; an excellent short case study of
rural populism in action is Anthony Leeds, "Brazil and
the Myth of Francisco Julião," in Politics of Change
in Latin America, ed. Joseph Maier and Richard W.
Weatherhead (New York: Praeger, 1964), pp. 190-204.

9. Alberto Guerreiro Ramos, A crise do poder no Brasil
    (Problemas da revolução nacional brasileira) (Rio
    de Janeiro: Zahar, 1961), pp. 45-93, for example,
    rightly saw populism as declining, but he wrongly felt
    it would cede to interest-group and/or class-
    ideological politics rather than to an authoritarian
    military regime.

10. For a range of   views set forth at a conference on
    the worldwide phenomenon of populism, see "Populism:
    A Discussion . . .", Government and Opposition, III
    (Spring 1968), pp. 137-180; and Ghita Ionescu and
    Ernest Gellner, eds., Populism: Its Meaning and
    National Characteristics (New York: Macmillan, 1969),
    including a chapter on Latin America by Alistair
    Hennessy, pp. 28-61.

11. The distinction between ideologies and mentalities is
    Theodor Geiger's, as elaborated in Juan J. Linz, "An
    Authoritarian Regime: Spain," in Cleavages, Ideolo-
    gies, and Party Systems: Contributions to Comparative
    Political Sociology, ed. E. Allardt and Y. Littunen
    (Helsinki: Transactions of the Westermarck Society,
    1964), p. 301; see the debate over whether populism is
    an ideology or a movement in "Populism: A Discus-
    sion . . .", op. cit., pp. 168-171, and Chapters Six
    through Ten of Ionescu and Gellner, op. cit.

12. An excellent brief analysis of Perón's thought and his
    justicialist philosophy is Alberto Ciria, Perón y el
    Justicialismo (Buenos Aires: Siglo Veintiuno, 1971),
    pp. 122-143 and passim; a hostile but perceptive
    discussion of the philosophical underpinnings of
    justicialism is George I. Blanksten, Perón's Argentina

(New York: Russell and Russell, 1967, c1953),
pp. 280-298. Interested readers will find citations
to major expositions of Peronist thought in Ciria.

13. James W. Wilkie, The Mexican Revolution: Federal Expenditures and Social Change Since 1910 (Berkeley:
University of California Press, 1967), pp. 188, 194.

14. Miguel Murmis and Juan Carlos Portantiero, Estudios
Sobre los Orígenes del Peronismo (Buenos Aires: Siglo
Veintiuno, 1971), pp. 59-129.

15. For similar observations in the Bolivian context, see
Malvin Burke and James M. Malloy, "Del populismo
nacional al corporativismo nacional: El caso de
Bolivia," Aportes, No. 26 (October 1972), pp. 66-73;
for the political factors underlying the economic
collapse of Perón's Argentina, see Eldon Gordon
Kenworthy, The Formation of the Peronist Coalition
(Ph.D. Dissertation, Yale University, 1970),
(Ann Arbor: University Microfilms, 1970), pp. 245-275.

16. V. I. Lenin, "What Is To Be Done?", in Lenin on Politics
and Revolution, ed. James E. Connor (New York:
Pegasus, 1968), p. 35; Frantz Fanon made a similar
observation about the basically populist African
independence movements: ". . . the great danger that
threatens Africa is the absence of ideology." Toward
the African Revolution (New York: Grove Press, 1967),
pp. 186-187.

17. See Table One and Jorge Basurto, "Populismo y movili-
zación de masas en México durante el régimen carden-
ista," Revista Mexicana de Sociología, XXXI (October
1969), pp. 853-892.

18. Wilkie, op. cit., pp. 72-73; William P. Glade, Jr. and
Charles Anderson, The Political Economy of Mexico
(Madison: University of Wisconsin Press, 1963),
pp. 120-121; Frank R. Brandenburg, The Making of
Modern Mexico (Englewood Cliffs, New Jersey: Prentice-
Hall, 1964), pp. 88-90.

19. Fernando Henrique Cardoso, Ideologías de la burguesía
industrial en sociedades dependientes (Argentina y
Brasil) (Mexico: Siglo XXI, 1971), pp. 206-211.

20. Guillermo A. O'Donnell, Modernization and Bureaucratic
Authoritarianism (Berkeley: Institute of International
Studies, University of California: 1973), p. 82.

21. For a brief description of this process, see Celso Furtado, "Political Obstacles to the Economic Development of Brazil," Obstacles to Change in Latin America, ed. Claudio Veliz (New York: Oxford University Press, 1965), pp. 145-161.

22. Leôncio Martins Rodrigues, Industrialização e atitudes operárias (São Paulo: Brasiliense, 1970), pp. 165-166 and passim; the model for this study is drawn from Alain Touraine, La conscience ouvrière (Paris: Le Seuil, 1966).

23. L. Rodrigues, Industrialização . . . , op. cit., pp. 165-166. Significantly, Rodrigues applied his questionnaire in 1963, the heyday of Brazilian populism, so the post-1964 authoritarian repression did not influence the attitudes described.

24. Erickson, op. cit., Chapter 3.

25. Consolidação das Leis do Trabalho, Article 514.

26. Weffort, "Política de massas," op. cit., p. 162.

27. Reinhard Bendix, Max Weber: An Intellectual Portrait (Garden City, New York: Doubleday Anchor, 1962), pp. 299-328.

28. Ramos, op. cit., p. 55; Juárez R. B. Lopes, "Some Basic Developments in Brazilian Politics and Society," New Perspectives of Brazil, ed. Eric N. Baklanoff (Nashville: Vanderbilt University Press, 1966), pp. 63-68.

29. Weffort, "Estado y masas . . . ," op. cit., pp. 65-66; Weffort, "Raizes sociais . . . ," op. cit., passim.

30. Major strikes and labor activity in this period are evaluated in Erickson, op. cit., Chapter 6.

31. See Raymundo Faoro, Os donos do poder; formação do patronato político brasileiro (Porto Alegre: Globo, 1958), p. 262 and passim.

32. João Café Filho, Do sindicato ao Catete (Rio de Janeiro: José Olympio, 1966), I, pp. 275-297; quote, p. 282.

33. The number of students enrolled in Brazilian higher education was exceedingly small during the period under study, and nearly all of these students came

from upper-class or middle-sector families. Of the 18-21 year-old population in Brazil in 1930, 1940, 1950, and 1960, respectively, the percentage enrolled in higher education was: .63, .58, 1.07, and 1.74 percent. Robert J. Havighurst and J. Roberto Moreira, Society and Education in Brazil (Pittsburgh: University of Pittsburgh Press, 1965), p. 187.

34. Biodata on the ministers are summarized in Erickson, op. cit., Chapter 4.

35. Brazil, Ministério do Trabalho, Indústria e Comércio, Documentário foto-biográfico dos ex-ministros que ocuparam a pasta do Trabalho, Indústria e Comércio (Rio de Janeiro: MTIC, 1955).

36. Getúlio Vargas, O Govêrno Trabalhista do Brasil, II (Rio de Janeiro: Departamento de Imprensa Nacional, 1953), p. 60, as reported in Thomas E. Skidmore, Politics in Brazil, 1930-1964 (New York: Oxford University Press, 1967), p. 365.

37. Diário Carioca, 14 June 1953, p. 12; Correio da Manhã, 16 June 1953, p. 1.

38. The differences between the styles of the two were highlighted by their speeches at Goulart's inauguration. Text in Brazil, MTIC, Boletim do Ministério do Trabalho, Indústria e Comércio (Nova Série), III (July-September 1953), pp. 23-28.

39. Correio da Manhã, 23 June 1953, p. 12; Diário Carioca, 19 July 1953, p. 4; 20 August 1953, p. 1 and 2; 21 August 1953, p. 12.

40. Diário Carioca, 5 July 1953, p. 1; 13 October 1953, p. 2 and 12.

41. Confidential interview. Ministerial regulations (portarias) show that Goulart changed the composition of 21 of the 22 Minimum Wage Commissions in Brazil during his six-month ministry. Brazil, MTIC, Boletim do Ministério do Trabalho, Indústria e Comércio (Nova Série) III (July-September 1953), pp. 91-92; III (October-December 1953), pp. 201-202; and IV (January-March 1954), pp. 231-232.

42. Text of memorandum in Oliveiros S. Ferreira, As fôrças armadas e o desafio da revolução (Rio de Janeiro: Edições GRD, 1964), pp. 122-129. The officers' comparison does not take into account the many fringe benefits which they receive.

43. Data from Getúlio Vargas Foundation in Nathaniel H. Leff, _Economic Policy-Making and Development in Brazil, 1947-1964_ (New York: Wiley, 1968), p. 89.

44. A brief English-language history of Brazil in this period is Thomas E. Skidmore, _op. cit._

45. All of the financial data below are from the national budget (orçamento), published annually in the _Diário Oficial_ at the time of its passage by the legislature, or from the national accounts (Balanços Gerais da União), which are drawn up by the Contadoria Geral da República in the Ministry of Finance several years after the close of each fiscal year. These data are summarized in Erickson, _op. cit._, Tables 4.4, 4.5, and 4.6.

46. Celso Furtado, _Dialética do desenvolvimento_ (Rio de Janeiro: Fundo de Cultura, 1964), pp. 83-85; Robert E. Ward made a similar observation when dealing with the expansion of participation in Japan in "Political Modernization and Political Culture in Japan," in _Political Modernization: A Reader in Comparative Political Change_, ed. Claude E. Welch, Jr. (Belmont, California: Wadsworth, 1967), pp. 101-102. See also E. E. Schattschneider, _The Semi-Sovereign People_ (New York: Holt, Rinehart and Winston, 1960), p. 3.

47. Furtado, _op. cit._, p. 86.

48. Lei No. 3807 of 27 August 1960, regulated by Decreto 48.959-A of 19 September 1960. Subsequent modifications, particularly those after 1964, are compiled in Ronaldo Waldemiro Groehs, _A lei orgânica da previdência social_, 4th ed. revised (Porto Alegre: Sulina, 1967). The impact of the 1960 law went far beyond the domaine of social security administration. Indeed, it contributed in a major way to the political mobilization of the early 1960s, yet the Brazilian press gave its passage scant coverage at the time, and no case study has since examined it. It would make an excellent topic for a short research grant.

49. Brazil, DASP and IBGE, Serviço Nacional de Recenseamento, _Censo dos Servidores Públicos Civis Federais, 31 de maio de 1966, Resultado Preliminares_ (Rio de Janeiro: IBGE, n.d.) (Mimeographed), p. 2; Brazil, IBGE, _Anuário Estatístico do Brasil--1965_ (Rio de Janeiro: IBGE, 1965), p. 470.

50. Carlos Veríssimo do Amaral, "As Controvertidas Nomeações para a Previdência Social em 1963: Estudo de um Caso," in Política e Administração de Pessoal, ed. Carlos Veríssimo do Amaral and Kleber Tatinge do Nascimento (Rio de Janeiro: Fundação Getúlio Vargas, 1966), pp. 24-33.

51. Erickson, op. cit., Chapters 6 and 7.

52. Jornal do Brasil, 24 April 1963, 6.

53. Employee data in Brazil, DASP and IBGE, op. cit., p. 11; insured and budget in Brasil, IBGE, Anuário Estatístico do Brasil--1965 (Rio de Janeiro: IBGE, 1965) p. 367.

54. Jornal do Brasil, 17 March 1963, p. 5.

55. Jornal do Brasil, 19 May 1963, p. 14.

56. Details in Erickson, op. cit., Chapter 7.

57. Skidmore, op. cit., p. 277, for example, ignores this move by Goulart and states that the president had abandoned what Brazilians called the "positive left," implying that he had moved farther left toward the "negative left."

58. J. A. Rodrigues, op. cit., p. 69.

ECONOMIC ORGANIZATION AND SOCIAL CONSCIENCE:

SOME DILEMMAS OF CUBAN SOCIALISM[*]

Bertram Silverman

Introduction

The confrontation between the past and the future is never more visible than in periods of revolutionary transition. During the revolutionary phase what is possible seems unlimited as the weight of oppression and tradition is lifted, and in the euphoria of newly discovered power the present appears as an unbounded future. But the morning after is not too long in coming. As Marx so aptly wrote, "the tradition of all the dead generations weighs like a nightmare on the brain of the living. And just when they seem engaged in revolutionizing themselves and things, in creating something that has never yet existed, precisely in such periods of revolutionary crisis they anxiously conjure up the spirits of the past . . . ."[1]
This tension between revolutionary will and historical constraint has been an ongoing dialectic of the Cuban revolution. In response to the economic difficulties through which Cuba is now passing, the advocates of greater conformity to tradition are again raising their voices inside and outside Cuba. Declining worker productivity[2] is seen as a product of romantic attempts to radically alter social consciousness and to develop new systems of motivation based on social (socialistic) rather than material (capitalistic) incentives. Recently Professor Leontief argued that:

> "In Cuba as in other socialist countries such moral incentives failed in their effectiveness to measure up to more conventional individualistic self interest . . . .[3] In prompting an average laborer, sales clerk, manager or technician to exert himself day in and day out in steady purposeful, i.e., productive work nothing seems as effective as a steady flow of material benefits closely commensurate with the results of his individual effort . . . this is not to imply however that human nature cannot change in the long run."[4]

---

[*]I would like to express my appreciation to Leo Kaplan and Murray Yanowitch for their critical evaluation and assistance.

Yet, there is no evidence presented to show the
correlation between moral incentives, per se, and declining worker productivity. Indeed, material incentives
were used extensively through 1965 and worker productivity
declined during this period. Certainly one would not conclude from this evidence that material incentives are
ineffective. The relationship between moral incentives
and worker productivity is more complex, and cannot be
disassociated from the economic organization of which it
is a part.[5] This paper is primarily concerned with examining how pragmatic responses to the problems of the Cuban
transition to socialism influenced economic organization
and the ideological commitment to moral incentives.[6]

Marxian analysis suggests two fundamental criteria
in the transformation of economic organization within a
socialist society. On the one hand economic organization
must be consistent with the stage of development of the
social forces of production, that is, technology, skills,
education, work habits, etc. On the other hand economic
organization must also be consistent with the formation
of socialist values and behavior. Since all socialist
revolutions have occurred in relatively backward economies,
an inevitable contradiction exists between the organizational forms held to be most consistent with communist
goals and the capacity to establish such an economic organization. Generally, traditional economic analysis has
tended to obscure the relationship between economic
organization and social character. The rationality of
economic organization has been defined primarily in terms
of an efficiency criterion   (e.g., the rational allocation
of scarce resources among competing ends.) And the market
and mercantile relations were the most effective means of
achieving those ends.[7]

Cuba's rejection, after 1966, of an economic organization based on the money motive reflects strong commitment to revolutionary principles and socialist ethics.
Further, Cuba's revolutionary ethics does not mean an end
to ideology in the Marxian sense. Cuban economic organization and developmental strategy have been closely tied
to Cuban praxis, and ideology has frequently served to
rationalize practice and economic policy goals. While
ideology has played an important role in mobilizing mass
commitment to social and economic goals, it has also had
the effect of obscuring real underlying forces. Unravel-
ling the actual social and economic relationships that
have governed the developemnt of economic organization
may help to "demystify" Cuban ideology: to bring theory
and practice into a more conscious harmonious correspondence, i.e. to comprehend socialism in the way that Marx
comprehended capitalism.[8]

From Praxis to Principle:
The Development of Cuban Economic Organization

The evolution of socialist economic organization, in
this period of the transition to socialism, has historically
been the dynamic resultant of a previously adopted socialist ideology and a pragmatic response to experience. Consequently, the theory of a particular experience has frequently served as the ideological veil to justify or rationalize that experience. Ideology has been an ex post
response to experience as well as an ex ante guide to
practice.

Cuba's pragmatic style has been a recognized characteristic.[9] "But an absence of theory 'lends an air of
crisis' to the present situation in socialist countries.
The apologetic nature of the pragmatic theory of economic
practice obscured many fundamental problems that today have
become paramount."[10] No doubt Alberto Mora, the former
Minister of Foreign Trade, had Cuba in mind when he wrote
this comment in 1965. Cuba began her economic experiment
without a well-developed theory of economic organization.

During this first phase (1959-1961), the rapid
nationalization of the strategic sectors of the Cuban
economy presented the government with serious problems of
economic control and planning. The rapid nationalization[11]
began with the first Agrarian Reform that led to confiscation of the latifundia and sugar centrales. This was
followed by a confrontation with the United States that
resulted in the confiscation of United States holdings.
Simultaneously, the nationalization process was accelerated
by the confiscation of domestic enterprises that had
openly collaborated with Batista or who were resisting the
economic programs of the regime. At this time many owners
simply abandoned their businesses. Spontaneous action by
workers, led by an aggressive trade union leadership
demanding immediate changes in the distribution of income
and privilege resulted in increased labor conflict. These
early struggles frequently led to government intervention.
According to Luis Alvarez Rom, the former Treasury Minister:[12]

> Toward the end of 1960, the revolutionary govern-
> ment had to confront its first practical economic
> and financial problem. The problem had to do with
> the need to take charge of the administration and
> control of nationalized enterprises that had been
> recuperated or intervened.

The Industrial Administration Department of INRA
(National Agrarian Reform Institute) headed by Che Guevara

had to deal immediately with problems of financing the
production of economic units as complex as petroleum re-
fining or as simple as shoe workshops. The centralization
of financial control, the keystone of Cuba's organizational
model, emerged from a number of related experiences and
problems.[13] First, during the initial phase of nationalization the banking system was still in private hands.
Credit restrictions were frequently used as a method of
opposing government policies. Moreover, the State sector
still had to pay interest on loans to finance a growing
government deficit. Second, there existed in Cuba highly
advanced forms of cost accounting which gradually emerged
as a model for the Ministry of Industry (that was subsequently established in 1962). There was (and still is) a
strong bias toward adopting the latest administrative
techniques.[14] Third, central control provided a method
of integrating and controlling small and medium size
workshops, gradually elininating inefficient shops and re-
locating labor to other sectors. Fourth, centralization
of financing permitted the state to confront the enormous
demands for funds associated with the sugar harvest without total dependence on a private banking system. Fifth,
the centralization of finance, permitted production units
to focus their attention on physical output rather than
on financial matters.[15]

Finally, the revolution had unleashed dramatic shifts
in the administrative structure. The old managerial and
staff personnel began leaving as the revolutionary process
accelerated. Accountants and financial experts who were
trained in the latest United States techniques left the
country with transferable skill. Consequently those with
the most specialized skills, and who were committed to the
revolution, assumed staff positions at higher administrative
levels. Therefore, managerial functions particularly at
the production level were increasingly left in the hands
of more reliable political cadres. Initially, the actual
transfer of power to workers and peasants with relatively
little formal training symbolized the dramatic transformation of the social structure. This process of permitting
the free emigration of old civil servants, and the managerial and administrative strata is a distinctive feature of
the Cuban revolution. It permitted a relatively peaceful
transformation of the social structure and at the same
time avoided the dominance of the State by the old bureaucracy.[16] But despite their political reliability, the
cadres did not fully understand economic problems and the
need for a rational distribution of scarce resources that
required economic controls and measurement. Thus, central
finance and accounting also provided a method of economic
control over "overenthusiastic" cadres. There were also

innumerable problems due to the inconsistency of the budget
program and poor record keeping. Initially many concrete
operational problems made it difficult for enterprises
to follow the budget program and as a consequence many
enterprises accumulated large unplanned deficits.[17] The
standardization of the system of central budgeting did not
take place until 1961.

During this initial period specific events and problems transformed conflicts about the development of organizational forms into central issues of principle. This
occurred after 1961 when Cuba entered its socialist phase.

The "Great Economic Debate" over
Economic Organization. Phase II

The ideological and theoretical controversy over
market socialism versus centralized planning began in Cuba
with the formulation of the first economic plan in 1962.
Economists from socialist countries, particularly
Czechoslovakia were invited to aid Cuban planners. Many
advisors placed considerable importance on financial planning and particularly on "profitability" as a measure of
economic efficiency.[18] But these suggestions were in
conflict with the methods that were developing in Che's
Ministry of Industry.

The economic crisis in that year also raised questions about Cuba's organizational methods and economic
development. In August 1961, the Minister of Economy,
Reginald Boti, predicted that in ten years Cuban living
standards would be comparable to those of any European
country.[19] But instead of increasing, Cuban national output may have declined by 10 per cent between 1962 and 1963.[20]
It is likely that initially, declining productivity may be
an inevitable phase of socialist development in an underdeveloped society. Still, Cuba had rapidly transformed
her important economic institutions. However, individuals
without previous experience, technical know-how, or reliable information were directing an economic system. In
part, Cuba's difficulty stemmed from an initial economic
strategy. The regulated national and international market
had made the coexistence of idle land and labor rational
from the viewpoint of the large scale capitalist farmer.
By abolishing capitalist production these constraints on
land and labor utilization were exploded. It was now
argued that an expanded and diversified agriculture could
increase and stabilize employment while providing foreign
exchange for expanded industrial development. This in turn
would absorb a high and rising proportion of urban unemploy-

ment. The theory broke down, however, as the import content of the new industries turned out to be higher and
their productivity lower than expected while agricultural
productivity in the new crops was disappointingly low
and sugar production dropped precipitously. As a result
a growth strategy designed to reduce Cuban dependency
resulted in a tendency toward "economic stagnation via a
growing strangulation of foreign trade."[21]

   As a consequence production bottlenecks arose with
greater frequency and other economic problems became
apparent: a serious supply problem led to rationing in
1962; shortages increased the political and economic
resistance of the peasants, which in turn led to the
Second Agrarian Reform in 1963 that nationalized all land-
holdings above 165 acres; the reemergence of bureaucratic
inefficiency led to a breakdown in economic coordination.
As a result, the economy seemed to be running por la libre,
that is without effective controls.[22] The first response
to these problems was an abrupt revision of Cuba's
developmental strategy -- a return to agriculture and sugar
as the turnpike to development, a turn that was to have
serious implications for Cuban economic organization.

   Some Cuban leaders and foreign advisors began to
argue that Cuba's economic difficulties were rooted in
Cuban economic organization. What began as a response to
circumstances was transformed into "the Great Debate" over
fundamental issues of ideology and revolutionary principles.[23]
The participants included most of the members of the Council
of Ministers.[24]

   In opposition to central direction and control in the
industrial sector, another system of economic organization
was emerging in agriculture under the direction of Carlos
Rafael Rodriguez, and in Foreign Trade under Alberto Mora.
This system of self-finance of self-management was given
official sanction in 1962. In order to understand the
basic differences between the two systems it is necessary
to distinguish between them in their ideal form.[25]

   Under the system of self-management enterprises are
juridically independent. They trade their products with
different enterprises through the market and profitability
is the basic measure of their success. Although each
enterprise has considerable financial independence, it has
to cover its current expenses through banks that provide
interest-bearing credits. Bank loans are closely supervised so that the banks play a critical role in evaluating
and controlling the enterprise. Basic output and investment decisions are set by the Central Planning Agency but
within the aggregate constraints enterprises have independent
decision-making functions. Most significantly, managerial
incentives and labor income are based primarily on material
incentives.

Under the system of Central Budgeting, enterprises
are more seriously circumscribed by the national plan.
Rather than being legally independent, each firm is considered a part of a larger productive unit -- the public sector as a whole. Therefore, the movement of products from
one enterprise to another is an intermediary step, and
products acquire the characteristics of commodities only
when they leave the socialized sector and are sold in the
market, (i.e., in the private sector, to consumers or to
other countries). Profitability plays no role in the evaluation of the enterprise, and all net income is deposited
with the Treasury, which centrally allocates funds to various enterprises. Each enterprise is directed by the central plan, and as its function fulfills the targets set by
the plan. Rigorous financial control is established through
a central organization, Empresas Consolidadas, that coordin-
ates the accounts of enterprises in a particular sector
(e.g. textiles). Finally, moral rather than material
incentives is emphasized as the prime form of motivation.
Thus, in the system of central budgeting, the "administration of things" provides greater possibility for eliminating
mercantile and economic incentives. In 1963, two systems
of economic organization and ideology were emerging representing different sectors of the Cuban economy. A confrontation was inevitable. The central issue was the viability of market socialism as an organizational model
during the transition to communism.

The Great Debate over economic organization represented two divergent views concerning the transition to
socialism. While each group accepted comprehensive planning, they disagreed about the economic laws regulating
the socialist transition and the institutional forms that
best corresponded to those laws.[26]

Supporters of a greater reliance on the market,
decentralized economic organization and decision-making
and material incentives argued that the law of value operated
in all sectors of the Cuban economy. In their view so long
as the productive forces were unable to provide for the
distribution of consumer goods according to need, the stage
of commodity production could not be willed away through
changes in juridical forms. Centralized organization
designed to circumvent the market were beyond Cuba's current
level of technological and administrative capacity. Consequently centralization would result in the misallocation
of resources, inefficiency, bureaucracy and ultimately in
the breakdown of planning. Economic organization was an
aspect of the relationship to production and could not be
"higher than the historically determined level of the productive forces.

The Guevarist opposition rejected both the "economism"
of their argument as well as the applicability of the law of

value to the transition to socialism. The basic elements
of their argument were: First, the law of value was not
merely an expression of a universal problem of relative
scarcity but an historical phenomenon that reached its
fullest development under the capitalist mode of production. Therefore, changes in juridical relationships
that resulted from the socialization of the means of
production did affect the law of value. Second, the pursuit of socialist values required interference with the law
of value and the implicit ethics of the marketplace. Once
the law of value was distorted through planning, how could
you determine what it was? Third, the ethics of communism
based on non-market relationships could only be realized
under a centralized system of administration. But Guevara
never fully explored the connection between centralization
and worker participation in decision-making. Fourth,
contradictions between the relationship to production and
the forces of production were inevitable during the transitional phase. But they could be overcome by the development of administrative and technical skills and through
the growth of revolutionary consciousness. Thus, Guevara's
aim was to consciously use the process of socialist economic
development as a force to create a new socialist morality.

Fidel never formally entered the debate, although in
1965 he seemed to display impatience with the controversy
when he argued "our obligation as revolutionaries is not
to theorize in the field of philosophy." Moreover, in the
same speech, his support of material incentives seemed to
suggest opposition to Guevara.[27] Nevertheless, beginning
in 1966 Cuba moved decisively to adopt Che's organizational
model and by 1967 all organisms were operating under
radicalized versions of central budgeting. Fidel not only
adopted Guevara's ideas but carried them forward more rapidly
and in ways that went beyond the arguments of his comrade.

The Radicalization of Economic
Organization: Phase III

1966 marked the beginning of a new phase in the
evolution of economic organization. During the earlier
period, economic organization was linked to the practical
problems of nationalization, social justice and the transition to socialism. The new period seemed to signal a
conscious effort to develop a communist society and create
el hombre nuevo (The New Man).
During this phase the transformation of social
consciousness (social character) was linked very closely
to organizational forms. Market socialism was regarded
not merely as a contradiction in terms, but a road to

capitalism. Thus Fidel argued:[28]

>The problem is not in equalizing salaries and
>placing emphasis on the distribution of incomes.
>If one limits oneself to that, one does not yet
>break with the conception of a society founded
>on money. What we wish is to demystify money
>and not rehabilitate it. We propose to abolish
>it totally.
>
>Man will liberate himself completely from his
>lust for money only when all his necessities
>are able to be satisfied outside his wages.
>But it is not possible to prepare the advent
>of this period of communism of abundance while
>continuing to apply the method of the old society.

The emphasis upon the money motive has had special consequences for economic organization.

1. The New System of Economic Management:[29]

    The introduction of the new system of economic
management in 1967 radically extended Che's system of Central Budgeting. The new system of economic management
eliminated transactions between unidades within the socialized sector. Under the guidelines set by the annual plan,
firms entered into direct contractual relations but no
monetary or credit relations were involved. Records of
receipt and transfer of goods were kept but no payments
were required. Mercantile relations still occurred in
foreign trade, in final sales to consumers, in wage pay-
ment and in the private sector but in the latter three
cases they were, as we shall see, seriously limited. Since
unidades received materials for production without monetary
exchange, a major function of banks and the treasury was
eliminated. Domestically, the major purpose of financial
planning was keeping the wage fund in balance with the
value of consumer goods -- a task made exceedingly difficult because all taxes were eliminated under the new model.
Moreover, the deemphasis of money undermined consciousness
of financial controls.
    The new system of direction raised significant prob-
lems for economic control and measurement. Under this
system traditional economic measures became obsolete. Thus,
analysis based on production costs and revenues were useless and misleading. This was due to two related factors.
First, the price freeze and rationing had destroyed any
real relationship between value and price. Moreover, value
of final goods were designed to reflect social rather than
market factors. Second, labor policy called for the

separation of the relationship between wages and output (work). Thus, the new system of economic management had to confront the complex problem of devising new economic measures that were applicable to this economic model (an exceedingly complex task that has not yet been achieved).

The immediate consequence has been to place prime importance on physical rather than value measures. As a consequence Cuba's reliance on accounting, including cost accounting has been virtually eliminated, and in its place the system has turned logically to statistical analysis of data, such as delivered output, consumption of raw materials, inventories, etc., expressed in physical units. The goal is to develop a statistical system that would facilitate highly centralized planning.

The new system of economic direction is a logical extension of centralization of economic planning. Therefore, Cuba has moved rapidly to introduce advanced mathematical techniques into its planning apparatus. The latest computer technology is planned to process information and coordinate decisions. Indeed, a visit to the top levels of the planning hierarchy leaves an impression of a relatively technically advanced system. Yet, even on this level contradictions are apparent. By 1968, Cuba had not yet codified her principal products and activities, essential elements of input-output analysis. But more significantly, a unit of account of economic cost, which makes aggregation and comparison possible, had not been developed. In practice, monetary measures are still used to estimate costs, and shadow prices are employed to calculate the "actual" cost of production, particularly to account for changes in the price of imported materials that play such an important role in Cuban production costs. But even this procedure is still in its infancy and is only employed for selected goods. Ultimately, Cuba's organizational model is leading economists to experiment with a non-monetary measure of relative costs such as man-hours of labour time. Cuban economists have begun experimenting with a unit of account that would translate all output in terms of a unit of simple labour necessary to produce a given quantity of sugar -- a commodity that accounts for approximately 85 percent of export earnings.

Ideologically, Fidel has argued that the commodity myth must be exploded if man is to fully appreciate the social and community implications of productive relationships. Human labour would then be expressed in real terms, rather than in money, its fetished commodity form. But monetary measures still remain the simplest way to deal with the complexities of modern economic relations. And, more significantly, the real test of demystification lies in the real relationship to production that the new system has introduced. And to this we shall shortly turn.

2. Technical versus Political Cadres

The new system of management had special significance for administrators and technicians, particularly at
the unidad level. On the one hand, the leadership placed
increasing emphasis on revolutionary and political
commitment. President Dorticos argued:

> We don't conceive . . . the possible usefulness
> of an economist that is not absolutely and fully
> identified with the objectives of this revolution
> and with its defined conception. . .
> And consequently, it is just and valid to affirm
> that we don't think an economist is either useful
> or usable if in addition to being a good techni-
> cian he is not, above all, a good revolutionary
> in theory and in practice . . . . It is a task
> that can be understood not only with an adequate
> technical preparation but moreover with an
> attitude and a positive presence before the
> difficulties that can only be developed by an
> independence from personal temperaments with
> the presence of revolutionary faith and of an
> absolute conviction in the correctness of the
> Cuban revolution.[30]

On the other hand, the Cuban revolution has stressed the
importance of technical development and education. The
shortage of technical and administrative cadres has always
been singled out by Fidel and Che as the major constraint
on economic development. Of course, the ideal administrator
should be technically competent as well as a revolutionary.
Yet, at this time Cuba's model places special importance
on political rather than technical criteria in the
management of the production unit.[31] Thus, in 1969, it
became obvious that little economic analysis took place
at the work place. Statistical data were sent to the
Empresa, or regional level, for analysis, comparison,
aggregation. Thus, economic control and responsibility
were removed from the production units and transferred to
technicians who were less likely to be militants.

This procedure was consistent with the functional
requirements of the model. Since material incentives no
longer guided managerial and worker behaviour, the major
function of management was to mobilize worker participation
in the major economic efforts of the regime; freed from
"paper work" and "money illusions," the manager can concentrate on the problems of work and social consciousness.

But there is a relationship between social consciousness and economic control and responsibility, a factor
that has not been fully appreciated in the development of
Cuban economic organization.

3. Moral versus Material Incentives

A motivational system based on economic rewards and penalties was inconsistent with the new system of economic management and centralized planning. As a result, Cuba moved rapidly to eliminate many of the remaining material incentives that had been part of Che's central budgeting system. The separation between work and wages was rapidly introduced. Thus, bonuses or penalties for fulfillment or nonfulfilment of work norms were eliminated. Piece rates were rapidly phased out and, where they were part of traditional seasonal work patterns, attempts were made to develop steady year-round employment. Income differentials were narrowed through efforts to reduce the high salaries for new entrants in the labour force and to raise the income of the lowest groups.[32] There were strong tendencies to reduce the use of economic penalties to enforce labour discipline, and the system of work norms, while still in effect, seemed, at least in 1969, to be loosely enforced. How could one norm a worker's conscience? Organized efforts in 1969 led to the virtual reunuciation of overtime pay. The salary scale developed prior to 1966 providing differentials was still in effect, but restrictions on personal consumption reduced their motivational significance.

Conscience or moral incentives were the means through which work and sacrifice would be induced and economic development fostered. Essentially moral incentives have been used as a lever for mass mobilization and to convey the idea that work is a social duty rather than a means of personal advancement. In Cuba, the "moralization of work" has replaced the carrot of material incentives as the means of modernization. Thus economic development would grow simultaneously with social consciousness, social commitment and egalitarianism; essential elements in constructing communism.

The renewed emphasis on moral incentives, particularly in 1968, was reflected in new experiments with socialist emulation. The emulation system that had emerged after 1962 was suddenly abandoned in 1966. Bureaucratic and complicated regulations had provided few possibilities for worker participation or recognition of particular problems within individual enterprises. Moreover, the Stakhanovite aspect of the system led to competition among managers for prizes and status, and motivated them to falsify reports.

The transition to a new system began in 1966 and 1967 with the development of industrial efficiency plans. General goals were set up by individual ministries. These general targets were then translated into concrete plans by individual firms. After six months of experimentation, a decision was made to tie the efficiency plans to socialist emulation. The previous bureaucratic structure and complicated point system was abandoned. Although competition between plants was still occasionally practised, the central idea was self-emulation where individual workers and unidades set their own compromisos (goals) and tried to fulfill them. In 1968 emulation plans were connected to historic periods in Cuban history, culminating, on July 26; with the possibility of winning the Moncada flag. Thus, theoretically, every enterprise could win a flag. Winning did not mean being better, but rather, fulfilling one's compromisos (i.e., efficiency plans).

The role of Cuban trade unions (CTC-R) seemed unclear in 1969. They were assigned a major task of fulfilling socialist emulation goals. But their bureaucratic structure and limited function in the plant seriously undermined their effectiveness. There was considerable speculation that Cuba would soon eliminate or replace the trade unions whose function seemed unclear under the new system of management. Experimentation was underway to establish an Advanced Workers Movement that would replace the older system of selecting vanguard workers. In 1969 the Advanced Workers Movement had replaced the local trade union in some factories. These experiments were aimed partly at revitalizing mass participation in the work centre. But in general these efforts were mainly concerned with mass mobilization and increasing work efficiency rather than worker participation in social and economic decisions.

But moral incentives have radically extended the original commitment to social equality and ruralism. First, rationing reduced the consumption patterns that had separated upper income groups from lower income groups. While, paradoxically, scarcity tended to magnify small differences, in general, shared austerity also reduced the disparities in the distribution of consumption and guaranteed minimum standards of living for the entire population. Second, the new orientation de-emphasized private consumption and expanded collective goods and services made available free or with slight charges. This included the continued extension of education, medical and health care as well as free local public telephones, transportation for funerals, weddings, recreation, and sporting events. Collective meals were served at work centres and schools. Rent, which was already abolished for many consumers, was eliminated for all families with per capita incomes under twenty-five pesos per month. Fourth, mass mobilization has significantly affected the Cuban social structure and re-emphasized the rural bias of the revolution. Large "armies" of volunteer labour participate in the Zafra and in thousands of microprojects. Youth and communist brigades have been created. Mass Education has been increasingly concerned with problems

of economic and technological development and students,
teachers, intellectuals, and urban workers have been
intimately involved in rural development; thus reducing
occupational and regional distinctions. The plans to
bring the schools to the country, and, more recently, to
remove the university from its urban base and connect
more closely to the work environment, are all part of the
same pattern.

But these policies are not seen as ends in
themselves. Thus education, economic and technological
change are essential pre-requisites for a communist society.
Only in the technologically and economically advanced
society would the "moralization of work" end. The work
ethic -- work as a social duty -- would be replaced by
the identification with work as a creative activity.

4. Revolutionary Offensive: The Death of the Private Sector

It is inconceivable that Cuba's organizational
model could operate effectively within an economy having
a significant private sector. Yet in 1966, the beginning
of the radicalization process, a considerable private
sector existed (see Table 1). Thus a large proportion of
the labour force was not only outside the economic
organizational model but working in the private sector,
either in retail trade, service, light industry or
agriculture. This not only undermined the centralized
planning system but provided an ideological alternative
to Cuba's radical model. Indeed, under the condition of
severe shortages, the private sector provided an illegal
source of consumer goods and was competing successfully
for scarce resources and labour. Thus, the prototype of
the "consumer goods society" worked within the heart of
the Cuban system, playing on the inherent contradictions
and inefficiencies within the socialized sector.

On March 13, 1968 the Revolutionary Offensive was
launched to eliminate the remaining private sector,[33] and
to significantly limit the role of private enterprise in
agriculture as well as to intensify the ideological
campaign for revolutionary commitment. It demonstrated
Fidel's commitment to radicalize the revolution despite
serious economic difficulties. Thus, he rejected the NEP
alternative, that is, market socialism. But the Government
added to its difficult organizational problems the necessity
of planning and managing the many small enterprises in
services and retail trade.[34] In many cases this simply
meant the reduction or termination of neighbourhood stores.

The move to end private enterprise in agriculture
has also become part of the Revolutionary Offensive --
but this has proceeded more cautiously and less publicly.
In 1968 the Cuban Government revealed that private
agricultural production was supervised by and included in

TABLE 1

DISTRIBUTION OF THE LABOUR FORCE BETWEEN THE
PRIVATE AND PUBLIC SECTORS
JANUARY, 1965*

Total Labour Force	2,492,919
Unemployed	376,293
Employed	2,116,626
Public	1,355,259
Private	761,367
By Sector	
Industry	
Public	281,755
Private	105,425
Construction	
Public	93,404
Private	20,247
Transport	
Public	71,585
Private	10,987
Communications	
Public	11,690
Private	979
Commerce	
Public	208,661
Private	53,606
Agriculture	
Public	364,508
Private	304,299
Other Productive Activities	
Public	8,608
Private	70,238
Services	
Public	287,085
Private	202,516

* Source: Ministry of Labour, Balance de los Recursos
Laborales, January, 1965.

the nationwide development plans   what Dumont has called
the Third Agrarian Reform.   Dumont summarized the process
as follows:

> Until 1967 a controller of ANAP (National
> Association of Small Farmers) asked peasants
> their forecasts with respect to planting.   In
> the year 1967 the ANAP suggested modifications
> that seemed desirable.   In 1968 he gave them
> orders established by the regional agricultural
> plan.   In 1968 there began a campaign of exclusive-
> delivery to the State of all available production.
> First presented as purely voluntary, it was then
> made obligatory with the publication of sanctions
> against those who did not participate.[35]

Moreover, peasants were forbidden to hire their own labour.
In effect, peasant land holdings were incorporated within
the large granjas.   In exchange, the State provided
labour, machinery, and technical advice.   A campaign was
initiated during this period for peasants to voluntarily
sell their land to the State.   Model projects such as
San Andres were also given considerable publicity.   They
have been held up as examples of the voluntary integration
of the campesino into socialist agriculture.   But, rural
workers are permitted one hectare of land for subsistence,
which has influenced their effort.
   As a result of the Revolutionary Offensive, Cuba
could report that in less than a decade it had become the
socialist country with the highest percentage of state-
owned property.   Yet, the Revolutionary Offensive and its
strong ideological undertones reflected deeper underlying
social and economic forces, to which Cuban economic
organization was a response.

Ideology and Reality

1.   Economic Organization and Socialist Accumulation

   In part, the radicalization of Cuban economic
organization was a response to problems immanent in the
Cuban model: the spontaneous growth of the private sector
and the corresponding rise of the black market; the
exposure of corruption at the highest levels of the army
and trade unions; the persistent growth of bureaucracy
as well as the apparent contradiction between demands of
the accounting procedures of Central Budgeting and the
available cadres at the base.   These problems were not
unrelated to the growth of criticism among some members
of the old Communist Party within and outside Cuba, who
saw both Cuba's domestic and foreign policies as romantic

and naive. But in particular, response to economic
problems was necessary as GNP in 1966 declined by more
than four percent.[36] The radicalization of Cuban economic
organization was closely linked to the decision to intensify
the rate of economic development. The unfolding economic
strategy of the post-1966 period reflected a determined
effort to confront the persistent problem of economic
stagnation and inefficiency.

The new strategy originated in 1963, when a
deepening balance of payments crisis forced a shift away
from industry to agriculture as the leading economic
sector. Essentially, the strategy called for capital
accumulation through sugar exports. This would provide
needed foreign reserves -- first, to develop agriculture
in which Cuba had a comparative advantage, and later, after
increasing agricultural productivity, to transfer this
surplus to industrial development. The greater potential
yield in agricultural investment was explained primarily
in "terms of the productivity-increasing potential of
applying advanced techniques to activities such as cane
and animal husbandry, where previously considerable long-
term practical experience coexisted with a traditional
primitive technology."[37] The post-1966 period marked a
rapid increase in the rate of capital accumulation, leading
symbolically to the production of ten million tons of
sugar in 1970.

The most significant effect of the policy was to
rapidly convert Cuba's labour surplus into labour shortage.
The unemployment problem disappeared and a new problem of
discovering sources of labour reserves emerged. This was
particularly troublesome because the initial income policy
of the Government had set in motion a large migration of
labour from rural to urban employment, particularly
services. In part, this was the result of the growth of
small towns and state farms in the interior of the
country where social and educational services were rapidly
expanding. The reduction in the number and productivity
of the traditional cane cutter -- a seasonal worker --
was particularly troublesome. Thus the rural poor were
either moving to the higher income centres of the towns
or taking part of their increased income and economic
security in additional leisure. The rapid expansion of
the service sector from one quarter to one third of the
labour force, a sector with considerable disguised
unemployment, reflected the rapid expansion of the
bureaucratic apparatus, as well as the expansion of
social services (see Table 2).

Moreover, the increase in the rate of gross investment from an average 18 percent in the period 1961-1963
to 31 percent of GNP in 1968 required a reduction in
personal consumption. As a result, rationing -- established
in 1962 -- was extended to include virtually all consumer

TABLE 2

ACTIVE POPULATION BY PRODUCTIVE SECTOR IN CUBA,
1958-1965*
(000's)

Sector	1958/59	1960/61	1965
Agriculture	813.0	862.0	838.0
Industry and Mining	378.5	411.8	390.0
Construction	82.8	71.7	123.0
Transport	80.6	86.5	90.1
Commerce	284.3	265.5	258.8
Services and Others	558.3	572.7	846.1
Total	2,197.5	2,270.2	2,546.0

* Source: Republic of Cuba, JUCEPLAN, Central Statistics
Department. Resumen de Estadisticas de
Población, No. 2, Havana, 1966, p. 120.

goods, as well as a reduction in the variety and quantity
of commodities available for personal consumption. By
1969 personal consumption of durable goods virtually
disappeared and most nonfood items, such as clothing, were
distributed irregularly. Thus, Cuba's strategy implied a
rapid expansion in employment co-existing with a planned
reduction in percapita personal consumption. It was this
apparent contradiction -- the need to increase work,
expand and shift the labour force while reducing personal
consumption -- that set the stage for Cuba's distinctive
growth strategy: economic development with moral incentives.
    First, in 1966 Cuba was faced with a decline in
agricultural labour at a time when extensive growth of this
sector was planned. Reversing rural-urban migration through
a programme of resettlement made little sense since economic
plans called for a technological revolution in agriculture
that would shortly reduce agricultural labour requirements.
Therefore, the short-run solution required the redeployment
of urban labour to agriculture, particuarly during planting
and harvesting. The type of labour required was the most
menial and unskilled. Material incentives would have had
to be unusually high to induce urban labour into these

occupations. Moreover, the use of wage differentials made little sense because the transfer was frequently of workers from more skilled and productive activities to less skilled, that is, from industry to agriculture. The moralization of work under these circumstances is quite rational and reliance on unpaid voluntary labour is reasonable. Since 1962 Cuba has increasingly relied on this method to mobilize labour for agriculture. In 1968 perhaps 15-20 percent of the agricultural labour force was made up of nonagricultural labour.[38] Such a transfer of labour could only make economic sense if it was based on moral rather than material incentives. Moreover, such a transfer of labour inevitably disrupted other sectors of the economy. Under these circumstances of extremely tight factor supply, market socialism was untenable.

Second, the planned reduction in personal consumption made expansion of employment possible, only through the worker's heightened sense of social commitment and conscience. Furthermore, the already low level of available consumer goods made increased capital accumulation possible primarily through the expansion of unpaid labour. Therefore, Cuba seemed to be in a stage where the dangers of "primitive accumulation" -- a period in capitalist develop-ment where force was used to extract the economic surplus -- was possible.

Yet, if additional labour can be supplied voluntarily, that may be a more consistent translation of the concept of primitive accumulation in a socialist society than that used in the Soviet experience. The translation of primitive accumulation to socialist accumulation was an essential element of the organizational model. But if moral incentives fail then the ominous necessity of coercion must be faced. While the commitment of the Cuban population to the revolution has reduced the reliance upon force, conciencia is also a scarce resource and the failure to use it efficiently may be one of Cuba's fundamental problems.

Finally, the sharp decline in personal consumption made reliance on material incentives politically dangerous. An emphasis on material incentives during a period when workers were asked to increase hours worked, and to reduce personal consumption, would merely serve to heighten the sense of economic sacrifice and exaggerate economic distinctions and privileges. Politically, under these circumstances an emphasis on collective efforts toward social goals was more reasonable.

2. Cost of Social Conscience

The ideological preoccupation with the commodity fetishism problem and its relationship to economic organiza-tion becomes comprehensible when related to Cuba's economic

strategy. But it is precisely the contradictions between
Cuba's economic strategy and economic organization that have
challenged Cuba's ideological goals. Conversely, ideology
has frequently become a rationalization for economic and
social policy. In order to fully understand these
contradictions, as Charles Bettelheim has suggested, "it
is necessary . . . to bring to light the real social
relations that are revealed and hidden, at the same time,
by the forms of representation and the elaborated ideological
notions based on them."[39]

Cuba's economic strategy made the reliance on
material incentives and market relations inoperable. In a
system of organization based on moral incentives which
eliminates the direct connection between individual
performance and reward, the individual's motivation for
increasing his economic performance must come from a
heightened identification with the goals of the nation
(internalization of social goals). Paradoxically, over-
zealous political leaders can undermine this commitment.
This had become in 1968-1969 a serious problem since
economic decisions at the base were politically rather than
economically motivated. This problem had been compounded
by an over-ambitious economic strategy associated with the
ten million ton goal which overburdened Cuba's fragile
economic controls and planning structure.

Economic controls, through a system of planning, must
serve as a substitute for the market and economic incentives.
Yet, if national output and efficiency do not increase, a
cynical attitude may develop which undermines the worker's
identification with the system -- an essential ingredient
of the model. As of the moment, effective planning and
economic controls are extremely weak in Cuba. Economic
decisions depend on a bureaucratic planning structure that
must translate information about physical output collected
from the base into operational instructions. Managers
under this sytem are seriously circumscribed from making
independent decisions based on economic analysis (nor do
they often have the skills to do this). As a result, the
data collected have little meaning to management and are
therefore frequently inaccurate and under-utilized.
This is reflected in the hostility sometimes expressed
about the useless information that is sent up to the
Empresas or Ministries that, the managers felt, is rarely
used. On the other hand, instructions from above are
frequently beyond the competence and skills that exist at
the local level. Moreover, Havana-based administrators
have no real knowledge of local problems. Despite romantic
feelings, a man with a sixth grade education has difficulty
collecting and using the simplest statistical data. This
is particularly problematic in such critical sectors as
agriculture where large-scale state farms have become the
basic organizational unit. As a result, success is frequently
measured simply by fulfilment of gross output targets
expressed in physical terms and by the conservation of scarce

raw materials. The fragile planning is further undermined by "overcommitment" of resources, frequently a product of revolutionary enthusiasm and the uncertainty of foreign supplies. The inevitable has occurred: first, shortages and bottlenecks have reduced industrial capacity and worker productivity; second, the decision making process has been plagued by bureaucracy, so that a parallel planning apparatus that bypasses the existing bureaucratic structure has been created to ensure the fulfilment of special or urgent strategic economic goals; these special plans are under Fidel's personal direction. Third, there has been a large turnover of managerial and administrative personnel. Problems similar to 1962 have re-emerged.

To meet these inefficiencies, managers have frequently called upon the worker's conscience, that is, labour's willingness to work overtime without pay. Thus, moral incentives have served to compensate for the inefficiencies and irrationalities of the economic organization. Indeed, moral incentives often foster the irrational uses of labour and capital, since managers do not feel compelled to complete tasks that could be done during the normal work day. Nor do they feel compelled to explore sources of inefficiency. Administrators frequently considered overtime or voluntary work costless, and were often perplexed when asked whether they had wasted conciencia in fulfilling their goals. The same attitude was prevalent in agriculture. Since no production unit assumed the cost of voluntary work, more labour was frequently demanded than was needed in order to guarantee results. Often, the irrational use of moral incentives results in problems of worker apathy and discontent. The cost of conciencia (Cuba's most precious resource) needs to be considered.

3. Conscience and Compulsion: Some Dilemmas of the Cuban Model

In the face of these difficulties Cuban economic organization has undergone some significant changes. First, the search for organizational efficiency has led to some imitation of the military model. The military is the most efficient organization in Cuba and considerable talent has been shifted to this sector. Recently, military techniques have been used in organizing large production units and directing large units of labour. Command Posts have been set up throughout Cuba that resemble the operational headquarters of an army. These techniques should not be confused with regimentation. Their purpose is to establish more effective controls over the organization and deployment of labour and capital, particularly in agriculture. Moreover, labour brigades have frequently employed military techniques and schedules. However, the model has not effectively dealt with the problems of bureaucracy, particu-

larly in developing greater responsibility and self-
reliance at the production level. Nor has it effectively
helped foster real participation in the decision making
process. Inefficiency and the absence of effective control
still plague Cuban economic organization.

A second response to inefficiency is reflected in
labour force controls. According to Risquet, the Labour
Minister, previous labour legislation that penalized
workers with discharge and loss of salary had become
outmoded.[40] At first, increased moral pressures were to
be used. A labour file was created for each worker where
merits and demerits are to be entered after his work
record has been discussed at semi-annual assemblies. The
second phase was the promulgation, in 1971, of an anti-
loafing law aimed at dealing with absenteeism and bringing
all able-bodied men between the ages of 17 and 60 into the
labour force. The penalties for absenteeism ranged from
working under the vigilance of other workers and revolutionary
organizations, to working in a rehabilitation centre for up
to one year.[41] Thus Cuba's economic model posed the
serious issue of using coercion in pursuing economic
development.

In an interview in Havana, Regino Boti argued that
after a socialist revolution a period of primitive accumulation may be inevitable. A socialist revolution inevitably
leads workers to reduce their efforts because they think
that the end of employer control means less work. Therefore, he argued, all socialist revolutions face the
inevitable dilemma between economic development and consent.
In Cuba this problem has been complicated because the
initial welfare and redistribution policies of the Government had retarded the rate of investment and created
illusions about the relationship between work and economic
development. The question therefore, Boti argued, then
becomes how do you get workers to increase their efforts
and discipline. Thus Boti's analysis raised some critical
questions: Does Cuba's experiment suggest that compulsive
work requirements are the inevitable consequences of an
organizational model based on socialist values? Is low
worker productivity and absenteeism functionally related to
Cuba's radical efforts to eliminate material incentives?
The economic problems that were admitted in a remarkably
candid speech by Fidel in 1970 have reopened these questions.

Our analysis suggests that the roots of Cuba's
economic problems must be found in deeper sources than moral
incentives. In the first place Cuba's economic strategy
required massive increases and deployment of labour. This
created an overcommitment of available labour resources.
Part of the difficulty can be explained by the particular
nature of surplus labour in pre-revolutionary Cuba. In
large measure under-utilization of labour was a seasonal
problem. Thus, during the months of peak labour requirements,

the "reserve army of labour" was sharply reduced or
disappeared. The revolution over-estimated the labour
surplus.[42] Consequently, increasing numbers of outside
workers, students, and the military, are needed to fulfil
agricultural targets, disrupting production schedules in
the industrial and service sectors. One of the results
is the need to exhort workers to work longer hours or
move, when needed, to critical sectors. But these efforts
are frequently frustrated because of bottlenecks of poor
planning. Thus, workers may spend many hours in the factory
or in agriculture but considerable time is wasted or
misused. And despite the large increase in land cultivation,
"season after season, . . . the administrators of numerous
state farms were obliged to decide which harvests should be
sacrificed entirely, or, at least, which crops should be
harvested outside their optimal time-period at the cost of
a decline in their volume and/or value."[43] Such pressures
on labour resources lead to uneconomical hoarding of
labour and a work ethic that may contradict the goals of
the revolution. It creates a cynical attitude on the part
of workers toward the Government's exhortations about
labour discipline. The process of primitive accumulation
is not a "law" of social development but rather a function
of policy decisions.

A second aspect of the strategy required a reduction
in personal consumption while expanding (relatively)
employment. Under these circumstances it is quite logical
for workers to take part of their real income in the form
of reduced effort and increased leisure. Increasing
aggregate personal consumption has nothing to do with a
system of differential economic incentives. As Ernest
Mandel, a defender of moral incentives, has argued, "raising
the producer's standard of living is a major way to stimulate
output and raise labour productivity."[44] Ideological preoccupation with the disappearance of money is, to a degree
then, a rationalization of austerity.

The decline in money as a medium of exchange reflects
a decline in real personal income, that is, shortages of
consumer goods. Its consequences show up in worker
resistance and cynicism. Thus, shortages tend to undermine
the system of moral incentives by undermining social
conscience.

Moreover, rather than diminishing in importance,
scarcity reinforces the desire for material goods. True,
rationing does provide a more equitable distribution of
subsistence than would exist under a free market and many
basic services are virtually free. But under conditions of
severe shortages, small decreases and additions to consumption assume great importance. As a result informal markets
exist where goods are bartered or traded at unofficial
prices. The decline in consumption is related to the high
rate of planned investment. Unlike the shortages that emerged

in 1962, Cuba claims that the present phase of austerity
has been planned. But there is a relationship between
rate of capital accumulation and the rate of compulsion.

Third, Cuba's development strategy required a
highly centralized organizational model where material
incentives were inappropriate. Economic incentives could
not move hundreds of thousands of workers into the Zafra.
Political rather than technical cadres direct the productive
process under the new system of economic management. Thus
far, the results have seriously undermined effective
economic control. There is considerable evidence that a
highly centralized economic organization is beyond Cuba's
present administrative capacity. Political enthusiasm is
no substitute for technical and organizational knowledge.
This is reflected in the high rate of turnover of politically-
committed administrators. Nor does the winning of the
Moncada flag necessarily imply economic efficiency.

But what types of economic controls are compatible
with moral incentives? The issue becomes apparent when
confronting the problem of labour discipline. Economic
planning depends on a reliable labour force. High labour
turnover and absenteeism are inimical to planning and
efficiency. But since economic rewards and penalties have
been rejected, only social pressures, and ultimately
compulsion, remain as methods to deal with these problems.
Policies that lead to premature controls and direction of
the labour market may lead to unnecessary compulsion. A
supporter of Che's defence of moral incentives cautioned
that "to abolish the private ownership of labour power
before the society can assure the satisfaction of all its
people's basic needs would actually introduce forced
labour."[45]

In the face of these contradictions there is a
natural tendency for the Government to increase the use of
ideological instruments to develop greater expression of
social commitment. This is the basis of the Revolutionary
Offensive and the "radicalization" of Cuban ideology which
has virtually declared a moratorium on public debate over
economic and social policies. These developments have
resulted in the externalization of revolutionary ethics.
But a system of incentives that relies on directives from
above becomes just another form of repression. As Alberto
Mora, a participant in the debate over moral incentives
warned:

> We must at the same time assure that the super-
> structure is so organized as to prevent the
> substitution of the money motive by the power
> motive.[46]

Thus, worker-resistance is also reflected in the absence
of real participation in decision making. While mass

organizations such as the Committee for the Defence of
the Revolution and the Federation of Cuban Women have
recruited large numbers of para-professionals in the
extensive dissemination of health, welfare, and child-care
services, these organizations remain primarily transmission
belts for centralized party decisions. Mass meetings are
used primarily to gain support for policy decisions
already made. Fidel seemed to understand this shortcoming
when he recently said:

> We have been able to unleash the energy,
> interest, and will of millions. Now we
> must channel this energy into greater
> participation in decisions that affect
> their lives.

The economic crisis of 1970 has opened a new phase in the
discussion about economic organization. Castro's speeches,
since July 1970, have revealed considerable frankness about
economic and social problems. These initial problems are,
after all, part of an early process of experimentation;
Cuba's organizational model is only five years old.
Certainly an insignificant period to test its efficacy;
nor do productivity statistics include the large investment
in training and education. Nevertheless, if our analysis
is correct, Cuba faces a serious dilemma in the immediate
future. Some modification in Cuba's ambitious economic
strategy and organization to provide greater local
responsibility will be necessary, if the link between
socialist consciousness and economic development are to be
encouraged and the connection between economic development
and compulsion dissolved. This will also require a greater
concordance between ideology and reality.

There are some indications that the demystification
process has already begun as _praxis_ once again triumphs
over ideology. Thus, 1970 seems to mark the beginning of
a new phase in the relationship between moral incentives,
economic organization and economic development. This new
chapter will have much to instruct us about the relationship
between socialist economic development and _conciencia_.

NOTES

1. Karl Marx, <u>The Eighteenth Brumaire of Louis Bonaparte</u>,
    New World paperback, p. 15. The same tension between
    revolutionary will (voluntarism) and recognition of
    historic constraints are exhibited in the Eighteenth
    Brumaire. A few pages after this citation Marx
    writes: "The social revolution of the nineteenth
    century cannot draw its poetry from the past, but
    only from the future. It cannot begin with itself
    before it has stripped off all superstition in
    regard to the past. Earlier revolutions required
    recollections of past world history in order to drug
    themselves concerning their own content. In order
    to arrive at its own content the revolution of the
    nineteenth century must let the dead bury their
    dead. There the phrase went beyond the content;
    here the content goes beyond the phrase."

2. Cuba has named 1971 the year of productivity.

3. Leontief, W., "The Trouble with Cuban Socialism," <u>The
    New York Rieview of Books</u>, January 7, 1971, p. 22.

4. Ibid. For a similar view see the writings of Carmelo
    Mesa-Lago. Inside Cuba the view is expressed by
    those who were supporters of the system of self-
    management.

5. See Benjamin Ward, <u>The Socialist Economy</u>, Random House,
    1967, pp. 36-37, who argues that questions of
    incentives within the socialist context have hardly
    been explored.

6. In this paper I have not considered the many important
    political factors influencing policy (e.g., U.S.
    imperialism) nor have I attempted to describe in
    any detail the changes in the structure of economic
    organization and planning. For the latter see
    Juceplan, <u>La planificación economica en Cuba</u>,
    Santiago de Chile, 1968.

7. This is particularly evident in the discussion about
    the economic rationality of socialist economy. In
    dealing with the Misses-Lange et al. controversy
    Professor Dobb argued that "most of the socialist
    critics of Professor Misses have argued, in one key
    or another, that a socialist economy can escape the
    irrationality which is predicted of it if, but only
    if, it closely imitates the mechanism of the
    competitive market and consents to be ruled by the
    <u>values which this market affirms</u>." (my emphasis)
    Maurice Dobb, <u>Political Economy and Capitalism</u>,

International Publishers, 1945, p. 273. Of course, there have been outstanding social scientists who have seen this relationship, e.g., Marx, Weber, Polanyi, Fromm, Riesman to name just a few.

8. Marx's analysis of ideology is illustrated in the following passage:
In considering such transformations (social revolutions) the distinction should always be made between the material transformation of the economic conditions of production, which can be determined with the precision of natural science, and the legal, political, religious, aesthetic, or philosophic -- in short, ideological forms in which men become conscious of this conflict and fight it out. Just as our opinion of an individual is not based on what he thinks of himself, so can we not judge such a period of transformation by its own consciousness; on the contrary, this consciousness must rather be explained from the contradictions of material life, from the existing conflict between the social forces of production and the relations of production. (Karl Marx, A Contribution to the Critique of Political Economy, in Feuer (ed.) Marx and Engels, Anchor, p. 44.) Marx's approach was evident in his earlier writing, thus: "The immediate task of philosophy, one the saintly form (religion) of human self-alienation has been unmasked, is to unmask self-alienation in its unholy forms (ideology)." (Karl Marx, Toward the Critique of Hegel's Philosophy of Right, in ibid., p. 263.)

9. C. Richard Fagen, "Continuities in the Style and Strategies of Cuban Revolutionary Politics" (mimeographed) 1970.

10. Alberto Mora, "On Certain Problems of Building Socialism," in Bertram Silverman (ed.), Man and Socialism in Cuba, Atheneum, 1971, p. 329.

11. For a description of the natioanlization process see: Dudley Seers (ed.), Cuba: The Economic and Social Revolution, The University of North Carolina Press, 1964. James O'Connor, The Origin of Socialism in Cuba, Cornell, 1970, Chs. 5 & 6.

12. Luis Alvarez Rom, "Finance and Political Development," in Silverman (ed.), op. cit., p. 271.

13. Many of these observations are based on conversations with Cuban economist during the period 1968-1969 in Cuba and on JUCEPLAN, Notas sobre el nuevo sistema de dirección (mimeographed) 1968, hereafter, noted as Junta Report. For additional evidence that the

initial development of central finance did not
arise out of the need to develop the worker's
conscience see Alexis Codina, "Experiences of
Control Under the Budgetary System," in Silverman
(ed.), op. cit., pp. 204-206.

14. Ernesto Che Guevara, "On the Budgetary Finance System,"
in Silverman (ed.), op. cit., p. 130.
From a technological standpoint, we should
borrow the most advanced forms of economic administration available, from whatever source, so long as
they can be adopted for use in the new society . . .
the same rule applies with regard to technical
standards in production control and administration
. . . We might say, then, that as a technique the
predecessor of the budgetary finance system was
imperialist monopoly as it existed in Cuba . . .

15. Interestingly, Cuban planners cite ECLA advisors for
influencing their bias toward physical and structural rather than financial analysis -- see Junta
Report.

16. See Moshe Lewin, Lenin's Last Struggle, Vintage, 1970,
for discussion of these problems in the Soviet Union.

17. Codina, op. cit., pp. 206-208.

18. Junta Report, op. cit., p. 2. See also comments by
outside observers such as Rene Dumont, Cuba
Socialism and Development, Grove, 1970.

19. Obra Revolucionaria, No. 30, 1961.

20. These were Charles Bettelheim's estimates. See
Carmelo Meso-Lago, Availability and Reliability of
Statistics in Socialist Cuba, University of Pittsburgh,
1970, p. 50.

21. Based on H. Pollitt, "Employment Plans, Performance
and Future Prospects in Cuba," Overseas Studies
Committee Conference, 1970, University of Cambridge,
1970, pp. 11-12. Also C. Romeo, "Acerca del desarrollo
economico de Cuba," Cuba Socialista, December, 1965.

22. For a description of this earlier period see Edward
Boorstein,"The Economic Transformation of Cuba,"
Monthly Review Press, 1968.

23. For a compilation and discussion of the Debate, See
Silverman (ed.), op. cit.

24. See Dumont, op. cit., esp. pp. 115-133. The debate included some outside observers, and Dumont was one of the first to criticize centralization.

25. For a good description of the two systems see Sergio de Santis, "The Economic Debate in Cuba," International Socialist Review, August 1965. Neither system ever functioned in this ideal form. Nor did the system of self-finance become operational except in a restricted form during the 1963-1965 period.

26. For a more complete discussion of the -ebate see my introduction to Man and Socialism in Cuba: The Great Debate, op. cit.

27. See Fidel Castro's speech "Criterios de Nuestros Revolución," Cuba Socialista, September, 1965. In this speech Castro reveals a pronounced long-term commitment to moral incentives that probably accounts for Gerassi's suggestion that Fidel supported Che's position (see Venceremos, Clarion, 1968, p. 20). But Fidel's pragmatic approach strongly suggested the need to use material incentives. In the same speech he argued that it would be idealistic to assume that the large majority of workers cut cane from a sense of duty. Therefore, it is logical to use economic incentives for work that is of critical importance. As a consequence Mesa-Lago in his book, The Labor Sector and Socialist Distribution in Cuba, Praeger, 1968, p. 124, suggests that Fidel rejected Che's thesis.

28. Junta Central de Planificación, Sobre el Salario y la Organización del Trabajo, Habana, 1968. See also R.S. Karol, Guerrillas in Power, Hill and Wang, 1970, pp. 342-345.

29. Based on Junta Report, op. cit., Juceplan, La planificación en Cuba, op. cit., and interviews with Cuban economists.

30. Unpublished speech presented at Economic Institute in Havana, 1969.

31. For a recent discussion see Cuba Internacional, Febrero, 1970, p. 30.

32. The highest salary cited was 300 pesos for engineers.

33. "La Nacionalización de los Establecimientos Privados en la Ofensiva," El Militante Comunista, June, 1968. See also Gramma Weekly Review, March 31, 1968.

34. For a critical view of this approach see Mandel, op. cit., p. 81.

35. René Dumont, Cuba: Est-il Socialiste?, Paris, 1970, p. 92.

36. Mesa-Lago, op. cit., p. 51.

37. Based on Pollitt, op. cit., pp. 12-13.

38. More than fifty percent of the labor force was working in agriculture in 1969. See Gramma, April 1, 1969.

39. Charles Bettelheim, "The Transition to Socialism," Monthly Review, December, 1970, p. 5.

40. Verde Olivo, August 17, 1969, pp. 12-13.

41. For complete text see Gramma, Weekly Review, March 28, 1971, p. 2.

42. Pollitt, op. cit., p. 20.

43. Ibid.

44. Mandel, in Silverman (ed.), op. cit., p. 81.

45. Ibid.

46. Mora, in Silverman (ed.), op. cit., p. 334.

47. Fidel Castro Speech in Gramma, Weekly Review, August 25, 1971.

OPPRESSION BY ANY OTHER NAME: POWER

IN SEARCH OF LEGITIMACY IN GUATEMALA

Thomas Melville

and

Margarita Bradford Melville

Anthropologists have long had to distinguish between real and ideal culture in order to make sense of the universal dichotomy that exists between what people do and what they believe they do. John Beattie (1964:40) says that "social relationships are really quite complex abstractions from people's behaviour, implying both a factual, behavioral aspect, and an ideal, conceptual one . . . As constituents of systems of action they have consequences, and as constituents of systems of ideas they have meanings."

This essay deals primarily with a partial system of ideas, the ideology of the powerbrokers or so-called ruling class of Guatemala. It is not our intention to attempt to demonstrate what portion of the social scene in Guatemala is due to or rationalized by this ideology, but rather to demonstrate that the differential interpretation of the dominant concepts of this ideology by different segments of the population is a necessary prerequisite for that degree of integration in the centuries-old power configuration that persists.

This is not a novel approach. It was suggested to us by Edmund Leach's interpretation of ritual and myth in his Political Systems of Highland Burma. Leach states that such differential interpretation, as we mention:

> does not lead to intolerable
> misunderstandings and is due to the
> essential vagueness of all ritual state-
> ments. Ritual and mythology represent an
> ideal version of the social structure.
> It is a model of how people suppose their
> society to be organized, but it is not
> necessarily the goal towards which they
> strive (Leach 1954:286).

In other words, the same verbal symbols, important ideological terms and phrases are used by different segments of the population to interpret and justify activities and concepts that are logically contradictory.

Victor Turner, following Sapir, distinguishes between referential and condensational symbols and states:

> While referential symbolism grows with
> formal elaboration in the conscious, con-
> densation symbolism strikes deeper and
> deeper roots into the unconscious, and
> diffuses its emotional quality to types
> of behavior and situations apparently far
> removed from the original meaning of the
> symbol (Turner 1967:29).

Even though he would generally include verbal forms as falling within the domain of referential symbols, Turner does recognize that "symbols are at one and the same time referential and condensation symbols, [and] each symbol is multi-referential rather than unireferential." It is in terms of such multireferential symbols that we interpret the ideology of Guatemala's power structure.

Many of the recognized studies dealing with the national social structure of Guatemala grant primary importance to three prominent institutions as providing much of the basis for social control and its justification: the national Army, the Catholic Church, and the traditional aristocracy of the large landowners. Since some of these studies do not adequately clarify the distinction between an institutional structure and the people who comprise it, there is a tendency to represent the articulation of these three institutions as based on conspiratorial personal relationships that might be translated, at least occasionally, into economic or monetary terms.

It is our intention to demonstrate that this articulation is not consciously economic (it definitely has profound and favorable economic consequences for all three), is not conspiratorial (except in individual cases), and is based instead on a differentiated and ambivalent interpretation of various ideological symbols that spell an adequate ideological power equation which includes all three institutions. This is not to say that these three institutions are not intentionally united in maintaining the structural status quo, as well as the raison d'etre of its existence and function and therefore their justifications, are quite different.

In other words, these three institutions have distinct ideologies and it is not correct to attribute to them a common social or political philosophy as the basis for their articulation in a power alliance.

We do not hesitate to refer to the traditional land-owning aristocracy as a unique and unified institution on the same order of abstraction as the Catholic Church and the Army. Barraclough (1966:50) defines land-tenure as "the institutionalized system of relationships among groups of

individuals in the use of land and labor and control of their
products." Any agrarian society such as Guatemala must have
an institutionalized land-tenure pattern if it is to have a
workable, if not a stable, political and economic order.
Guatemala's present tenure system was established in essence
and effect at the time of the Spanish Conquest and its
single-minded defense is the bond that unites the large landowners today. Thus it is that the National Association of
Cattlemen, the National Federation of Sugar Growers, the
Association of Vegetable Oil Producers, the Association of
Poultrymen, together with the National Association of Coffee
(ANACAFE), are all joined together in the General Association
of Agriculturalists (AGA). It is, therefore, justifiable to
refer to the large landowners as an institution unto itself,
with clearly defined, persisting and organized relationships,
the existence of which is an empirically demonstrable fact.

We do not exclude the financial-industrial sector from
Guatemala's power alliance. Rather, we agree with the
Guatemalan anthropologist, Humberto Flores Alvarado, that the
development of this segment since World War II is the result
of

> an 'advanced' sector of the agrarian
> bourgeoisie that has begun to invest a
> part of its juicy income in other fields
> of economic activity in the nation, into
> mechanizing its crops, into the manufac-
> turing or industrial processing of the
> agricultural products they themselves
> grow, or even into financial speculation
> (Flores Alvarado 1968:119).

With the exception of rare individuals, the interests of the
financial-industrial sector cannot be divorced from the
interests of the large landowners--they are largely the same
people.

A comprehensive understanding of Guatemala's power
structure demands that we also consider one other segment of
the population, the peasantry, which is the principal object
of the exercise of social power. By peasantry, for the purposes of this paper, we mean those rural dwellers engaged
mainly in subsistence agriculture, whether as small landowners, migrant laborers, sharecroppers, or tenant farmers,
who often supplement their incomes with seasonal labor on the
large plantations. Although the urban working class cannot
be excluded from a complete analysis of Guatemala's power
structure, for present purposes we are obliged to pass it
over. Nor is this omission unjustified. Over 75 percent of
Guatemala's population still lives in the rural sector; much
of the urban population, even as a significant minority, is
only one generation removed from rural life. Also, many of
those whom the 1964 census classifies as "urbanites" are

still engaged in subsistence agriculture outside their
"urban" dwellings, living in small villages in the heart of
the rural zones.[1]

Some of the major ideological commitments of the
peasantry which have facilitated the largely unchallenged
control of their lives by the aforementioned institutions in
the past must also be examined. The use of the term
"segment of the population" in reference to the peasantry and
"institution" to designate the other three groupings is
intentional, since it is precisely because of the lack of
horizontal organization, whether formal or traditional, that
the peasantry is the docile object of power manipulations,
rather than the executor of same.

One final introductory point: differential ideological
commitments to the status quo can threaten to lead to fundamental structural changes if a substantial segment of any of
the three power blocks perceives the discrepancy between the
ideological symbols it uses to define its social philosophy
and the social reality it pretends to describe. This is apt
to happen especially in the context of any type of power
confrontation, when verbal symbols must serve not only as
ideology but as propaganda. Such a confrontation can be
precipitated by ideological shifts occurring first within the
peasantry itself, as a result of its changing historical conditions, effecting changes in its relationship to any or all
of the three power blocks. Such a shift seems to be taking
place in Guatemala and the anticipation of a structural
realignment is of paramount preoccupation to the three power
institutions.

Max Weber defines power as "the probability that one
actor within a social relationship will be in a position to
carry out his own will despite resistance regardless of the
basis on which the probability exists" (Weber 1964:152).
Although there are probably as many different definitions of
power as there are power theorists, we accept the essence of
Weber's definition as our own, with a single caveat, i.e.,
the emphasis on resistance in the power relationship. Those
power relationships involving influence, what Richard Schermerhorn (1961) calls relationships of "positive emotional
orientation" such as mutual friendship (symmetrical relationships) and popularity (assymmetrical relationships), do
not contain the negative element of resistance.
C. J. Friedrich says that:

> Power, though often spoken of as thing,
> is actually nothing of the kind. It is

---

[1]In the 1964 census an artificial distinction between
rural and urban is calculated as follows: rural areas are
considered villages of 2,000 people or less (1,500 if a village has running water) and anything above this figure is
considered urban population.

> as the Hobbesian definition suggests,
> oriented toward things and anything can
> become the basis of power. A house, a
> love affair, an idea can all become
> instruments in the hand of one seeking
> power. But in order to convert them into
> power, the power-seeker must find human
> beings who value one of these things
> sufficiently to follow his leadership in
> acquiring them (1950:22-3).

Power, then, is that aspect of a social relationship between
two or more individuals where one (or more) are in possession
of a substance or quality capable of influencing the behavior
of the others party to the relationship. The "substance or
quality" on which the power rests runs the gamut from love to
physical force. Political theorists have concentrated their
attention on the use of physical force and the process of
legitimization of such force demanded by a "stable" political
system, even as we ourselves do in this essay. But to limit
ourselves to the exclusive consideration of the negative
aspects of power would be to obscure the nature of the
Catholic Church's ideology in legitimizing those very negative power manipulations by the Guatemalan Army and landed
aristocracy and would distort its rationale of self-
justification. By first examining the Army, the primary
wielder of physical force on the Guatemala national scene,
especially as it operated within the Mendez Montenegro government (1966-1970), we hope to present an empirical demonstration of our thesis of differential interpretation of a
power ideology.

In popular theory, social control by the use of
physical force in modern societies falls primarily to the
police operating with the authority of and under the control
of the civilian representatives of the civil population. In
Guatemala, as in many other modern nations, this function has
been appropriated to itself by the Armed Forces.

The responsiveness of the Army to direct civilian
control in Guatemala is often non-existent, except for mutually beneficial cooperative alliances with certain power
blocks of the civil population. The sometimes uneasy, but
effective alliance between the Armed Forces and the large
landowners enables the 2.1 percent who own more than
72 percent of the cultivatable land to rule over, or over-
rule, the rest of the population.

With few exceptions the officer corps is made up of
aspiring members of the middle class who would like to take
their place within the upper or ruling class before or after
their retirement from the military establishment. It is in
their best interest to cooperate with all those people who
can facilitate that process.

The uneasiness of the power alliance comes from the civilians' inability to judge the extent of power a given officer wields within the Armed Forces. The alliances and counter-alliances make the military something other than the perennially monolithic structure that some civilians seem to think it is. It was therefore indispensable for President-elect Mendez Montenegro to visit each Army commander throughout the country and publicly proclaim his personal respect for each and every one of them, and not to confine himself to relating to their boss, his Minister of Defense. The President-elect's condition of dependency on the various military commanders was obvious to the public who observed him making his visits around the country, a .45 calibre pistol strapped on his hip, while his Minister of Defense, Col. Arriaga Bosque, just two steps behind, was noting with care everyone Mendez Montenegro spoke to and what was said. The insightful joke was made, not without subsequent evidence of truth, that the .45 calibre pistol was carried by Mendez Montenegro to protect himself more from Arriaga Bosque and the latter's Army clique than from any would-be revolutionary.

The primary alliances within the Armed Forces are based on what is commonly called personalismo (personal relationships). This is not to say that there is no generalized ideological content to such relationships. Rather, the ideology is not of a political or societal nature, but is one of proper behavior toward one's military companions based on concepts of class loyalty and manliness. Richard N. Adams, in Crucifixion By Power (1970:258), notes that Yon Sosa, the hunted guerrilla leader, was welcomed to a party given by his military classmates from the Politecnica, the military academy, even while being one of the government's most hunted enemies. Luis Turcios Lima, another well-known guerrilla leader, with a $25,000 price tag on his head, moved with near impunity among his military friends in Guatemala City during 1962-66 until his death in an automobile accident.

The competing alliances among military officers can sometimes be used by a clever politician to his advantage. Mendez Mentenegro, while not a particularly astute politician, was able to take advantage of a huge political blunder committed by his enemies and, counting on the cross-cutting loyalties within the military establishment, was able to rid himself of his biggest political (not to say physical) threat. This blunder was the kidnapping of Archbishop Mario Casariego of Guatemala City in March, 1969, an act which was seen by much of the Guatemalan press and people as obvious collusion between Right-wing terrorists, operating on the payroll of the large landowners, and the Army. The Government immediately accused Left-wing guerrillas of the kidnapping but this was popularly viewed as a smokescreen.

It was not hard to guess who was responsible, it was only a question of their motivation.

Mario Monteforte Toledo, sociologist and former President of the National Congress in the Government of Juan José Arévalo (1945-50), says that there were three reasons for the kidnapping of the Archbishop: Casariego did not align himself with the Liberation Party (the landowners party), and thereby with the privileges of the wealthy, as did his predecessor, Archbiship Rossell; Casariego had not lent himself to the constant anti-communist campaign, nor to condemning the guerrillas as if they were the only ones responsible for the deplorable national conditions--as a matter of fact, he had imprudently embarrassed the Government by publicly petitioning it to turn over to the proper tribunals 273 people who had been arrested and had disappeared while in police custody--(El Imparcial, a Guatemalan daily newspaper, December 14, 1967: hereafter Imp.); and, most important, the kidnapping would produce an outpouring of public revulsion and thus the citizens, expressing their lack of confidence in Mendez Montenegro, could have publicly demanded a military coup that would then have been easily executed (CIDOC, Document 68/61).

The plan backfired for several reasons. Church authorities remained calm and asked the country to do likewise. Archbishop Casariego is not a particularly popular man in Guatemala due to his heavy-handed political maneuverings, and even among the clergy the kidnapping was greeted with some amusement and little outrage.

The Right-wing terrorist/military collusion was effectively confirmed after a few days when it was discovered that the Archbishop had been held prisoner in the home of the former Secretary of Information of the Castillo Armas military Government, Dr. Carlos Cifuentes Diaz. Furthermore, any doubts that may have lingered were dissipated when the Minister of Defense refused to heed President Mendez Montenegro's request to cut short his visit to the United States and return home. At the time, Arriaga Bosque was visiting the Pentagon and other U.S. military installations (Imp., March 13, 1968) where Guatemalan social-control experts were being trained, while he made public statements denying his relationship to Right-wing terrorist groups (Washington Post, March 15, 1968). He prolonged his visit five days beyond Casariego's kidnapping and in effect told the President that he would return only when the Army requested it, and not as Minister of Defense, but as head of a new military Government.

Mendez Montenegro moved fast. Congress censured the Vice-President, Marroquin Rojas, a staunch backer of Arriaga Bosque and a vociferous defender of Right-wing terrorism, for his editorials in his family-owned newspaper justifying the kidnapping. Then Mendez sought and obtained promises of support from various quarters, said to be the

Air Force, the Mariscal Zavala Brigade in the Capital, and
the U.S. Embassy. Finally he called in three men who were
most often linked to the Right-wing extremists: Col. Rafael
Arriaga Bosque, who, as Minister of Defense, was responsible
for the indiscriminate arrests and executions perpetrated by
the Army; Col. Carlos Arana Osorio who made efficient use of
terrorist bands against purported guerrilla sympathizers in
the Zacapa area; Col. Manuel Sosa Avila who was accountable
for the hundreds of arrested citizens who could not be
located in any police detention center.

From the day he was sworn into office, the President
had found these three men to be his most persistent opponents
on the Right. When the Liberation Party issued a repeated
call to the country to join the "national crusade in order to
demonstrate to the Castroite subversives that the Government,
the people and the Army, have joined to form a single combat
force" (El Gráfico, Guatemalan daily newspaper, May 16, 1967;
hereafter Gra.), the true meaning was only vaguely hidden:

> In view of the Government's indolence in
> confronting with decision the challenge
> of the armed rebels, and in view of the
> leniency of the Courts in judging them,
> diverse sections of the citizenry,
> reacting justifiably to the growing
> Leftist offensive, have spontaneously
> organized themselves, have adopted a
> posture of self-defense, and have begun
> to respond to the enemy with the same
> arms and the same tactics.

It had been openly commented by both the radio and
the Press that the Army and police force were involved in
Right-wing terrorist activities sponsored by various large
landowning groups. The relationship could hardly be hidden.
Why else the law of amnesty passed as the final act of
Peralta Azurdia's military Government (1963-1966), "for all
members of the Army, all policemen and their superiors, for
those acts committed in the repression of subversive activities?" (Imp., April 28, 1966). Arriaga Bosque himself came
close to admitting the relationship in December 1966, when
he stated that he was "grateful to the public for their help
in fighting communism" but added that he could not make
deals with these secret organizations since this was "pro-
hibited by the Constitution" (Imp., December 12, 1966). The
kidnapping of Archbishop Casariego, however, was just one
act, although the most blatant, in a whole series of
terroristic Right-wing activities that could not have been
accomplished without the active cooperation of military and
police authorities, and often under their very auspices.

The President told the trio that he has removing them
from their posts: Arriaga Bosque would go as Consul to Miami

and Arana Osorio as Ambassador to Nicaragua. Both places are
centers of intrigue and plotting, the temporary homes for
political exiles from many Latin American nations. Arriaga
Bosque made a last effort to save himself, appealing to the
Armed Forces to "remain united in their fight against communism" (Imp., March 29, 1968). The ploy did not work and no
one rallied to his side. Mendez Montenegro, in an attempt to
salvage some of the tarnished image of the military,
explained the changes as "democratic removals" that occur
regularly within the Armed Forces (Imp., April 9, 1968). Few
were deceived.

The seeming ascendancy of the President over the
Arriaga Bosque/Arana Osorio axis was short-lived. By
November, Col. Arana Osorio, speaking from Nicaragua, was
announcing that he was the Liberation Party's (the landowners' Party) candidate for the presidency in the 1970
elections (Imp., November 29, 1968). He had been in Nicaragua
only eight months, but this was sufficient time to make some
necessary alliances. By coincidence, the same day as Arana's
announcement, Mendez Montenegro visited the CONDECA headquarters (Central American Defense Command) and was quoted as
saying: "Central Americanism is not just a platitude, but a
reality" (Imp., November 29, 1968).

CONDECA had ostensibly been established to facilitate
cooperative military training exercises and to coordinate an
appropriate military response in case of a foreign invasion.
Its efforts were more concerned with internal security,
however, and it was acknowledged that the participating
governments would aid one another where the pacification of
the citizens of one or other nation was more than the respective governments could handle. Guatemala's Minister of
Defense, Col. Chinchilla Aguilar,[2] when he was named President of CONDECA in July 1968, stated:

> CONDECA embraces not only actions that
> are purely military for the defense of
> democratic institutions of our countries,
> the maintenance of our territorial integ-
> rity, independence and liberty, but it
> also involves the maintenance of an
> environment of peace and security that
> will permit the respective governments
> and inhabitants to begin [sic] the devel-
> opment of economic, social and cultural
> programs (Imp., July 1, 1968).

----

[2]Many considered that Col. Chinchilla Aguilar,
previously Minister of Education, was being groomed as the
next Partido Revolucionario candidate for the presidency, and
the one favored by the U.S. Embassy. He succeeded Arriaga
Bosque, but later fell from grace within the counter coup.

CONDECA, then, is really an international police force meant to be used to keep the citizens of Central America in line. An effective demonstration of CONDECA in action occurred during the attempted coup in El Salvador in March, 1972. Napoleon Duarte, head of the Christian Democrats, and Col. Benjamin Mejia collaborated in attempting to overthrow Col. Fidel Sanchez after the latter sponsored the "massive, straightforward fraudulent elections" (Latin America, Vol. 6, No. 41, p. 327) that gave the presidency to his close friend, Col. Arturo Armando Milina. Latin America, a respected weekly published in London, remarked of the "decisive" air power that Guatemala's President lent to the Salvadorean Government to put down the rebellion:

> Whether or not Guatemala was involved
> (since Guatemala vociferously denied it),
> there may be a lesson for Central
> American golpistas trying to seize power
> from a position left of the established
> regime: there are powerful forces outside
> the country as well as inside which have
> a strong interest in stability that such
> a coup will not be allowed to succeed
> (Latin America, Vol. 6, No. 13, p. 97).

The feat was repeated in March of 1974, when the Christian Democratic candidate in Guatemala, General Rios Montt, seemed to have dramatically outpolled his colleague on the Right, the MLN's (Party of National Liberation) General Kjell Laugerud Garcia. If Arana Osorio had any doubts about nullifying the results of the election and turning the Government over to Laugerud, they were immediately dissipated by a quick trip to Guatemala by President Anastasio Somoza of Nicaragua, only two days after the election, a dramatic display of Somoza's intentions.

But avoiding left-of-center elections and coups is not CONDECA's only function. Individuals or groups who are political fugitives from the internal security forces of their own country know that they will be pursued across neighboring borders with no ensuing international incident. They also realize that if they are captured in a neighboring country, their fate is no more likely to be determined by legal considerations than if they were back home. Thus it is that the international alliances established among the individual military commanders of Central America (also containing a component of personalismo) are certainly secondary to the domestic alliances, yet do play an important role in determining the power position of a particular officer in his native country.

It is only in the light of these military alliances, especially with the Armed Forces of the Somozas, that Arana's ambassadorship to Nicaragua and his subsequent

political comeback can be understood. Mendez Montenegro's
statement, on the day Arana's candidacy was announced, contained a bitter core of truth for the President: "Central
Americanism is not just a platitude, but a reality."
     One year after his "exile" Col. Arana Osorio was back
in Guatemala conducting his political campaign with the self-
confidence of a man already elected. Roberto Alejos, a
landowner who had lent his plantation to the CIA for training
the Bay of Pigs invasion force, had withdrawn his candidacy
for the PID (Independent Democratic Party) Party in favor of
Arana Osorio in order to form an "alliance of all the anti-
communist and patriotic sectors of the nation." Arana Osorio
lashed out at Mendez Montenegro's Revolutionary Party and
blamed them for dragging their feet on suppression of the
guerrillas, barely excluding the President from his attacks
(Imp., May 12, 1969). Daily his pronouncements on sundry
subjects were repeated in full detail in the press. One day
he was condemning the new immorality of motion pictures and
the next he was announcing that the MLN and the PID would
co-sponsor the bill in Congress for the exoneration of export
duties on coffee.
     The real measure of Arana's new power was demonstrated
on June 11, 1969. The Liberation candidate visited the
President, accompanied by many of his high-level backers.
After an hour alone with Mendez Montenegro (his retinue
waited in the foyer), the Colonel told reporters "We
exchanged impressions in order to find a formula that would
permit the coming elections to take place in a climate of
peace and tranquility" (Imp., June 12, 1969).
     The next day it became clear of what the climate
consisted. The Liberation Party sent a declaration to the
newspapers:

> The MLN views with sorrow the increase of
> negative forces which, aided by the
> little efficacy or total lack of it on
> the part of the authorities charged with
> maintaining order and security, frightens
> the citizenry preparing for the 1970
> elections. If these groups continue in
> this destructive and discouraging work,
> the citizenry itself will have to take
> into its own hands the means of self-
> protection and then Guatemala will enter
> the worst of anarchies (Imp., June 13,
> 1969).

     The Liberation Party's accusations of lack of efficacy
in suppressing the revolutionary guerrillas were aimed at the
Minister of the Interior, Mansilla Pinto. It was to him that
Arana Osorio had referred in his first attack on the Government and it was he whom the Colonel had demanded be replaced

in his meeting with the President on June 11. There were
immediate rumors throughout the Capital that Mansilla Pinto
was out and that none other than Col. Manuel Sosa Avila was
back in power, not as Head of the National Police, but now
as Minister of the Interior.

Mansilla Pinto had been a target of the Right-wing
extremists since his appointment. The Mano Blanca, the
principal Right-wing vigilante organization of the landowners, but one whose connections with the national police
were particularly strong, published a flier stating:

> Is not President Mendez Montenegro
> responsible for what happens when his
> Minister of the Interior is shown to have
> obvious sympathies for communism and is
> completely incapable of fulfilling his
> obligations? Licenciado Mansilla Pinto
> is undermining the stability of the gov-
> ernment with his incompetence and it is
> absurd to think that the Revolutionary
> Party is not aware of the dissatisfaction
> and lack of tranquility that is notice-
> able among the people (CIDOC, Dossier 21,
> p.4/283).

The publication went on to state what it believed to be the
proper attitude of the Minister of the Interior or any other
Government official:

> The question that the MANO poses is this:
> on which side is the Revolutionary Party?
> A third position will not help to solve
> the problem. Either one aids the commu-
> nists or one is against them. This
> bloody situation, this war unto death,
> will only terminate when one of the two
> bands in this struggle triumphs com-
> pletely over the other.

When, only three days after Arana Osorio's visit, the private
secretary of the President announced the appointment of
Col. Sosa Avila as the new Minister of the Interior, he qualified the change of Ministers as a "routine appointment in a
democratic system" (Prensa Libre, June 16, 1969: hereafter
P.L.), reminiscent of the very words used a year before when
Sosa Avila and his two companions had first been fired.

The new Minister took office promising to do all in
his power to establish "law and order". He denied any connections with Right-wing terrorist groups, but not everyone
believed him. The University Students Association protested
against the appointment (P.L., June 17, 1969). And up in

Miami, Cuban exiles with strong economic and political interests in Guatemala were openly jubilant about what they referred to as "our first coup."

Arana Osorio, strengthened by his military alliances, did not overthrow Mendez Montenegro in the last year of his administration only because he felt that he could lend an air of legitimacy to what he did by going through the motions of an election. Guatemala's military establishment continually has to face the problem of legitimization of the Army's use of physical force on the domestic scene. When Col. Enrique Peralta Azurdia replaced the overtly corrupt civilian regime of ex-General Miguel Ydigoras Fuentes in 1963 with a military dictatorship, the popular opposition to the government stiffened despite the universal dissatisfaction with Ydigoras' blatant manipulations of public finances. Peralta Azurdia's regime was religiously honest by all accounts, and yet popular opposition grew. His installation of a rubber-stamp Congress was not sufficient to gain him the legitimacy he wanted or needed. Meanwhile, the guerrilla revolutionary forces organized popular opposition and gained control over much of the Northeastern party of the country.

By March, 1966, Peralta Azurdia permitted presidential elections to take place because his "military honor" forced him to live up to his own constantly reiterated protestations of honesty (he called his government "Operacion Honestidad") and because of popular resistance to his military rule. If Peralta Azurdia had not been too proud to accept the proffered counter-insurgency aid of the U.S. Embassy;[3] popular resistance would not have been so serious a problem.

When Mendez Montenegro unexpectedly won the 1966 elections over the military's handpicked candidate, Col. Juan de Dios Aguilar, it was decided, with more prodding from the U.S. Embassy, that a "civilian" regime led by Mendez Montenegro but under effective Army control, could gain legitimacy more quickly and thereby be able to deal more efficiently with the rebels in the Northeast sector of the country as well as elsewhere than could a self-proclaimed military regime. When "democratic elections" cannot be used as a legitimizing factor for one reason or another (e.g., midway through the term of a "democratically elected" government), the Army has been relatively successful in legitimizing its domestic use of direct force to monopolize governmental functions by the clever manipulation of verbal symbols, guaranteed to bring support from several legitimizing agencies.

The most valid of these symbols, in terms of the Army's true function, is "sovereignty." "Sovereignty" is

---

[3]One of the authors was witness to several condemnations of the Peralta Azurdia regime for this attitude by U.S. AID officials in Guatemala City during 1965.

used to justify repressive terror tactics against the
restless rural population because rural unrest can easily be
attributed to foreign intervention, especially Cuban in
recent years.

Another verbal symbol of legitimization is the term
"anti-communism" used in much the same way as "sovereignty".
The Army attributes social unrest to the influence of
"foreign and atheistic doctrines" rather than to the existing
social structures and conditions of Guatemala. "Anti-
communism" is probably the number one symbol of legitimization manipulated on the domestic scene. It quickly and
effectively enlists the aid of two sources of prestige and
authority that serve as the primary agencies of power-
legitimization, i.e. the Church hierarchy and the large
landowners. It was Peralta Azurdia's inability to use
"anti-communism" as a believable rationalization for his 1963
military coup (Ydigoras was also an anti-communist ideo-
logue), that was at least a contributing factor in denying
him the needed public support of these two legitimizing
agencies.

"Constitutionality" is the verbal symbol most
difficult for the military to manipulate, though they continue to do so. Guatemala has lived under four different
constitutions in the last thirty years. Military governments
violate and rewrite the national constitution in Guatemala
as much as other countries disregard the U.N. Charter. It is
not as easily apparent what institution or group is the
intended target of the "constitutionality" banner, since it
is not an effective symbol inside Guatemala. We can specu-
late that the proclamation of "constitutionality" is intended
for international consumption, particularly for the U.S.
Embassy, where "constitutionality" is the prime index of
political development and the most important symbol for
including Guatemala among the nations of the "free world."
Since the subsidiary verbal symbols, "freedom" and
"democracy" are religiously included whenever the Guatemalan
constitution is rewritten, the claim of "constitutionality"
assures membership in the international community of "free
nations ruled by law."

Legitimization of secular power can properly be
thought of as one of the most important social functions of
the Catholic Church's hierarchy. Without the clergy's
ministrations to the peasant population, the ideological
integration of the rural population into the national social
structure would be largely non-existent. It was Archbishop
Mariano Rossell's pilgrimage with the "Cristo de Esquipulas"
through the countryside in 1951-52 and his public declarations against Communism that, more than anything else,
diminished the authority of the Arbenz government and
consequently its ability to effectively marshall support to
repulse the CIA-sponsored invasion by Col. Castillo Armas.

The support of Archbishop Rossell and the Papal Nuncio for the Castillo Armas military "crusade" and his subsequent military government played an important role in legitimizing the policies of the "liberator" among much of the rural population. Archbishop Rossell went so far as to publicly declare Castillo Armas as numbered among the Church's "saints," a not insignificant contribution to the legitimization process.

When Mendez Montenegro was about to take over the Presidential Palace in July of 1966, he recognized that he lacked a meaningful power base among the populace from which to operate. He went first to the Church hierarchy, even before approaching the Army high command. He asked Archbishop Mario Casariego (Rossell had died some years before) for the hierarchy's public support. Casariego promised him support only if Mendez Montenegro would acquiesce to "rectify" his marriage in a Catholic ceremony which the Archbishop would celebrate in his private chapel. The President-elect had never been considered a devotee of the Church, but the arrangement was agreed upon and the wedding took place in almost total secrecy. Shortly thereafter, a letter went out from the hierarchy to the clergy requesting they lead their congregations in public prayer for the health and success of the new President.

Such ecclesiastical cooperation is not always so easily forthcoming nor do we assert that legitimization of military power flows only from the Church's blessing. But it is probably no exaggeration to assert that legitimization of military power in Guatemala in the face of overt Church opposition would be most difficult, if not impossible.

As noted above, the cry of "atheistic communism" is sufficient for the Church to cooperate with both the Army and the large landowners in the process of legitimizing a so-called "anti-communist" power alliance. But this important verbal symbol cannot be employed merely to cloak outright and obvious repression, for the Church preaches justice and charity as well as anti-communism and peace (stability). If an overt conflict develops from the ambiguous utilization of these symbols, the Church begins to drift away from the alliance, much as Casariego did by publicly asking the government to answer for the disappearance of 273 police detainees.

Another ambivalent symbol mutually shared and differentially interpreted by the landowners and the Church hierarchy is that of "poverty". Catholicism, particularly Guatemalan Catholicism, is imbued with a spirit of resignation that preaches "everyone in his place" and that one's life condition is largely the result of God's will. This is a doctrine ardently embraced by the plantation owners. "Thou shalt not covet thy neighbor's goods" is used by the landowners and the wealthy in addressing themselves to the destitute in an attempt to keep them from becoming

dissatisfied with their lot. So, too, the Archbishop of
Guatemala City could say to the poverty-stricken people of
La Limonada, one of Guatemala City's cardboard and tin
barrios:

> You, the humble ones of this colony, are
> the most cherished by me; I was poor like
> you; you live in shacks like that of
> Bethlehem that housed the Infant God, but
> you are happy because where there is
> poverty, there is happiness (Imp.,
> February 24, 1967).

La Limonada is one of the numerous colonies that have sprung
up around Guatemala City in the ravines that encircle it.
They are called the 'Crown of Thorns' and house the tens of
thousands of landless peasants who have come to the City
hoping for work, for a livelihood. Often they have to turn
to crime or mendicity to stay alive, and just as often they
fail at this.

When in early 1968, Time magazine published a letter
from the authors referring to the poverty of Guatemala's
masses, AGA (Guatemala Agricultural Association, large
landowners) demanded equal space and offered this rebuttal:

> Guatemala, under no circumstances, is the
> most impoverished nation in the world,
> nor are we indifferent to wanting to
> improve the conditions of our poor. The
> program "Against Poverty" of President
> Johnson shows that many fellow citizens
> of Thomas Melville live in greater neces-
> sity and poverty than many Guatemalans.
> We have here more than 417,344 owners of
> plantations and lands, and if each of
> these represents a family of five mem-
> bers, it signifies that more than half of
> our people own their own lands (P.L.,
> February 20, 1968).

Thus AGA, representative of the landowners' mentality,
consoles itself that Guatemala is not the poorest country in
the world, and that some U.S. citizens are worse off than
some Guatemalan citizens, both facts that cannot be denied.
But the disingenuousness of this defense can be seen in the
claim that more than half of all Guatemalans are property
owners, while there is no mention made of the extent of these
holdings, nor whether they are sufficient for supporting a
family. No recognition is made that only 7.3 percent of
these holdings are legally registered, thus facilitating
extemporaneous expulsions and thefts, nor of the almost
50 percent of the population that owns no property. Thus,
when the newspapers report a lack of corn in Huehuetenango on

the Western highlands, with its corresponding hunger (Imp., August 8, 1967), no relation is made to Guatemala's land-tenure pattern. So too, in Chiquimula, on the Eastern highlands, it was observed the same month that "the peasants want to give away their children in order to save them from hunger" (Imp., August 28, 1967) and the problem can be attributed to the Will of God. Every year, as first more corn, and then rice, has had to be imported, the basic cause of the problem is still ignored. For the first time in its history, Guatemala imported black beans in 1967 (Imp., November 11, 1967), thus completing a shortage of all three of the peasants' basic staples.

When someone describes the extent of the problem, he is promptly labeled a communist and an agitator and becomes open game for Right-wing vigilantes or for the Government itself. Ydigoras refused to allow the publication of a study that attributed 50,000 infant deaths a year to malnutrition, as a "communist document" (Imp., January 6, 1964).

Poverty is a negative concept, a lack of something, a difficult symbol upon which a power alliance can be integrated. Yet "poverty" is a very important part of the Church's definition of itself in virtue of which it can encourage poverty among the poor, as did Archbishop Casariego in La Limonada. Every cleric in the Catholic Church takes implicit or explicit vows or oaths of poverty, chastity and obedience. In terms of these vows or oaths, "poverty" is understood, not as the renunciation or lack of material goods, whether of subsistence, leisure or prestige, but rather as the renunciation of ownership, the "right of deposition." This right is granted to the corporate Church, through its representative, the Bishop or religious superior, who must then see that those under his care do not suffer material want. In this sense, it was unusual for the Archbishop of Guatemala City to tell the inhabitants of La Limonada that he "was once poor," because the usual interpretation of the vow or oath is that all clerics "are poor," even though one may live in a "palace" (if he is an archbishop), have chauffers and maids and dress in silks.

The concept of poverty that the Church asks the landowners to embrace is somewhat similar to its own--a "spirit of poverty," a lack of ideological attachment to material goods. The Opus Dei and Cursillos de Cristiandad, organizations principally of wealthy Catholic laity, preach this type of "poverty" to their members, though its practical effects are not always evident.[4]

---

[4]The authors know at least one wealthy Opus Dei member who made a vow of poverty, putting all his worldly possessions in his wife's name. It did not affect his style of life.

The poverty that the peasant is asked to accept, however, is quite different. It is the poverty of hunger and sickness, it is the poverty of insecurity, it is the poverty of ramshackle rural slums on the plantations, "like that of Bethlehem that housed the Infant God."

But there are indications now that the ideology of poverty does not have the number of adherents that it once did, and that even among the Church clergy, there are those who see the differential interpretation of this verbal symbol as fundamentally contradictory and no longer acceptable.

"Poverty," and the "spirit of poverty," are not the only verbal symbols that serve to unite the landowners and the Church hierarchy in an ideological relationship that spells power. There are two others that also fulfill this role: "private property" and "free enterprise." They are actually two sides of the same coin.

To the landowners, "private property" means unlimited access to personal wealth, devoid of any notion of social responsibility or social justice. In fact, the MLN (the landowners' Party) managed to block all references to the "social function of property" in the 1965 military constitution as their defense of the right to unlimited private property. They took their lead from Guatemala's Chamber of Industry which stated, "social justice is a dangerous ambiguity. For the communists and socialists, social justice is administered by the State; for Catholics, social justice is left to the conscience of every individual" (Imp., February 26, 1965). The Coordinating Committee of the Association of Landowners, Businessmen, Industrialists and Bankers demanded that all references to social justice be struck from the constitution: "We are not against social justice but rather against the demagogic way this term is used. Private enterprise might collapse if we augment the burdens of the owners" (Imp., May 27, 1965). When this version of the constitution was finally approved by a vote of 79 to 1, the Archbishop's representative, Monsenor Giron Perrone, complained, not about this omission, but that "no special rights, which duly correspond to the Church, have been democratically conceded" (Imp., September 14, 1965). He was answered by Congressman José Calderon Salazar of the MLN: "Seven months we fought over this Magna Carta and not a word out of the Church; even when we discussed the topic of social justice, the Catholic Hierarchy could be found toasting at a reception, turning their backs on the religious reality of Guatemala" (Imp., September 14, 1965). The justification for the exclusion of such concepts had earlier been given by Congressman Menendez Sandoval of the MLN:

> That evil phrase, "the social function"
> of property, gave birth precisely to
> Decree 900 (1952 Agrarian Reform Law)
> which was on the point of carrying

> Guatemala to the greatest disaster in its
> history, this both in practice and in
> theory, because the real agrarian problem
> of Guatemala is not the scarcity of
> lands, but rather that the lands be made
> to produce more (<u>Imp</u>., October 30, 1964).

So, too, "free enterprise" is used as a similar defense
against all those who might claim that the government has a
right, indeed, an obligation, to prevent the economically
powerful from excessively exploiting the economically weak.

The Church lost its right to own property under the
reformist Liberal government of Justo Rufino Barrios in the
1870's, and only managed to regain that right under the new
constitution established by the Col. Castillo Armas military
Government. Its churches, rectories, convents and schools,
not to mention its historical position as a large landowner
and the contemporary analogue of that position, a large
investor in industrial enterprises, give the Church reason
enough to support the concept of private property.

There is another reason for the Church's support of
this concept, one more fundamentally ideological. Catholicism is a salvific religion whose basic ideological
orientation is the salvation of souls in the afterlife. As
such, its fundamental dogmatic conceptualization is concerned
with the individual being, i.e., soul, and the soul's
essentially private relationship to God. This private
relationship to God is a function of the unencumbered free
will of every individual, immune to coercion (but not
temptation) from all quarters, including the Devil. Because
of this orientation, the Church has no consistent intellectual tradition capable of dealing with collective social
responsibility and social structures, other than the social
encyclicals of the last three-quarters of a century. But
even these have not managed to deal with social problems
except in terms of individual freedom and responsibility.

When the Guatemalan landowners raise the banners of
"private property" and "free enterprise," they elicit a
sympathetic vibration from the Church's hierarchy. Any
ideology thatputs the solution of social problems beyond the
pale of the individual's will and responsibility is a threat
to the most fundamental tenets of Catholicism. "Social
engineering," unless it is some kind of psychological
reductionism, is often seen to be as threatening as Marxism,
while Marxism is equated with atheism and the devil. On the
other hand, free enterprise and private property are equated
with free will and individual responsibility; and these are
of the essence of Catholicism. The differential interpretation of these verbal symbols is evident and the smooth
ideological interpenetration of these two power blocks is
the result.

Just as the large landowners and Church hierarchy see
private property and free enterprise as essential components
of their world-views, so the Army high command sees the
negation of these symbols as its potentially gravest threat.
Communism, of course, represents the gravest threat to the
ideology of unlimited access to personal wealth and power,
and is, by the Army's definition, foreign. Communist ideas
are, therefore, a threat to Guatemala's sovereignty and a
direct challenge to the Army. "Private property" in these
terms is every bit a component of the Army's ideological
definition of itself, just as it is for the Church and large
landowners. It is logical, therefore, that the MLN, the
landowners Party, nominated Col. Arana Osorio as their presidential candidate for the 1970 elections. His "anti-
communist crusade" against disaffected peasants and "potential guerrilla sympathizers" in Zacapa in 1966-67 was
essentially a war to maintain the twin ideals of the
landed-aristocracy, unlimited private property and freedom
to exploit the economically weak. His defense of Guatemala's
"sovereignty" also happened to be a battle for "freedom of
conscience" and the expression of "free will," sine qua non
of Christian virtue.

It is not our purpose here to go into the Marxian-
Weberian debate concerning the direction of the causal
relationship between religious ideology and social structures, but only to demonstrate how the functional articulation of these two components of social life is accomplished
in Guatemala. We do not maintain that this articulation is
without conflict. On the contrary, contemporary Guatemala
cannot be considered a society in "equilibrium," whatever
that term may mean to some social scientists. We have
described elsewhere[5] in detail what these conflicts are and
the attempts being made by various blocks to suppress or
resolve them. We wish only to point out here a number of
developments that can be considered both causes and effects
in relation to a dramatic, on-going shift away from the
peasant ideology of poverty and submission to "God's will"
that probably presage a substantial structural re-alignment
in Guatemala's economic and political structures.

Eric Wolf (1955:456) describes the "closed corporate
peasant community" of Mesoamerica as one which "represents a
bounded social system with clear-cut limits, in relation to
both insiders and outsiders." Thirty-three years ago, Sol
Tax attributed the cultural diversity of the indigenous
populations of Guatemala to the "impersonal character of
social relations of all kinds, both within the community and
between people of different communities" (1941:34). Kalman
Silvert has said, in reference to the rural Guatemalan Indian

---

[5]Thomas Melville and Marjorie Melville, Guatemala: The
Politics of Land Ownership (New York: Free Press, 1971).

populations, that "their outwardly directed political
activity was managed by others" (1954:2) and Benson Saler
says that we can "trace Indian inferiority in power rankings
back to the traumata of the Conquest" (1967:97).

All of these knowledgeable observers of Guatemala
recognize the situation of political and economic inferiority
of the Guatemalan Indian population, a people composing
more than 43 percent[6] of the nation's total. They also
recognize that the ideological commitments of the peasant
masses, especially of the Indians, have been an important
factor in maintaining the situation of dominance that has
existed since the Conquest.

It is not our intention to attempt to judge the
breadth and depth of the changes in peasant ideology that
could serve as an index of potential rebellious or revolutionary movements among them. Even if it were within our
competence to so judge, we would not publish such information
since it would betray our own ethical standards by serving
the interests of the oppressors and may thereby help obstruct
the chances of a successful redistribution of power. We
can, however, repeat here some evidence that is already in
the public domain.

Dramatic realignment of social groups is occurring in
Guatemala today, and the extent of the repression employed
by the Army during the Mendez Montenegro regime, tactics
that have been, if anything, escalated under the present
Arana Osorio government, is perhaps the best indicator. The
government has mounted a repressive extra-legal apparatus of
historic dimensions at the hands of which as many as 10,000
Guatemalans, according to a variety of sources, have died in
the last ten years. The vast majority of these deaths have
been those of peasant leaders, labor organizers, spokesmen
for social change, suspected guerrilla sympathizers, actual
guerrillas and non-involved bystanders. The U.S. Senate
Subcommittee for Latin American Affairs of the Senate Foreign
Relations Committee, a source that certainly cannot be
considered sympathetic to revolutionary movements in Latin
America, recently stated,

> opposition estimates of thousands of innocent
> peasants brutally murdered may well be exaggerated,
> but in any event, Zacapa was pacified and Arana
> rode it to the presidency. The Mendez administra-
> tion also saw the beginning of terror from the right
> carried out by clandestine organizations
> which were at least to some

---

[6]The 1950 census registered 55 percent of the
population as Indian, while the 1964 census lists only
43 percent, a drop due to a governmental desire to demonstrate "progress" rather than abandonment of Indian ways.

>extent inspired by the Army and manned by
>"off-duty" [quotes in the original] Army
>personnel (December 30, 1971:3).

The State of Seige from November 1970 to November 1971 placed
the country on a virtual war footing so that the government
could repress its own people without maintaining the trap-
pings of democratic government. The denial of civil liber-
ties and "constitutional rights" was Arana's persistent
method of governing.

The pastoral response of the Church to peasant unrest,
as well as its difficulty in approving such repressive
measures even in the name of "private property" or the
"virtue of poverty," is becoming more and more evident among
individual bishops and clerics. When Bishop Gerardo Flores
blocked the appointment of Teodoro Díaz in February 1971, as
vice-president of the Asociación pro Desarrollo Integral
Cristiano against the wishes of Bishop Martínez de Lejarza,
because of Díaz's involvement in right-wing terrorist
organizations, the latter proceeded to desecrate Bishop
Flores' church in Izabal as a warning. Even Archbishop
Casariego's kidnapping can be seen as an indication of the
malfunctioning of the still-existing power alliance. And
these men do not stand alone in their pastoral opposition to
government repression tactics. It is evident that the
government will necessarily have to continue to increase the
coercion component (direct Army intervention) of its rule to
maintain the status quo even as its authority and legitimacy
decreases, much as did President Justo Rufino Barrios in the
1870's as a result of his persecution of the Church.

A singular difference between the 1870's and the
1970's is that governmental persecution is not aimed directly
at the Church, but only at those individuals who align themselves with the intended targets of governmental repression,
the dissident peasant and laborer. There is a growing
reluctance among some clerics closely associated with the
urban and rural poor to continue preaching the ideology of
poverty and submissive obedience. It can be cogently argued
that this change is as much a response to the changing
peasant ideology as it is the result of ecclesiastical
interest in social questions sparked by the encyclicals of
Pope John XXIII, the Documents of Vatican Council II, or the
declaration of the Latin American Bishops in Medellin,
Colombia in 1968.

Another index of the changing ideology of the peasants
is the fact that the attempted anti-government coup sponsored
by young military officers in November 1960, was converted to
a truly revolutionary movement by peasant support of the
defeated and fleeing golpistas (Melville and Melville, 1971).
This movement gained such control over the northeastern
departments of Zacapa and Izabal from 1963 to 1966 that the
revolutionary forces were able to defy the government by

conducting political education campaigns that saw them remain
in the same area for two or three days at a time, holding
public meetings, sponsoring slide-shows, and even challenging
the local soccer teams to contests. Such feats were as much
an effect of the wide-spread support given to the revolutionary movement as they were of the guerrillas' audacity.

The efficient causes of these changes in peasant
ideology are many and complicated. We underline here only
those we see as the most important, and do so with the
knowledge that the government also recognizes them as such.
Any serious attempts to eliminate these causes either implies
the revolutionary changes sought by the guerrilla movements
or a reversal of the processes of history by a strategy of
genocide.

The increasing demographic pressures on the land,
created by a rising birth rate and a declining death rate,
must be considered a major factor. Both are products of
modern preventive medical techniques introduced into the
countryside by missionaries and the government. The
Guatemalan census (1964:14) lists the most populated departments as the department of Guatemala, having 366 inhabitants
per sq. km.; Sacatepequez, 170 per sq. km.; Quezaltenango,
136 per sq. km.; Totonicapan, 134 per sq. km.; and Solola,
102 per sq. km. All of these departments are located on the
altiplano, where the lands are poorest.

It is true that with the exception of Guatemala City
in the department of Guatemala, none of these areas have seen
a marked degree of revolutionary activity. Some would
attribute this to the large proportion of indigenous people
in the highlands still committed to the ideology of submissive acceptance of oppressive poverty and repressive power
manipulation as the natural order of the world. We find this
interpretation outdated.

Although much of the guerrilla activity sponsored
and/or supported in the departments of Zacapa and Izabal came
from Ladino (mestizo) peoples, it has not been exclusively
so. The indigenous population in that area is more accul-
turated at the Spanish heritage than in the Western highlands, but acculturation is a gradual process, and cannot be
seen as an either/or selection of a cultural totality. On
the other hand, revolutionary activity in the Departments of
Escuintla, Retalhuleu and San Marcos on the South coast can
be traced to indigenous migrations out of the highlands in
search of new lands, especially those sparked by the Arbenz
agrarian reform program of 1951-2. Even to this day, the
Government recognizes San Marcos, with a high proportion of
indigenous population, as one of its most difficult areas to
pacify.

According to a FGEI (Frente Guerrillero Edgar Ibarra)
publication, one of its three major components was made up
entirely of Cakchiquels, the majority from the Department of
Baja Verapaz. Both Alta Verapaz and Baja Verapaz have been

focal points of guerrilla activity and the Government has
acknowledged publicly the indigenous inspiration of these
activities. It can hardly maintain otherwise, since the
leader of the FAR (Fuerzas Armadas Rebeldes) movement in the
area, Emilio Roman Lopez, was a well-known Cakchiquel leader
from Rabinal, killed at the end of 1966 in armed combat with
the national Army.

The history of Roman Lopez' conversion from a
Protestant pastor to an armed revolutionary is indicative of
another major factor contributing to the ideological change
among the indigenous masses. He was an earnest worker in
the agrarian reform program of President Jacobo Arbenz in
1951-52, working at the side of another indigenous leader,
Tomas Tecu Chiquito. The Arbenz government managed to give
expropriated and unused lands to more than 100,000 landless
peasant families. When Castillo Armas, after his CIA
sponsored overthrow of Arbenz, reversed this process, the
vast majority of these people lost their lands. Hundreds
were killed in the turn-around, among them, Tomas Tecu
Chiquito. The North American rural sociologist, Nathan
Whetten, in noting the dynamics created by this reversal of
historical processes, says:

> There are many campesinos who received
> lands under the agrarian law of 1952 only
> to have them taken away again after the
> fall of the Arbenz government. They
> might be receptive to any revolutionary
> scheme that promises to restore to them
> the land of which they were the proud
> possessors for such a short time
> (1961:356).

Just as the repressive activities of the Castillo
Armas government were instrumental in awakening the peasants
to a new view of their relationship to the Army and government, the even more repressive and less discriminate tactics
of the Mendez Montenegro and Arana Osorio governments will
probably have similar results.

Sociologist Alejandro Portes, referring to the
repressive alliance between the landed aristocracy and the
terroristic para-military groups made up of Army and police
personnel, states categorically:

> Since lumpen repression is inefficient at
> locating true revolutionary foci, main-
> taining a state of excitement necessi-
> tates the continuous broadening of the
> definition of the "enemy" [quotes in
> original] to assure a supply of visible
> and easily punishable victims . . .
> Moderate sectors increasingly see

themselves as forced to choose between
absolute apathy or revolutionary
violence, as their leaders are
suppressed, exiled, or driven to despair
of ever implementing peaceful alternatives (1972:48).

Even in terms of constitutional measures, it is an
army of peasant footsoldiers who must ultimately comb the
mountains in search of the guerrilla bands. Though the Army
high-command is assiduous in assigning peasant soldiers to
duty in areas far from their native villages, the same kind
of dynamic might be expected to develop among them that
occurred to Luis Turcios Lima and Marco Antonio Yon Sosa.
Just as these two guerrilla leaders were forced to ask themselves the "why?" of U.S. interest in their counter-
insurgency training, the answer to which helped lead them to
use their new knowledge against the sponsoring institutions,
so Guatemalan footsoldiers are not only being trained in the
methodology of insurgency, they are being forced to think of
the ideology that supports it. The assumption that they
will be left intellectually and morally untouched by the
experience is presumptuous.
        Two other factors that contribute to the changing
ideological position of Guatemala's peasant masses are the
introduction of large numbers of indigenous peoples into the
money economy in the last few years by the development of
new high-yield wheat seeds for the western highlands, and
governmental emphasis on a program of national integration
that insists on popular education, learning of Spanish,
reading and writing. Such participation in the money economy
and the broadening of popular education has developed a
process of communication on a regional and national scale
never before experienced in Guatemala. It is becoming harder
and harder to locate a community in Guatemala that approximates Eric Wolf's description of a closed corporate
community. It is no longer possible to view these peasant
communities as ideological or even organizational isolates.
        To say that this communication will directly
contribute to a revolutionary movement would be precipitous
at this point. But because there can be no question that
these are contributing factors to a change in values and to
a greater understanding of the world beyond the village, it
would be even more precipitous to suppose that they will
contribute to prolonging the customary peasant ideology of
submission. All indices point in the opposite direction.
        So it is that the verbal symbols that have
traditionally functioned to integrate three institutionally
distinct sub-cultures in a power alliance; "sovereignty,"
"constitutionality," "anti-communism," "democracy,"
"freedom," and "private property," are now becoming part of
the political lexicon of the peasantry. But the peasantry

are finding more than a little dissonance in attempting to
fit these words into a context that is also defined by
symbols such as "poverty" and "obedience." This dissonance,
in turn, produces new insights, new understandings. There is
no way that peasant interpretation of these concepts can
produce the illusion that they are speaking the same language
as the power structure. As they attempt to apply these
concepts more and more to their own social conditions, widespread disillusionment with present structural relationships
result. The process develops much structural tension that
presages profound structural realignment. We cannot, nor
would we, venture to say if and when it will reach revolutionary proportions. But because these verbal symbols are
still part of the political ritual whereby the large landowners, the Church hierarchy and the Army high command all
define their position in Guatemala's social structure and
their world views, and because these three have the ideological and military backing of the U.S. government, even
minimal shifts will be made at a high cost in peasant blood.

The authors wish to acknowledge the
permission of The Free Press, New York,
for extensive use of Chapter 17 from
their book, Guatemala: The Politics of
Land Ownership.

For more information about Guatemala, see
the latest book by Jonas and Tobis (1974).

REFERENCES

Adams, Richard N. Crucifixion by Power. Austin: University
of Texas Press, 1972.

Barraclough, Solon and Domike, Arthur. "Agrarian Structure
in Seven Latin American Countries," in Land Economics,
XLII:4 (1966), pp. 391-424.

Beattie, John. Other Cultures. New York: The Free Press,
1964.

CIDOC. Document 68/61. Cuernavaca, Mexico, 1968.

Flores Alvarado, Humberto. La Estructura Social Guatemal-
teca. Guatemala: Rumbos Nuevos, 1968.

Friedrich, C. J. Constitutional Government and Democracy.
Boston: Ginn and Co., 1950.

Jonas, Susanne and Tobis, David. Guatemala. New York:
NACLA, 1974. (available from Box 57, Cathedral
Station, New York, New York 10023)

Leach, Edmund. Political Systems of Highland Burma. Boston:
Beacon Press, 1954.

Melville, Thomas R. and Melville, Marjorie. Guatemala: The
Politics of Land Ownership. New York: The Free Press,
1971.

Portes, Alejandro. "Guatemala's Right-wing Terror." The
Nation, January 10, 1972.

Saler, Benson. "Nagual, Witch and Sorcerer in Quiche
Village." In Magic, Witchcraft and Curing. Edited by
J. Middleton. New York: Natural History Press, 1967.

Schermerhorn, Richard. Society and Power. New York: Random
House, 1961.

Silvert, Kalman. A Study in Government: Guatemala. Middle
American Research Series 21, 1954.

Tax, Sol. "World-view and Social Relations in Guatemala."
American Anthropologist 43 (1941).

Turner, Victor. The Forest of Symbols. Ithaca: Cornell
University Press, 1967.

U.S. Senate Subcommittee for Latin American Affairs.
    Guatemala and the Dominican Republic. Washing-
    ton, D.C.: U.S. Government Printing Office, 1971.

Weber, Max. _Theory of Social and Economic Organization._
    New York: Free Press, 1964.

Whetten, Nathan. _Guatemala: The Land and The People._
    New Haven: Yale University Press, 1961.

Wolf, Eric. "Types of Latin American Peasantry." _American
    Anthropologist_ 57 (1955).

INDEX

298

Peppe, Patrick V. 5, 90, 91,
92-109, 230
Peralta Azurdia, Enrique 274,
279-80
Peron, Juan Domingo 5, 61, 79,
201, 204, 205, 207, 208,
209
Peru 5, 31-54, 40, 41, 62, 65,
68, 69, 117
Pessao, Epitacio 211
Petras, James 100, 108, 215
Pimentel, Irineo 129
Pinto, Anibal, 109
Pinto, Robert 109
Political parties 40, 98, 100,
177, 182, 187
  Acción Democratica 187
  Acción Nacional Revolucio-
    naria (ANR) 131
  APRA 187
  Brazilian Labor Party (PTB)
    226-7
  Christian Democrat (PDC)
    95-100, 105, 276
  Colombian Communist Party
    194
  Comuneros 192
  Fuerzas Armadas REbeldes
    (FAR) 290
  Independent Democratic Party
    (PID) 277
  International Communist
    Party 194-5, 202, 252-3
  Left National Revolutionary
    Party (PRIN) 128
  Liberal Party 189, 191, 194
  Liberation Party 273, 275
  Mano Blanca 278
  Movimiento Nacional Revolu-
    cionario (MNR) 6, 124, 126-8,
    134, 136, 142, 146-63,
    175, 178
  MRL 195
  Partido Comunista de Bolivia
    (PCB) 130
  Partido Obrero Revolucionario
    (POR) 149-9, 154-5, 160-1
  Party of National Liberatin
    (MLN) 276-7, 284, 286
  People's Progressive Party
    (PPP) 73-5
  PIR 153, 155
  Popular Front 5
  Populist 5, 17, 124, 187,
    200-29

Radical Party 98
Revolutionary Cuban 74
Revolutionary Government
  (Mexico) 58
Revolutionary Party 278
Socialist Party 102
Tupac Amaro 192
Unidad Popular (UP) 71,
  105, 107
Pollitt, H. 264, 266
Polyani 263
Portes, Alejandro 109, 290-1,
  293
Portantiero , Juan Carlos 232
Portugal 214
Powell, John D. 166, 172
Prestes, Julio 211
Proletariat (see also class,
  working; labor) 2-4, 38,
    59, 106, 112, 117-8, 142,
    145, 149, 164, 194, 208
  rural 31-44, 59
  urban 33, 39, 92, 116
Puerto Rico 75

Q

Quadros, Janio 211, 216
Quijano, Anibal 90, 165

R

Radosh, Ronald 86
Ramos, Alberto Guerreiro 211,
  231, 233
Redfield, Robert 31
Reichel Dolmatoff, G. 192, 199
Reiser, 86
Religion 62, 71, 72, 114,
  119-22, 176, 185-6, 194,
  268, 270, 272-3, 280-6,
  288, 289, 292
Reno, Philip 89
Revilla, Arcenio 48, 54
  Ana B. 48, 54
Revolution 1, 40-1, 59, 64,
  78-9, 107, 111, 113, 118,
  124, 126, 128-37, 142-3,
  145-58, 163-4, 185, 187,
  188, 191, 200-1, 212, 214,
  217, 228, 237-61, 279,
  287-91
Rhodes, Robert 89

304